A PLUME BOOK

TOOLS FOR SURVIVAL

JAMES WESLEY, RAWLES, has been an enthusiastic survivalist since his teenage years. He is now a survivalist author and lecturer and the editor of SurvivalBlog.com. He has a bachelor of arts degree from San Jose State University with minor degrees in military science, history, and military history. He is a former U.S. Army intelligence officer who held a Top Secret security clearance and access to Sensitive Compartmented Information (SCI), and achieved the rank of captain before resigning his commission.

Since 2005, Rawles has edited SurvivalBlog. With rich archives on a wide range of topics available free to the public, SurvivalBlog is the nation's most popular blog on family preparedness.

Rawles lives on a ranch in an undisclosed location in the Inland Northwest. There, he faithfully attends a local church and homeschools his children. He and his family enjoy a largely self-reliant lifestyle by hunting, fishing, raising livestock, doing large-scale gardening, and beekeeping. His tools are always close at hand.

D0896956

TOOLS FOR SURVIVAL

WHAT YOU NEED TO SURVIVE WHEN YOU'RE ON YOUR OWN

James Wesley, Rawles

P

A PLUME BOOK

PLUME
Published by the Penguin Group
Penguin Group (USA) LLC
375 Hudson Street
New York, New York 10014

USA | Canada | UK | Ireland | Australia
New Zealand | India | South Africa | China
penguin.com
A Penguin Random House Company

First published by Plume, a member of Penguin Group (USA) LLC, 2015

P REGISTERED TRADEMARK—MARCA REGISTRADA

LIBRARY OF CONGRESS CATALOGING-IN-PUBLICATION DATA
Rawles, James Wesley,.
    Tools for survival : what you need to survive when you're on your own / James Wesley, Rawles.
        pages cm
    Includes index.
    ISBN 978-0-452-29812-5
1. Survival. 2. Self-reliant living. 3. Alternative lifestyles. I. Title.
    GF86R38 2014
    613.6'9—dc23   2014032904

Printed in the United States of America
10 9 8 7 6 5 4 3 2 1

Set in Palatino

DISCLAIMERS

SAFETY WARNINGS

Always wear the appropriate safety gear. For most of the shop processes described in this book, goggles, or at least safety glasses with side guards, are a must. Sturdy boots and a shop apron are highly recommended. Never work alone around fire and always keep a big fire extinguisher of the appropriate type handy.

Because I foresee the possibility of a "grid down" world, in this book I emphasize nineteenth-century tools and technology that don't require electricity. When using tools designed in that era or when referring to nineteenth- and early twentieth-century publications (and reprints thereof), keep in mind that the safety standards in those days were considerably more lax than those used today. So be *very* careful around harmful or explosive vapors, unshielded blades, unguarded drive belts and drive chains, flammables, poisonous and carcinogenic chemicals, and so forth.

CONTENTS

Disclaimers   v

Foreword   ix

Acknowledgments   xvii

Before We Begin   xix

Introduction   xxiii

Chapter 1 Setting Up Shop   1

Chapter 2 Food Preservation and Cooking Tools   10

Chapter 3 Gardening, Farm, and Ranch Tools   19

Chapter 4 Sewing and Leatherworking Tools   38

Chapter 5 Shop Tools and Tool Making   49

Chapter 6 Electrical and Electronics Tools   75

Chapter 7   Mobility and Countermobility Tools   95

Chapter 8   Welding and Blacksmithing Tools   112

Chapter 9   Fire Prevention and Firefighting Tools   131

Chapter 10 Timber, Firewood, and Lumber Tools   140

Chapter 11 Rifles, Shotguns, and Handguns   149

Chapter 12 Archery   189

Chapter 13 Medical and Sanitation Tools and
Supplies   202

Chapter 14 Knives and Traditional Hand Tools   216

Chapter 15 Lifelong Learning and Skill Building   233

Appendix A   Your Retreat Library   241

*Appendix B   Recommended Gunsmithing Service
Providers*   249

Appendix C   The Pre-1899 Antique Guns FAQ   257

Appendix D   Useful Formulas   259

Glossary   271

Index   307

FOREWORD

Starting with primitive stone and bone tools, hollowed-out gourds, bone needles and fishhooks, clubs, and arrows and spears, mankind has been fabricating tools for survival. It is our tools, combined with the skills and knowledge to use them, that enable humans to build and maintain a highly complex society that feeds, clothes, shelters, sustains, and entertains the more than seven billion people who populate planet Earth—a population that is several times what Earth could support were we all hunter-gatherers. In recent times, increasingly complex tools and technologies offer us nearly instant access to a dizzying variety of gadgets, clothing, and foodstuffs, along with a wide array of medical services and pharmaceutical drugs that enable us to attend to our short- and long-term medical needs. However, when disaster strikes, access to this seemingly unlimited supply of modern tools, gadgets, pharmaceuticals, and foodstuffs could evaporate in the blink of an eye. If a major calamity of significant scope and duration casts a shadow upon your portion of the world, causing serious disruptions in the electric power grid, supply chains, and central services lasting weeks or months, the tools, supplies, and skill set that you have on hand would be of utmost importance for the safety, comfort, and survival of yourself, your family, and your friends.

Just a few decades ago, before the advent of just-in-time deliveries precisely coordinated by the computerized flow of information across the World Wide Web, stores in major cities across America stocked their consumable goods nearby in giant warehouses, where roughly a month's supply of food and other critical items were stored at all times. Not so anymore. Just-in-time deliveries have allowed suppliers to cut costs by reducing local inventories of most consumable stocks to a mere three-day supply. Hurricane Katrina and the Indian Ocean tsunami showed us that when a major disaster covers a broad area, affecting millions of people, governments and local authorities are ineffective and overwhelmed, taking weeks or months to resolve long-lasting grid-down situations coupled with the resulting cascading failures of supply chains and central services that require grid power for their daily operation. In situations when the grid is down and central services have failed for a significant period of time, you are on what is referred to in prepping/survival circles as "YOYO time" (You're on Your Own). It is during YOYO time that access to quality survival tools and supplies, along with the knowledge and skills for their proper usage, can make the difference between life and death, or in less critical situations the difference between living in relative comfort and ease and living in extreme distress.

There are many different events, some of them man-made

and others due to natural causes, that can cause disruptions far larger in scope and duration than those wrought by Hurricane Katrina. For example, a well-coordinated terrorist attack on the U.S. electric power grid, or a naturally occurring super solar storm, or the detonation of a nuclear device at an altitude high above the continental U.S. with its resulting powerful electromagnetic pulse (EMP) could cripple the U.S. power grid for an extended period, causing the collapse of our world as we know it for a period lasting several months to many years. In many communities hard hit by Katrina, it was several weeks and in some cases months before basic services like phone service and electrical power were restored. Eight years later, there are entire neighborhoods that have not yet recovered. When the grid goes down, most cell phone towers will exhaust their backup battery power after three hours. Within three days, most central telephone switching stations, hospitals, and police stations will run out of backup power. Without power, air conditioners, elevators, and the Internet grind to a halt. Without power, there is no water treatment, no gasoline pumping, no bank machine access, and the sewage pumps stop working, causing city sewers to back up and flood low-lying streets. Without power, food spoils and rots in refrigerators and freezers, both at home and in the markets. Without power, where will millions of people in America's cities buy groceries, obtain drinking water, and defecate?

Solar storms of a magnitude that would cause catastrophic damage to our electric power grid are naturally recurring events, and scientific evidence indicates they tend to strike our planet an average of once every seventy-five to a hundred years. Since the last one of a magnitude that would collapse today's modern electrical grid took place ninety-three years ago (the Great Geomagnetic Storm of May 1921), statistically we are due for the next one. Odds are that grid collapse due to an extreme solar storm will take place sometime in the not-too-distant future (scientists predict a one-in-eight chance per decade for being struck by a geomagnetic storm of this magnitude), unless another event causes grid collapse first, or our government/private industry spend the roughly two billion dollars it would cost to install the devices to protect our grid from catastrophic failure in the event of either an extreme solar storm or an EMP attack.

Of course, solar storms and an EMP attack are not the only potential causes for grid collapse, which could also be brought on by situations such as pandemic, a well-coordinated terrorist attack, or an act of war. No one can plan ahead for every contingency, but a wise person will plan for events that have a significant chance of occurring. Between our changing climate, potential terrorists, antibiotic-resistant superbacteria, and the probability of an extreme solar storm, it is my opinion that we stand a good chance of seeing a widespread long-term disruption sometime in the next decade or two. Would you board a plane if you were told, "Don't worry, there is only a one-in-eight chance the plane will crash"?

Who am I? In addition to being a professional engineer, I am a carpenter and general building contractor. I grew up hunting, fishing, camping, and climbing in the backcountry of Vermont, New Hampshire, and upstate New York. I have been a hands-on kind of guy for most of my life. My interest in prepping and survival did not really take off until 1997, when an epiphany brought the realization that in spite of all my technical training and considerable skills covering a variety of fields, if the grid were to collapse for an extended period of time, I lacked the knowledge, tools, and skill set that would be needed to reproduce much of anything from our technological world. For example, back in 1997 if I had been dropped in the middle of the Amazon basin with just the clothes on my back, I might not have survived. I needed to stock a supply of high-quality, durable, and repairable survival tools along with detailed information for how to grow or fabricate, store, and repair the essentials for survival.

We live in the age of information. The Internet, iPads, iPhones, and a host of other electronic gadgets and gizmos provide us with instant access to veritable mountains of information, far beyond what was available just a generation ago. In order for information to be useful, it must be trustworthy, practical, and presented in ways that are easily understood. You also must have access to tools for applying that information, whether those "tools" are simply a pair of skilled hands, a well-stocked fabrication shop, or a network of friends and neighbors who have a considerable collection of barterable skills, tools, and raw materials.

When you're having a lively discussion with your friends, you don't need to worry too much about whether or not that information is particularly accurate or was derived from a trusted and well-known source because the stakes are low. However, when that information pertains to building a stock of survival tools that you, your family, and your friends may need to depend upon in some future critical situation, the accuracy and efficacy of that information is of utmost importance.

The book you have in your hands is a wealth of this type of invaluable practical information gained the hard way— through experience. It is most certainly worth its weight in gold. Many thousands of hours of practical hands-on experience provide the foundation for its recommendations and "how-to" advice, which have been gleaned from the collective experience of dozens of experts in various fields, plus hundreds of experienced preppers, survivalists, outdoorsmen, soldiers, and skilled artisans who shared their knowledge and experiences on the tremendously popular survival and prepping resource SurvivalBlog.com. With an average of more than fifty thousand independent daily reads, SurvivalBlog.com is the Internet's most popular—and most comprehensive—survival and preparedness forum.

For many years, Rawles and his family have lived a self-sufficient lifestyle at their remote ranch located in "an undisclosed location somewhere west of the Rockies." Between his military service, ranching, and dedication to Survival-Blog.com, Rawles *knows and lives* what he preaches. Even though he has developed an extremely accomplished and impressive array of knowledge, tools, supplies, and skills covering a wide variety of fields, Rawles is the first to admit that no single individual can know and do it all. Rest assured that the advice and recommendations offered in this book are based on Rawles's vast storehouse of personal experience blended with that of dozens of accomplished and seasoned experts, and many other contributors to Survival-Blog.com.

Most of us do not have the luxury of copious amounts of spare time, motivation, and money to devote to becoming an expert in all the fields covered by this book. It is far less expensive and easier to learn from those experts who are willing to share their wisdom and advice. Whether you are an experienced prepper or a neophyte, you will find considerable value within these pages. If you are just starting along this path, and have limited budget and experience, the selection of a few critical survival tools from the multitude of options, such as a practical firearm or chain saw, can be a daunting task. I suggest you use Rawles's recommendations to help select those tools best suited to your needs and at a price you can afford. Don't feel you have to do everything at once, but do *something*. Treat this book as if you've had a grizzled old mountain man offering you pearls of wisdom that someday may well save your life. And thank God that you have access to this treasury of collected wisdom while there is still time to do something about it.

MATTHEW STEIN

Matthew Stein is a design engineer, green builder, and author of two bestselling books: *When Technology Fails: A Manual for Self-Reliance, Sustainability, and Surviving the Long Emergency* and *When Disaster Strikes: A Comprehensive Guide for Emergency Planning and Crisis Survival*. He is a graduate of the Massachusetts Institute of Technology, where he majored in mechanical engineering. Stein has appeared on numerous radio and television programs and is a repeat guest on *Fox News*, *Coast to Coast AM*, Alex Jones's *Infowars*, Vince Finelli's *USA Prepares*, and *The Power Hour*. He is an active mountain climber, serves as a guide and instructor for blind skiers, has written several articles on the subject of sustainable living, and is a guest columnist for the *Huffington Post*. His Web sites are WhenTechFails.com and MatStein.com. He lives in the high country of the Sierra Nevada in Northern California.

ACKNOWLEDGMENTS

This book is written in memoriam to two men who were key formative influences in my life as a survivalist: Colonel Jeff Cooper (1920–2006) and Mel Tappan (1933–1980). Without them, I would not have fully recognized that I needed to substantively prepare and train. They also both helped me focus on essentials as opposed to nonessentials.

I thank the editors and readers of SurvivalBlog for their instrumental input and assistance with this book. In many ways I consider the readers of SurvivalBlog to be coeditors, since collectively their knowledge and expertise goes far beyond my own. Special thanks to Pat Cascio, Dr. Cynthia Koelker, and Michael Z. Williamson for their expertise and their kind assistance.

For advice on specific tools, I'd like to thank L. K. O. (SurvivalBlog's central Rocky Mountains regional editor). His input was crucial, particularly for Chapter 6, Electrical and Electronics Tools. My thanks also to Sir Knight (of the excellent *Paratus Familia Blog*) for his input on shop tools, gauges, and some traditional tools, and to both Kyle T. and my old friend "Dan Fong" for their contributions to the passages on welding.

I've also included excerpts from SurvivalBlog articles and letters written by A. T., Ben F., Calvinist Cadet, David in Israel, Mr. F., G. M., J. D. C. in Mississippi, J. I. R., Jodier, J. T. F., Lockstitch, Matt M., Mike in Seattle, Kory Mikesell of FrostCPR.com, "John Mosby" (of http://mountainguerrilla.wordpress.com), Muscadine Hunter, Nina in Washington, John Parker Jr., P. D., Robert B., R. V., Ted J., TFA303, Todd Savage (of Survival-RetreatConsulting.com), "Rick Smith," Tanker, Texas Rancher, and Z. M. (Their articles and letters included herein all first appeared under SurvivalBlog.com's copyright.)

Special thanks to those who did editorial reviews of the draft edition of this book: Joe Snuffy, Kyle T., and Bruce.

Kudos to my No. 2 Son, who took all of the photos for the book.

I must also give credit to the nonfiction and fiction writers who have influenced me the most in my development as a writer. They are: David Brin, Algis Budrys, the late Tom Clancy, Bruce D. Clayton, Colonel Jeff Cooper, Frederick Forsyth, Pat Frank, Gordon Dickson, Friedrich Hayek, Henry Hazlitt, Ernest Hemingway, Dean Ing, Elmer Keith, H. W. McBride, Ludwig von Mises, Dr. Gary North, Arthur W. Pink, John Piper, Jerry Pournelle, Ayn Rand, Lew Rockwell, Murray Rothbard, George R. Stewart, and of course Mel Tappan.

JAMES WESLEY, RAWLES

THE RAWLES RANCH, AUGUST 2014

BEFORE WE BEGIN

Before we jump into the nitty gritty, there are a few things I'd like to note about the format and style of this book.

A NOTE ON INTERNET REFERENCES

For the sake of brevity, Internet uniform resource locators (URLs) are mentioned in this book without the prefixes "http://" or "http://www." So, for example, the full URL for the Crescent Tool Company is: http://www.crescenttools.org. But in this book, that would be presented as just:

crescenttools.org

For some URLs, the prefix is necessary; you must enter the appropriate prefix, or your Web browser will *not* be able to access those pages. In those cases, the prefix will be included, and you must enter the appropriate prefix to access those pages.

TRUNCATED URLs

The Internet is an amazing resource, but the URLs for Web pages are often a mile long, and therefore tedious to key in if you are transcribing them from a printed source. Therefore, many of the long URLs mentioned in this book have been truncated, using the free SnipURL service (snipurl.com).

Just type **http://** and then the "snipped" URL, *exactly as shown*, and your Web browser will automatically jump to the original (usually much longer) referenced URL.

For example, the full-length URL http://www.survival blog.com/noncorrosive.html has this assigned SNIP URL: snipurl.com/27lzh2u.

So you would activate your Web browser, and then type in: **http://snipurl.com/27lzh2u**

(Note that with many current browsers, you can skip typing **http://**, and it will automatically fill that in.)

Your browser will then jump to that referring page. Quick and simple!

DEFUNCT URLs

Also note that the many URLs mentioned herein were working *at the time* this book was being edited. However, Web entropy is inevitable. When you do eventually find URLs that have expired, just do a topical Web search to find some current links. (The author and publisher cannot be held responsible for the lax Web page maintenance of third parties.)

I highly recommend that you continue to study and build

your skill set throughout your life. Even in the Internet age, it is important to develop a hard copy binder of references for each of your workshops. Knowledge is power. Gather it unto yourselves! (See Chapter 15 for more about lifelong learning.)

GLOSSARY

This book includes an extensive glossary of terms. Rather than describing and explaining each tool, term, and acronym in the main narrative of the book, I have pushed those definitions back to the glossary, as a reference. In this way, advanced students will not feel bogged down with minutiae, while at the same time novices won't feel overwhelmed with any assumptions about their knowledge of the basics.

INTRODUCTION: YOUR TOOLS FOR SURVIVAL

Familiarity with the appearance of tools, and seeing them in the hands of others will not be of any value. Nothing but the immediate contact with the tool will teach how to use It.

—J. S. Zerbe, M.E., 1914

Man is a tool-using Animal. . . . Nowhere do you find him without tools; without tools he is nothing, with tools he is all.

—Thomas Carlyle

This book describes tools for survival and their use. By "survival," I'm not just referring to how to stay alive if you find yourself stranded in the woods. I use the term in a more all-encompassing sense. In my nonfiction book *How to Survive the End of the World as We Know It*, I outlined a number of disaster situations in which law and order might break down, or civilization might revert to an earlier mode. Recent history has shown that even localized disasters can soon devolve into You're on Your Own time, or YOYO time.

My goal in penning this book is to set you on the path toward becoming a fully qualified twenty-first-century artificer. An artificer is someone who creates or fixes intricate objects. In my parlance, I extend this definition to anyone who has eclectic skills in design, fabrication, maintenance, and repair of tools and machinery. By adapting the tools and skills of previous centuries, you will become an indispensible asset for any community, especially if the power grids go down and stay down for an extended period.

BACK TO 1890

I take a nineteenth-century-emphasis approach to tools and self-sufficiency. That is entirely appropriate for the circumstances that survivalists envision. A world without grid power will mean reverting to doing a lot of things by hand. Modern conveniences disappear, and suddenly life gets decidedly inconvenient. Even with the right hand tools available, you can expect a lot of sore muscles.

SURVIVAL ISN'T ABOUT STUFF; IT IS ABOUT SKILLS

I often stress in my writing that a key to survival is not what you *have*, but rather what you *know*. Skills beat gadgets and practicality beats style. The modern world is full of pundits, poseurs, and mall ninjas. Preparedness is not just about accumulating a pile of stuff. You need practical skills, and those only come with study, training, and practice. Any armchair survivalist can buy a set of stylish camouflage fatigues and an M4gery carbine encrusted with umpteen accessories. Style points should not be mistaken for genuine skills and practicality. Yes, it is important to have the right tools. But this book is as much about knowledge and skills to use tools properly, safely, and effectively as it is about the tools themselves.

To expand on those precepts, consider the following.

Balanced logistics are important for everyone, but absolutely crucial for someone who is on a tight budget. If you have a three-year food supply, then a quantity miscalculation for one particular food item will likely be just an inconvenience. But if you only have a three-month supply, then a miscalculation can be a serious hazard. Be logical, systematic, and dispassionate in your preparations. You need to develop some detailed lists, starting with a List of Lists. Be realistic and scale your retreat logistics purchasing program to your budget.

Avoid going into debt to get prepared. A friend of mine who was a physician's assistant went way overboard in 1998 and 1999, stocking up for Y2K. The massive credit card debt that he racked up eventually contributed to a prolonged mental depression.

Buy used instead of new. It goes without saying that your money will go further if you concentrate on quality used tools, guns, and vehicles. Remember that preparedness is not a beauty contest. Owning gear with some dings and scratches is not an issue. Just be sure to inspect used items very carefully. In the case of buying a used vehicle, it is worthwhile to run a check on its history through a service like Carfax. This will reveal if the car or truck was repaired after a major collision. Also, hire a qualified mechanic to do some checks before you buy a used vehicle. That will be money well spent!

Clip coupons, watch and wait for seasonal sales, shop at

thrift stores, go to garage sales and flea markets, attend weekend farm and estate auctions and Defense Logistics Agency Disposition Services (DLA Disposition Services) auctions, and learn to watch Craigslist and Freecycle like a hawk. The only thing better than finding inexpensive used items is having them *given* to you. This is a common occurrence with Freecycle. For example, it is not unusual to have someone give you several dozen used mason-type canning jars. Just be sure to return the favor somehow, in the spirit of Freecycle.

Strike a balance between quality and quantity. I'm a big believer in the old adage "Better is the enemy of good enough." Why buy a $320 custom Chris Reeve folding knife when a used $30 CRKT or Cold Steel brand pocketknife bought on eBay will provide 98 percent of the functionality? Buying at one tenth the price means that you will have money available for many *spare* knives and other important gear and training.

Take advantage of free or low-cost training. The Western Rifle Shooters Association (WRSA), for example, offers shooting and medical training at near their cost. I've discussed other such training opportunities at length previously on SurvivalBlog. In my Precepts page, I noted several points.

Learn to distinguish between essentials and nonessentials. Do you really need cable television? Or eating out? Or snacks from the vending machine? Use the cash generated by these savings to buy the far more important things, like storage food.

When you don't have cash, then apply sweat equity. Do you need pasture fence or garden fence at your retreat property? Don't hire someone and "have it done." Do it yourself. Not only will you save money, but you will also learn valuable skills. You might even lose some of that flab around your midsection in the process. Also consider that folks are often willing to barter their excess tangibles in trade for your skills and time. Do you have an elderly neighbor with a big gun collection? Then offer to paint his house in trade for a couple of guns or a few of those heavy ammo cans that he won't live long enough to shoot.

Even if you have a millionaire's budget, you need to learn how to do things for yourself and be willing to get your hands dirty. In a societal collapse, the division of labor will be reduced tremendously. Odds are that the only skilled craftsmen available to build a shed, mend a fence, shuck corn, repair an engine, buck firewood, or pitch manure will be *you* and your family. Hiring someone to deliver three cords of firewood is a far cry from felling, cutting, hauling, splitting, and stacking it all yourself.

Our retreat is so well stocked because I have been systematically stocking up for thirty years. I gave up my Big City salaried job many years ago to concentrate on living self-sufficiently. Part of this was a conscious decision to raise our children in a more wholesome environment. The major drawback is that the Rawles Ranch is in such a remote area that we don't get into town very often.

As my late wife ("the Memsahib") aptly put it: "The good thing about living so remotely is there are no shopping opportunities." Even if I had the urge to indulge in some retail therapy, I'd have to drive more than two hours to do it. The next best thing you can do is cancel your magazine subscriptions. If you analyze the contents of most magazines, you will realize that they are designed to make you dissatisfied with your clothes, your home decor, garden, electronics, and autos because they aren't the latest, greatest, and most fashionable. I also highly recommend selling or Freecycling your television, for the very same reason. A couple of exceptions to our magazine rule are *Backwoods Home* and *Home Power*, since they are both light on advertising and heavy on practical skills.

Do the best you can with what you have. Be truly frugal. I grew up in a family that still remembered both our pioneer history and the more recent lessons of the Great Depression. One of our family mottoes is "Use it up, wear it out, make do, or do without." I thank my mother for passing that wisdom along to my generation, and I am doing the same with my children.

RAWLES'S RULES ON TOOLS

Here is my philosophy of survival tools in a nutshell:

- Buy **durable** tools and gear. Think of it as investing in the survival of yourself *and* your children and grandchildren. Keep in mind that there'll be no more "quick trips to the hardware store" after The Schumer Hits the Fan (TSHTF).

- Buy tools **economically.** Watch Craigslist, Freecycle, classified ads, and eBay for tools and gear at bargain prices.

- Strive for **balanced** preparedness that covers all bases, all scenarios.

- Buy tools that optimize **flexibility and adaptability.** (Some examples: Shop to match a 12-VDC standard for most small electronics, truly multipurpose equipment, multiball trailer hitches, NATO slave cable connectors for 24-VDC vehicles, Anderson Powerpole connectors for small electronics—again, 12-VDC).

- Retain the **ability to revert** to older, more labor-intensive low technology.

- With the right tools, **you can *make* other tools**.

- **Redundancy**, *squared*. One of my mottoes is "Two is one, and one is none." I jokingly call my basement Jim's Amazing Secret Bunker of Redundant Redundancy (JASBORR).

- Fuel flexibility.

- Purchase high-quality **used** (but not abused) gear, preferably when bargains can be found.

- Whenever possible, **buy American**.

- If given the option, buy true military specification ("**mil-spec**") gear.

- If in doubt, buy **the larger size and the heavier thickness**.

- If in doubt, then buy **two**. (Remember, two is one and one is none.)

- Buy **systematically**, and only as your budget allows. (Avoid debt!)

- Invest your **sweat equity**. Not only will you save money, but you also will learn more valuable skills.

- **Train** with what you have, and learn from the experts. Tools without training are almost useless.

- Learn to **maintain and repair** your gear. (Always buy spare parts and full service manuals!)

- Buy guns in commonly available calibers.

- Buy everything with a long service life in mind.

- Store extra for charity and barter.

- Grow your own and buy the tools to **make** your own—don't just *store* things.

- **Rust is the enemy**, and lubrication and spot painting are your allies.

- Avoid being an "early adopter" of new technology, or you'll pay a higher price and get lower reliability.

- Select all of your gear with your local climate conditions in mind.

- Recognize that there are **no style points** in survival. Don't worry about appearances—concentrate on practicality and durability.

- Don't skimp on tools. **Buy *quality* brand-name tools**.

- **Skills beat gadgets** and practicality beats style.

- Use group standardization for weapons and electronics. Strive for **commonality** of magazines, accessories, and spare parts.

- Gear up to raise livestock. Those are the investments that **breed**.

- Build your fences **bull strong and sheep tight**.

- Tools without the appropriate safety gear are just **accidents** waiting for a place to happen.

- Whenever you have the option, buy things in flat, earth-tone colors. This is important if you ever have to live in **stealth mode**, where camouflage will be valued.

- Plan ahead for things **breaking or wearing out**. Again, redundancy and ease of repair.

- **Always have a Plan B and a Plan C.**

MAINTAINING AND CARING FOR YOUR TOOLS

Proper sharpening, oiling, and storage are crucial for giving your tools multigenerational longevity. This is particularly important in damp climates. With the exception of some files, most tools should be kept well oiled. Let me repeat this, for emphasis: Keep tools well oiled. Keep tools well oiled. Keep tools well oiled! Depending on your climate, you might need tool chests with tight-fitting lids and plenty of silica gel. If you have any tools that are rusty, evaluate their condition. Minor rust can usually be removed with a wire wheel. But if any tools are badly rusted, consider either paying to get them bead blasted or, if need be, replacing them completely. Why? Because leaving one rusty tool in contact with your other tools that are in good condition will encourage "sympathetic" rusting, eventually ruining many more tools that are in close proximity.

Bead blasting is also a good potential part-time home business, if you have a side yard available to dedicate to it. (It is messy.) You could even carry on this business post-Schumer if you have a generator and/or a large alternative power system.

Filing and grinding should be done judiciously. With any machining process, always remember that it is easy to remove metal, but it is usually impossible to put it back without ruining a part. Proceed with caution and take your time. The old saying is "Haste makes waste." Or, as my father put it, "Haste makes expensive trips to the hardware store."

xxxii   Introduction: Your Tools for Survival

Keep in mind anytime you use abrasives that you aren't done with the job until you have removed all of the fragments and filings, since these can wear other parts or scratch protective finishes. For this, I often use a spray can of brake cleaner solvent (available at your local auto parts store). Be sure to wear rubber gloves, and of course relubricate the parts as you reassemble them, since brake cleaner will strip away all of the protective lubricant.

One other caution that I only rarely see mentioned: When cleaning the rust off an old motor or generator, *never* use steel wool. This is because minute residue from steel wool can short out the commutator plates.

Tools Without Training Are Almost Useless

Owning a gun doesn't make someone a "shooter" any more than owning a surfboard makes someone a surfer. With proper training and practice, you will be miles ahead of the average citizen. Get advanced medical training. Get the best firearms training that you can afford. Learn about amateur radio from your local affiliated American Radio Relay League (ARRL) club. Practice raising a vegetable garden each summer. Some skills are only perfected over a period of years.

Next, I'll discuss how to set up your workshop and the most important tool that you will need.

TOOLS FOR SURVIVAL

· CHAPTER 1 ·

SETTING UP SHOP

Law of the Workshop: Any tool, when dropped, will roll
to the least accessible corner.

—Jerry Smith

One of the first things you'll need to do as you embark on becoming more prepared is to set up a well-equipped workshop for yourself. Actually, you'll want to set up multiple workshops with dedicated purposes. Having one big combination shop is an invitation to a conflagration caused by negligence. Having sawdust and scrap wood from your carpentry projects in proximity to your welding bench is foolhardy. As you build up the assortment of tools in your metal and woodworking shops, resist the urge to have any of your tools—other than perhaps measuring and squaring tools—migrate from one shop to the other. Using a woodworking chisel on any sort of metal is sure to ruin it. And it is quite discouraging to see one of your metalworking files gunked up with sap from wood. Keep your tools separate, and insist that your children and teenagers do likewise. If possible, set aside separate shops or at least dedicated corners of a shop building for each purpose.

TIP

When designing your workshops, try to err on the side of (A) more closely spaced power outlets, (B) better ventilation, and (C) copious lighting.

SAFETY FIRST!

Keep safety in mind when designing and operating your shop. Keep power cords out of the way and minimize other hazards that might cause anyone to trip or slip. Use common sense when designing your shelving arrangement: Stow the heaviest objects at waist level (so you don't have to bend your back when lifting them), stow the moderately heavy objects down low, and stow the light objects up high. And of course keep anything flammable away from sources of ignition. Oily rags should be stored in a special fire-resistant bucket (such as a Justrite model 9100) that is positioned well away from walls or benches.

One good mental exercise is to try to picture a spunky, unrestrained, and curious yearling bull that has been set loose to go crashing around in your workshop. That gives you a rough approximation of the trouble that people (especially kids) can get themselves into. You will want all of your sharp tools secured, nothing to trip over, no hazardous protuberances (particularly at eye level), and nothing flammable in places of risk.

THE ESSENTIALS

There are five items that you need to keep close at hand at all times:

- A rack of eye goggles and safety glasses (a couple of pairs of each so you have absolutely no excuse for not wearing them)

- A first aid kit with tourniquet

- An emergency eye-wash bottle

- An ABC fire extinguisher

- Communications gear in case of an accident or emergency

Buy sets of these for *each* of your workshops and position them where they are in prominent view and within easy reach.

WORKBENCHES

I'm often asked about the ideal height for a workbench. That varies, depending on your own height. Most bench tops are between thirty-two and thirty-eight inches. The ideal height for a carpentry bench is palm height, just where your palms rest on the surface if you stand up straight and leave your arms hanging at your sides. I generally like woodworking and painting benches right at palm height, metalworking benches lower than palm height, and electronics and reloading benches higher than palm height—perhaps as high as forty-four inches. Of course, sometimes you will be sitting in an adjustable-height stool at the latter two benches. Find what's comfortable for you.

Before building (or buying) your shop benches, you might want to experiment with your existing kitchen countertops to see what height works best for you. Be sure to build your benches quite sturdy, solidly on all four legs, and with the bench top dead level. If the top is not level, then everything that you build on it will be, as I call it, Pelosi.

When building carpentry benches, I intentionally build them three-quarters of an inch low, and then install a sacrificial piece of three-quarter-inch interior plywood on top, attached with a few very deeply countersunk screws. This top sheet of plywood gets replaced once every few years after inevitably getting nicked, furrowed, and gouged.

Some carpenters build a separate bench for planing, sanding, and painting that is considerably lower than their other benches. By placing the work surface of this bench at around twenty-eight inches, you will gain more leverage for planing and a more complete perspective on your projects.

If you plan to use rubber shop mats (to reduce fatigue and to provide a nonslip surface), then you will need to include that thickness in your calculation for your workbench heights.

Your sawhorses should all be made the exact same height as your workbench so that they can support long pieces and hold them horizontal. Your table saw height should also be adjusted to match. If you are quite tall, then you may find that this height is beyond the range of travel for your table saw's legs. If so, you can fabricate long inlet wooden blocks to act as boosters for each side.

Wood vises should be installed so that their tops don't protrude above the bench height. That way, they won't interfere when you are working with oversize pieces on your bench top. Metal vises are of course expected to sit considerably higher, but for the greatest versatility, attach them with oversize wing nuts, so that they can be repositioned quickly if need be. For some years, I simply attached my machinist's vise with a pair of extra-large C-clamps. But this only suffices for very light work.

VISES: YOUR GO-TO TOOLS

A swiveling machinist's vise will be one of your shop's most often used and most versatile tools. It is the centerpiece of most workshops, for good reason. It is your go-to tool for umpteen projects. Most of the mass-produced workshop vises made since the 1940s have a coaxial pair of pipe-gripping jaws below the main (flat) jaws. The better-quality vises have removable upper and lower jaw blocks. This design allows you to replace a damaged block. It also lets you fabricate spare jaw blocks of brass, plastic, or wood so that you can work with delicate surface items that would otherwise be marred by steel jaws. Most machinist vises are now made in China, but some of the Wilton brand and Yost brand vises are still American made. Check carefully for the country of origin before ordering, at their respective Web pages (Wilton: snipurl.com/27lz8g3; Yost: snipurl.com/27lz8o5).

A machinist's vise typically also includes an anvil surface for light metalworking, but it is no substitute for a proper heavy-duty blacksmithing anvil.

A heavy-duty machinist's vise

I also recommend buying a miniature vise, commonly called a "fly-tying" vise. These are handy for detail work, such as when soldering electronic components. There are several brands of mini-vises still made in the USA, such as Atlas and Apex (Wolff Industries), Dyna-King, and Griffin Enterprises. These are usually attached to a workbench with a C-clamp, but some use a lever-actuated suction cup.

For blacksmithing and welding, a different style of vise is used. Instead of a precise jaw screw thread—with *many* turns required to move the jaws two inches—a blacksmithing vise has a quick throw lever, which is useful because time is of the essence when working heated steel. This sort of vise also has a leg that goes to the floor to absorb the shock of the hammer blows (without this feature there would eventually be damage to the screw threads).

THE HOT SHOP

Your "hot shop" can combine most of your high-temperature processes: a steel welding table and sundry apparatus, brass and aluminum casting equipment, pottery kiln, glassworking torch, and so forth. Needless to say, this shop should be physically distanced from all the sawdust generated by your woodshop. If both of these workshops must be in the same combination shop building, then they should be located at opposite ends of the building.

Your flammables (bulk fuel, paint, solvents, and reloading powder) should be stored **in a completely separate, freestanding building**. In my experience the best approach is to establish a small locking continental express (CONEX) steel multimode shipping container dedicated to storing flammables. (CONEXes are the ubiquitous ribbed metal shipping containers that you see carried on many 18-wheel trucks.) The dedicated petroleum/oil/lubricants (POL) CONEX has long been standard for military units, and for good reason. In the civilian world, these are often called "paint sheds." It is best to leave no more than one cylinder of each type of gas for your cutting torches, one bar of oxidizer (such as Solidox), and one cylinder of propane in your metal shop. All of the spares should be stored in your POL building. This shed or CONEX should be situated in an open area that is clear of grass and brush so that even if it were fully engulfed in

flames it would not endanger any other structures, wood
fences, or timber. The same CONEX or shed should be used
to store nearly all of your surplus oil, grease, gas cans, diesel
cans, transmission fluid, hydraulic fluid, spray lubricants,
and so forth.

Speaking of lubricants, one of my favorites is a brand
called Break-Free CLP. We buy a couple of pints at a time for
use here at the Rawles Ranch.

YOUR STOCKPILES

To be prepared for a worst-case situation wherein you may
have to live self-sufficiently for months or even years, you
will need to accumulate stockpiles of lumber, plywood,
scrap steel, plumbing pipe, wire mesh, sheet plastic (opaque
and clear), glass, lead, casting sand, leather, nylon webbing,
wire, and many other supplies. All of this must be kept out
of the elements for longevity, and out from underfoot for
safety. Furthermore, it has to be well organized, so that you
can immediately see what you have available.

Planning your stockpiles requires common sense. Just
think through what you might need, given a paucity of outside resources and the potential for a lot of houseguests for
an extended period of time. Plan on lots of aunts, uncles, and
cousins arriving, with little more than the clothes on their
back. How would you feed them? How would you house
them? How would you provide for their privacy? Think this
all through, and you'll likely come to conclusion that you
will need a *big stack* of plywood!

Since many of your stockpiled materials will only appreciate in value, stockpiling is like putting money in the bank, so

buy all you can afford and safely store. You also need to plan ahead to provide the raw materials for self-employment during an extended period of economic dislocation. My key bit of advice: Buy lots of tanned leather hides, sheets of Kydex, and rolls of nylon webbing, because your neighbors are suddenly going to feel the need to have slings and holsters for all their guns. Count on it.

In my book *How to Survive the End of the World as We Know It*, I describe a variety of situations that could force you to revert to a small-scale, home-based business to survive. Consider those possibilities and think through the tools and materials that you would need to operate such a business.

· **CHAPTER 2** ·

FOOD PRESERVATION AND COOKING TOOLS

And ye shall eat old store, and bring forth the old because of the new.

—Leviticus 26:10 (King James Version)

O f all the tools we own, it is usually our kitchen tools that are used the most often. Buy good-quality tools and they will give you a lifetime of service. The other tools that I'll discuss in this chapter are specifically for food-preservation tasks. They are crucial tasks for well-prepared families, putting perishable foods into a form that can be stored for many months or years.

KNIVES

Good kitchen knives are the most important tools that you will need for food preparation and preservation, so don't skimp on quality. My preference is J. A. Henckels, Wüsthof, Hoffritz, or any other genuine Solingen steel knives. Nearly everyone knows the quality and value of these knives, so they are not often available on the secondary market, even at estate sales. But if you watch Craigslist and eBay regularly, you can find some gently used Solingen steel knives at reasonable prices.

For sharpening, I prefer modern diamond sharpening stones, such as those made by DMT. I have one in fine grit and one in extra-fine grit.

FOOD PRESERVATION

Home canning is a subject that would take an entire book to explain in detail, so let me recommend a few good references. The first is *The Encyclopedia of Country Living*, by Carla Emery, from Sasquatch Books. Be sure to get the tenth or later edition.

The second book on canning that I recommend is *Keeping the Harvest*, by Nancy Chioffi and Gretchen Mead, published by Storey Communications.

No kitchen is complete without a copy of the *Ball Blue Book of Canning and Preserving Recipes*. This is the definitive reference of processing times, with calculations to allow for elevation differences.

CANNING EQUIPMENT

Here are a few guidelines to follow when purchasing canning equipment:

- Buy the largest pressure canner that you can afford.
- Tattler brand reusable canning lids are preferred.

- Don't rush the recommended cooldown safety time.

- **NEVER** put a hot pressure cooker under running water or in a sink of cold water to speed up your processing. Doing so might warp the top of your pressure cooker, or cause a rupture that would cause scalding burns.

- Don't rush opening a pressure cooker. Let it cool before you take off the lid.

- Do not guess or rely on your memory for processing time. The *Ball Blue Book* should be your standard guide.

- Don't use water bath canning for processes in which pressure canning is required.

- An inexpensive compact digital timer that clips to your clothes will save you from the potential disaster of forgetting a canner that is boiling on your stove.

- Think outside the box. Canning jars can also be used to store other items that must be protected from moisture, such as salt, spices, and lamp wicking. Just don't be tempted to store matches or ammunition in sealed glass jars, or you will unintentionally be making a grenade that will throw glass shrapnel.

- Mason jars are also great for dry-packing foods that come in flimsy cellophane or plastic packaging, such as beans or pasta. The shelf life if these foods can be further extended by vacuum-packing the jars.

DRY PACK CANNING IN #10 CANS

Here at the ranch, we have a 1980s-vintage hand-crank canning machine that is designed to seal #10 size cans. These cans, which hold almost a gallon, are ideal for long-term storage of rice, grain, and beans. Unlike plastic buckets, which are very gradually air permeable, steel cans are airtight. They are also vermin-proof. These cans are also suitable for long-term storage of ammunition. (Just toss in a

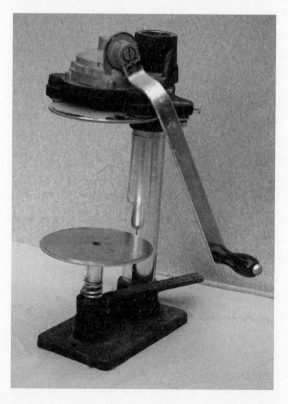

A dry-pack home-canning machine for #10 size cans

packet of silica gel before you seal each can to absorb any ambient air moisture.)

Our #10 canning machine is an Ives Way brand model 809 automatic can sealer. These are out of production, but if you watch eBay and Craigslist diligently, you can often find one for less than three hundred dollars. The cans and lids themselves can be bought wholesale in bulk (boxed in 144-can pallet loads). Be sure to specify cans that are BPA-free. The cans can be reused if the old seam lip is cut off, but they will lose a little height with each iteration.

DEHYDRATING

Home dehydrators are *very* useful! Over the years, we have used ours for everything from drying venison jerky, zucchini chips, and apples to "reanimating" silica gel rust preventive packets.

I recommend the Excalibur brand dehydrator. I would opt for their big 600-watt ED-2900 model. Because they are bulky, they are expensive to ship. So look for a used Excalibur dehydrator on Craigslist or Freecycle. We have an older model here at the Rawles Ranch that has been in regular use for about twenty years. And I expect it to last twenty more!

Most dehydrators require AC power and they draw a lot of current, so in anticipation of the grid going down, you should have a backup solar dehydrator, or at least all of the materials you will need to fabricate one after TSHTF. (Construction details can be found at snipurl.com/2953y3p or at many other Web sites.) Rolls of window screen are great to keep on hand at a retreat. In addition to replacing window screens, extra screening is invaluable for building a dehydrator, a springhouse, or a meat house. You can use the trays from your Excalibur in a properly dimensioned DIY solar dehydrator. Just don't get it over 250 degrees, or the plastic trays will melt.

VACUUM PACKING

For packaging the foods that you dehydrate, I recommend SorbentSystems, in Los Angeles. These vacuum packers use thicker bags than most, which are less prone to punctures and loss of vacuum. SorbentSystems sells a large selection of heavy-duty 6-mil-thickness Mylar bags and a very inexpensive vacuum machine that uses a snorkel to suck out the air. If you're going to be vacuum-packing wet foods, then put a piece of paper towel along the inside of the edge to be sealed to absorb any liquid.

Stock up on plenty of extra bags for your vacuum packer. We prefer to buy the bag material in continuous rolls. We just cut them to size as needed, and make bags of the desired length by sealing one end. We also use our vacuum packer to evacuate the air from canning jars using mason jar adapters. We use two-quart mason-type jars to vacuum-pack lots of foods—mostly grains, beans, and dehydrated apples and tomatoes.

As a backup for periods when grid power is not available, I recommend also buying a Tilia hand-pump sealer. It's a bit more time consuming to use, but it works well and costs just twenty dollars if you shop around.

To save money, it is probably best to buy your vacuum

packer used, through eBay. Just be sure that the seller guarantees it against being DOA (dead on arrival). Test it thoroughly immediately after you receive it. Be advised that vacuum packers are designed to seal only one particular thickness of plastic bags, and they have a limited maximum width. You should shop around for bags and bag material on the Internet, as prices vary dramatically.

THE SOFT ITEMS

In addition to core food supplies, you'll want to stock up on "soft" and perishable items. These include over-the-counter medications, vitamins, chemical light sticks, matches, paper products, cleansers, spices, liquid fuel, and so forth.

You need to exercise caution when stockpiling soft items. Here are some guidelines.

SHELF LIFE AND DETERIORATION

Some items, such as pharmaceuticals, batteries, and chemical light sticks, are best stored in a refrigerator. Keep in mind that items such as matches are vulnerable to humidity and therefore will not keep in a refrigerator or in a humid climate unless in a sealed container. Instead, store them in Tupperware, or in plastic bags—preferably using a vacuum sealer. This is also a great way to keep rubber bands (including elastrator bands) from deteriorating. Exposure to sunlight, heat, or moisture can be deleterious to soft goods.

BULKINESS

Paper products such as paper towels, toilet paper, and paper napkins are extremely bulky per dollar value. If you have limited storage space, then you will need to budget that space carefully. Paper towels are the most versatile, so stock those heavily. You will also want to lay in a large supply of washable cloth utility towels so that you can stretch your supply of paper towels.

FLAMMABILITY

You should think of your stored paper products as house fire tinder, and your stored liquid fuels as potential fire accelerants and explosives. One common mistake preppers make is storing numerous gasoline cans at home in an attached garage. Most garages have a hot water heater, often fired by natural gas or propane. If explosive vapors from your gas reaches the pilot light or a source of an electric spark (such as many electric motors), an explosion could result. Store gas cans, oil-based paint cans, and bulk lubricants only in a well-ventilated outbuilding that is far removed from your residence. Be sure to check your state and local fire codes for permissible limits.

OPERATIONAL SECURITY (OPSEC) RISK

The sheer bulk of stored paper products also makes them obvious to casual observers. This presents an OPSEC risk. If you have five hundred rolls of toilet paper and paper towels in your garage, someone is likely to notice. By the way, one

item that I've stored as a potential barter item is sheet plywood. Those extra plywood sheets, if properly positioned,
can keep prying eyes away from your stockpiles.

ABUNDANCE-INSPIRED WASTE

Human nature dictates that when something is scarce, it is
used frugally, but when it is abundant, it tends to get used
more wastefully. I've seen this happen with my children, in
target practice with .22 rimfire ammunition. If they know
that they have just fifty rounds apiece available for a shooting session, then they are sure to make every shot count. But
if there is a full "brick" of ammo sitting there, it soon starts
to sound like a day at the annual Knob Creek machine gun
shoot.

• CHAPTER 3 •

GARDENING, FARM, AND RANCH TOOLS

I foresaw that, in time, it would please God to supply me with bread. And yet here I was perplexed again, for I neither knew how to grind or make meal of my corn, or indeed how to clean it and part it; nor, if made into meal, how to make bread of it; and if how to make it, yet I knew not how to bake it. These things being added to my desire of having a good quantity for store, and to secure a constant supply, I resolved not to taste any of this crop but to preserve it all for seed against the next season; and in the meantime to employ all my study and hours of working to accomplish this great work of providing myself with corn and bread. It might be truly said, that now I worked for my bread. I believe few people have thought much upon the strange multitude of little things necessary in the providing, producing, curing, dressing, making, and finishing this one article of bread.

—Daniel Defoe, *Robinson Crusoe*

Most machinery used on a farm utilizes impact, cutting blades, mechanical advantage (leverage), or combinations thereof. If you expect to be able to feed your family in lean times, you can't just depend on stored foods. You need to be able to grow a large-scale vegetable garden. That will take gardening tools, stored non-hybrid seeds, good soil, plenty of water, adequate fencing, and lots of practice. It takes years to fine-tune a garden. Part of this is adjusting to the varieties that grow well in your particular climate zones. It also takes years to build up rich soil and to develop multiyear plants such as berry vines and asparagus beds, and especially to grow fruit and nut trees to maturity. Start developing your garden *now*. Don't expect to be able to magically start growing an abundant garden after things get Schumeresque.

HAND TOOLS FOR GARDENING

Reader "Calvinist Cadet" recommends the following for acquiring gardening hand tools:

> Primitive tasks require primitive tools. When endeavoring to prepare for an extended grid-down or without rule-of-law scenario one would do well to have on hand a ready mix of equipment and supplies which can meet the challenges requisite to providing for basic needs. Would-be survivalists often point to hypothetical situations in which they would gather water from some nearby source and make fire within their hastily crafted shelter beside their tilled, loamy garden bed, while butchering game, harvested casually in some illusionary, postapocalyptic Shangri-la. Without primitive or pioneer-type tools, basic human functions can become impossible. A simple and comfortable water pail may someday be a family's lifeline. An ax could be the only tool available with which to harness heat energy or to make shelter. An old and worn kitchen knife could be the only butchering tool.

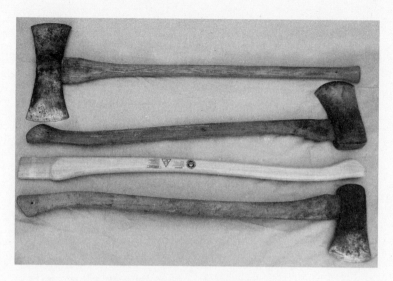

Axes. Don't forget spare handles!

A preparedness mind-set requires that we take advantage of the readily available resources of today and the pioneering knowledge and techniques of yesterday to ready ourselves for a return to the austere conditions our luxurious technologies have overcome. Today, we can walk the lawn-and-garden aisle of a local hardware store and for a couple hundred fleeting U.S. dollars acquire enough tools to provide for many of our needs. Someday soon we may wish we had laid up some of these basic tools. You have an ax, but do you have a maul and wedge? Do you have a froe and mallet (used for making shakes and squaring timbers)? Do you have a rotary grindstone on which to grind your ax, froe, and maul? You have a saw, but what kind? Is it a large crosscut saw for felling trees? Can it cut through metal or remove the head of an elk? A man needs several types of saws for performing these relevant survival tasks.

Today we have Honda-powered garden cultivators to make short work of the backyard garden patch. Now imagine clearing and amending a vegetable patch larger than your entire house lot, in order to feed your family staple foods. And if you manage to clear this area of turf and weeds and rocks enough to support seed plants, you must now weed and aerate and irrigate and fertilize and harvest this vast stretch of ground with just the tools you have in your garage. So you have a spade—do you have a mcleod (a cross between a rake and a hoe, used for ground clearing, trail building, and cutting fire lines), a Pulaski, a mattock, a turf spade, a stirrup hoe, a sling blade, a pitchfork, a grain scoop? These are just a few of the necessary hand tools, which were common on every homestead, even seventy years ago. Go back a few hundred years and the very same tools were also the only weapons on the farm. Take inventory now, acquire what you will need, start using these tools and techniques. Harden your hands and your backs. Ready yourself mentally, physically, and materially for what may lie ahead.

Do you have a sturdy watering can? You'll need one that will not clog or crack if left in the cold. How about a series of rain barrels from which to draw and water your crops? Now, we just move the hose and sprinkler around, twist the faucet, and believe our electric well pump—or, worse, municipal water—will flow and flow and flow. How many barrels do you have in your garage? Are you equipped to catch the rain or snowmelt from your roof? Could you build an elevated (tower) catchment system that could irrigate a broad expanse, without electricity and with the tools and lumber you have on hand? Planning on moving timbers for firewood or building structures? Make sure you have a peavey for log handling and a block and tackle to gain mechanical advantage.

With regard to harvesting timber, we currently lean heavily on our two-stroke chain saws. I know I do—we run a side business selling firewood from our retreat, ensuring that we always have at least ten cords on hand and continue to perfect local, low-tech harvesting and processing methods. Properly viewed, a good chain saw is a pioneer-type tool. The simple two-stroke motor has no circuit boards that would fail in an electromagnetic pulse (EMP) emergency. I would assert that if you have limited fuel-storage capabilities, you store premium, non-ethanol gasoline, mixed with a high-grade two-stroke oil. We have been able to start and run old Stihl two-stroke equipment that sat for years with a 50:1 mixture of Stihl oil and premium non-ethanol, 93-octane gasoline. This oil has a stabilizing ingredient in it, and non-ethanol gasoline is much better for long-term storage than the Al Gore alternative of ethanol "corn gas," which can gum up or go stale in less than six months. If this approach were embraced, a whole other essay could be composed on which two-stroke tools to acquire.

Imagine being able to barter your ability to fall and buck your neighbor's timber or run a two-stroke cultivator through his grass to save hours of shovel work turning a lawn into a garden. The two-stroke concept aside and returning to the basic premise of primitive, nonelectric hand tools for pioneering chores, the notion of bartering your services with these tools and techniques is strong. In the past, neighbors and churches got together to clear a field or build a barn. The Amish still cooperate around shared pieces of equipment and tools.

I consider small bottles of two-cycle fuel (premixed gas

and oil) ideal to keep on hand for barter. This has several advantages: It's compact, lightweight, premeasured, readily recognizable, and likely to be scarce, and it has long storage life and wide appeal.

Imagine the mission field of folks who can't do for themselves, but you show up with a unique tool or ability and exhibit beautiful Christian charity by lending a hand or lending the requisite tool. If the idea of starting now to accumulate all of the tools you may need is daunting, incorporate conversations with your group or family or church friends. Find out how your equipment complements that of others you will depend on in emergencies or after a collapse. Financial resources put into these pieces of equipment will benefit you tremendously even during peaceful and prosperous times. They provide the ability to improve your home, retreat, or garden. There are spiritual and physical benefits of working with your hands and getting a bit dirty. You're learning processes that can provide for your own needs and passing them on to children and friends, preserving the knowledge of the old way of doing things. Every task that was previously performed with the assistance of electricity or electronic modules can and should be rethought

Those individuals with stock animals capable of load work and the accompanying tack and gear will be so much better off. A mule, donkey, draft horse, or ox will be prized much more highly than the show horses and warm bloods that are the status symbols of today's equine societies. If you are a suburban or home-based prepper, be sure you have one or more sturdy wheelbarrows, carts, or sleds. Put away a bicycle pump for airing up the tires when you can't just run over to the filling station to inflate a flat garden cart tire in the spring.

Anything you do not have for survival after TEOT-WAWKI (the End of the World as We Know It) will have to be made, grown, harvested, scavenged, bought, or bartered. Hammers, pliers, pullers, bits and augers—it is almost unfathomable what we take for granted or do not use anymore due to the readily available, Chinese-made, disposable items we use to sustain our everyday comforts and needs. We can go online to Harbor Freight for the disposable equivalent of power tools. Dig a little deeper—we currently have many resources for finding the older, U.S.-made tools that continue to ably do the job they were made for. Pawnshops, Craigslist, garage sales, and even scrapyards can hold tools and equipment that today's consumers don't know the value of. For example:

- A washtub and washboard for clothes cleaning

- A hand-pumping well head and an inventory of piping or trough

- Traditional mechanical farm equipment like plows and threshers

- A drilling brace for drilling holes if your electric drill is useless

How many pounds of nails, screws, spikes, and pegs have you put up? Centuries ago, whole structures would sometimes be burned to the ground so that the nails that held them together could be gathered up and reused.

Remember all those old woodworking tools that your grandfather had and used, in an austere environment? And those primitive files, chisels, and planers will be invaluable. In the fields, all manner of rakes and shovels and picks will be used and broken, then mended or augmented to get the many tasks accomplished. Leatherworking and sewing, hide skinning and tanning, water gathering, shelter building and repair, gunsmithing and reloading, farming, silage harvesting, hauling, candle and soap making, all of these necessary tasks require specialty tools to complete, and in the absence of readily available grid power they become especially daunting. As we ready our retreats, homes, and farms for come-what-may, we must put on an attitude of confident can-do.

Consider realistically what it will take to provide the true necessities and keep the homestead going. When focusing on beans, bullets, Band-Aids, and broomsticks, do yourself, your family, and your community a favor and also prepare for the basic and historical tasks of a more primitive existence.

Five Essential Garden Tools

- Round-point shovel
- Hoe
- Spading fork
- Stiff-tined garden rake
- Trowel

GARDENING BOOKS

Gardening for self-sufficiency on small acreage is best accomplished with extensive use of composting and with either numerous raised beds and square-foot gardening or through the French intensive ("double-dug") method. Some gardening reference books that I recommend are:

The Complete Book of Composting, by J. I. Rodale and Staff

Gardening When It Counts: Growing Food in Hard Times, by
    Steve Solomon

*The Resilient Gardener: Food Production and Self-Reliance in
    Uncertain Times*, by Carol Deppe

All New Square Foot Gardening, by Mel Bartholomew

*Seed to Seed: Seed Saving and Growing Techniques for Vege-
    table Gardeners*, by Suzanne Ashworth

Small-Scale Grain Raising, by Gene Logsdon

A NICE PIECE OF HICKORY

One often-overlooked aspect of gardening tools for hard times
is the importance of laying in a supply of spare implement
handles. Tool handles are typically made of hickory wood.
These handles are difficult for most folks to improvise, especially if you live in a region where suitable hardwoods don't
grow. Buy plenty of spares—both for yourself and for barter
and charity. If stored out of direct sunlight and at moderately low humidly, your spare handles will last for decades.
And if you are blessed with living in a region with sturdy
oak and hickory trees available, then study tool-handle making and fitting under an experienced mentor.

PLOTMASTERS

To bridge the gap between small-scale hand-powered gardening and full-scale tractor farming, I recommend buying a
Plotmaster. This is a combination disk, rake, and grass seeder
that is designed to be towed behind an ATV, a garden tractor,

or a full-size tractor. It is ideal for planting grass or grain on small acreages (one to ten acres). So even if you can't afford to buy a full-size tractor, or even if your acreage is small (which makes running a full-size tractor difficult), you can still raise some grain.

Plotmasters are expensive (around four thousand dollars) if purchased new, but used ones can be found for far less. Back in 2008, we found a used one on Craigslist for just eight hundred dollars, but we had to drive almost two hundred miles to get it. Be forewarned that Plotmasters are *heavy*. You don't just lift one up into a pickup bed with two or three men. It is best to bring a trailer with a low ramp, so that you can roll it on. Even with that, bring plenty of help.

HI-LIFT JACKS

Hi-Lift jacks (also known as farm jacks or sheepherder's jacks) are incredibly useful tools. I find new uses for mine almost every year. I recommend that you buy nothing but the actual Hi-Lift brand jack manufactured by the Bloomfield Manufacturing Company.

Using Hi-Lift jacks is potentially dangerous. Heavy objects falling off of these jacks and out-of-control jack handles have killed a few men and injured many more. Don't allow anyone to use one unless they've been trained in their use. When lifting a load, keep your head or body from being directly above the handle. Make sure you move the handle through the entire range of travel and watch the walking pins to ensure they are engaging the beam holes and are walking up and down the way they should. After you've reached the

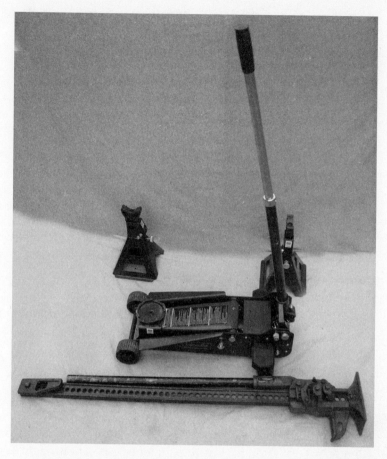

A pair of jack stands, a 3-ton floor jack, and a 48-inch Hi-Lift jack

desired height, *always* leave the handle in the fully up position. Then use a small bungee cord or a Velcro ski strap to secure it in this position. Lowering a load can be the most dangerous process of using a jack. Again, keep your head and body out of range of the throw of the handle. As the handle clicks into position at the bottom of the stroke, the entire load will literally be in your hands. Anticipate the load pushing the handle upward. (This is where most injuries occur.)

Remember that all post-type jacks are unstable. You will need to brace or block the load before you consider getting under a vehicle while using a Hi-Lift jack. Be sure to experiment with these jacks at home, on a level driveway, etc. before ever attempting to use one in the field.

You can download an operation and safety brochure in PDF format from the Hi-Lift site. See snipurl.com/27oll9d.

Don't risk your life using some cheap Chinese copy of a Hi-Lift jack, like those sold at discount tool shops—and good luck getting replacement parts for these! Bloomfield makes rebuild kits and replacement parts for all their products. Always keep a Hi-Lift jack rebuild kit in your vehicle. In addition to lifting your vehicle, these jacks can be used in combination with tow straps or tree straps and used as winches. They can also be used as oversize clamps, presses, and spreaders.

In addition to their vehicular use, we have found our aging but still quite serviceable pair of forty-eight-inch Hi-Lift jacks to be indispensable around the Rawles Ranch. Most frequently, we use them for pulling old fence posts. Bolting on a two-foot length of heavy chain just below the lifting surface (using a steel carabiner or a large grade 8 nut and bolt) adds tremendously to a jack's versatility for tasks like fence post pulling and as a makeshift "come-along" (ratchet cable hoist).

Again, it is important to keep a factory (white box) rebuild kit handy. But the most important thing to bear in mind is to always have the jack's pair of pins well lubricated and free of rust. Typically, owners abuse their jacks, often leaving them out in the rain. The pins rust, and consequently their motion gets stubborn. If a pin then gets stuck in the *out* position while you are lifting a load, it can be a very bad thing.

FENCES

Texas Rancher had the following advice regarding fences:

> We use twisted smooth wire (no barbs) for horse pens but to contain cattle, barbed wire is necessary. Good gloves are essential. Pigskin gloves are very barb resistant. You will be nicked by the barbed wire, so stay current with tetanus shots. Every vehicle on my ranch has a set of fencing pliers and other fence repair items because I have discovered making many small repairs over time to be much easier than waiting for things to get so bad entire fence sections need rebuilding. Making many small repairs over time is also much easier than continually tracking down stray cattle.
>
> Six-wire barbed wire fences are stronger and seem to function longer than those with fewer wires. They also catch more tumbleweeds and blowing debris that in high-wind conditions can act like a sail and bend T-posts. We go on tumbleweed patrol during sustained wind conditions. Many fencing problems are caused by not placing rigid poles (steel pipe, creosote-dipped wood, or cedar) at intervals in a T-post fence. We use six- to eight-inch oil field pipe either driven into the soil with a ram or set in concrete, both at low spots to keep a tight fence from pulling the T-posts up, and on ridges, which

seem to be weak places for wind- and animal-caused shear forces.

We take extra time with T-post clips to ensure both ends are securely wrapped around the barbed wire. This causes the wire to be pulled up tightly against the T-post. It can be tedious but I believe it greatly improves the integrity of the fence. Western Union and other types of splices can work with barbed wire, but I have found pairs of high-tensile crimp-style tube splices per wire splice to be more trouble-free in the long run. A well-built fence (and it must be surveyor straight—vertical T-posts with tops all aligned) will always need less care than a shoddy fence.

At every point where a barbed wire fence changes direction, we use six- to eight-inch pipe braces set in concrete. Such a brace consists of an eight-foot-long vertical pipe at the point of direction change (three feet buried in the ground) flanked by similar pipes in line with the old and new fence directions. The three vertical posts are connected by five-foot runs of horizontal pipe welded a foot below the tops of the vertical pipes. A front-end loader is essential because these thick-walled pipes when welded together into a brace may weigh a thousand pounds. Wooden posts are easier to work with and steeples are easy to use, but nothing lasts like thick-walled oil field pipe. We wrap several turns of a short piece of barbed wire around the vertical pipes, leaving two wire ends, one about two feet long and the other four feet long. The shorter free end is wrapped tightly around the longer end. The fence stretcher and splices are then used to connect the free end of this wire to the long run on down the fence line.

This is the only way I have found to ensure taut wire runs when using metal pipe braces. We strive to get it right the first time.

An assortment of fencing tools and a ratchet tensioner. Note the two different jaw widths on the tensioning tools.

A good-quality fence wire stretcher is also important. T-posts can be difficult to pull out of the ground if a fence line is being moved. We use a T-post puller. Everyone should have a Hi-Lift jack, which works well with a post puller, but if I'm moving a line of fence, I usually have a tractor with a front-end loader on site, so I chain the T-post puller to the front-end loader in order to pull up the posts. The loader bucket is also a good place to store the pulled T-posts. The higher on the T-post the puller is placed, the less chance of bending the post.

LIVESTOCK FENCING

Fencing is crucial for keeping wild critters out and your own critters in, to establish pastures, gardens, and large cultivated plots.

For versatility, my personal favorite fencing is forty-seven-inch-tall variable-mesh woven field fencing, tensioned on six-foot heavy-duty studded T-posts that are spaced ten to twelve feet apart. That is what we use at the Rawles Ranch. It will give you a fence that will hold sheep, some breeds of goats, most cattle, llamas, alpacas, donkeys, horses, mules, and more. I say "most" cattle because larger cattle, such as bison, will require stouter and taller fencing. And some ornery cattle will simply crash through and over a woven-wire fence unless you add an electric wire at the top. Needless to say, bulls of any breed require a very stout pen to contain them seasonally. (Unless you live in a very mild climate where having calves born in January wouldn't be a problem, then you will need to pen your bull for four to eight months of each year to prevent breeding at the wrong time of the year.)

H-BRACES

In my experience, used creosote-soaked railroad ties work fine for H-braces, anchor braces, and corner braces. Owning a proper post-hole digger will save you a lot of time. Ames and several other American companies make quality post-hole diggers. Beware of the newfangled "short stroke" clam-shell diggers, which have a mechanism that only requires the handles to be separated slightly to clamp the blades to-gether. All of these that I've seen are made in China, and they are not built to withstand rough use. Unless or until there is a sturdier alternative, just stay with a traditional clamshell digger. And depending on your soil, an auger might work better for you.

To tension the diagonal wires for the H-braces, I prefer to use steel ratchet tensioners, rather than the traditional "twisting stick" windlass arrangement. Here at the Rawles Ranch, I use ratchet wire tensioners for building fence corners and H-braces, and for tensioning our solar-charged electric fences. I was recently bemoaning the fact that the only tensioners I could find at my local feed store and hardware store were made in China, and priced at nearly four dollars each. So I did some searching and found a mail order company called Zeitlow Distributing Company in McPherson, Kansas (zeitlow.com), that specializes in electric fence products. They sell the Strainrite Tru-Test tensioners, which are made in New Zealand. Note that the Strainrite ratchet tensioners (called "cliplock strainers," in Kiwi parlance) are slightly wider that the typical American ones (such as the old Hayes brand), so you will need a tensioning tool (a.k.a. a ratchet handle) made by Strainrite, or one that is of compatible width.

Note: If you use railroad ties or other treated wood for your H-braces, be sure to wear gloves to avoid skin contact with the creosote, which is toxic.

DIGGING BARS

When building a fence in rocky soil, a seven-foot-long plain digging bar with hardened tips will be indispensable. A mushroom-head tamping bar is also quite useful.

If you get into an extremely rocky portion of ground along the intended fence line, you can construct aboveground "rock boxes"—a type that is commonly seen in eastern Oregon. These are cylinders of woven wire between thirty and thirty-six inches in diameter and four feet tall that you will fill with rocks anywhere from fist-size to bowling ball–size. Because the fence will have to be tensioned, make sure the side of the rock box that will contact the main fence wire has no rock tips projecting through the wire mesh that might hang up the main fence wire as it slides by during tensioning.

"Hot" Wires

Horses in particular tend to be hard on woven-wire fences. Especially in small pastures, they'll often lean their necks over them, reaching for grass on the other side. If you have horses, you can add a "hot" wire at the top of the fence that is energized with a DC charger. In anticipation of grid-down situations, a solar-powered fence charger (such as those made by Parmak, which we use here at the Rawles Ranch; see snipurl.com/27ntrev) is best.

Gates

I like steel-tube gates. If you strap on (or weld on) some woven wire or a hog panel, the gate will become "sheep tight."

For the best security, you should mount the hinge pins with at least one pointing upward and one pointing downward. Otherwise, an intruder can simply lift a locked gate off of its hinge pins. For even greater security, you can also tack-weld the nuts onto both the bolt threads and the gate's hinge sleeve assemblies to prevent them from being disassembled.

TENSIONING

Tensioning a woven-wire fence can best be accomplished with a forty-eight-inch "toothed" bar to hold the woven wire. These can be either bought factory-made or custom fabricated in your home welding shop. But for those without welding equipment, here is a simple expedient that can be made with wood, carriage bolts, and chain: Cut a pair of fifty-two-inch-long two-by-fours and install a row of protruding screws down the length of one of the wide sides. Drill a row of shallow holes in the other board, to accept the screw heads from the first board. (Like the teeth on a commercially made bar, these screws will evenly distribute the stress on the full height of the woven wire.) Drill through holes and position six-inch-long three-eighths-inch carriage bolts through both boards at both ends. Sandwich the woven wire between the two boards. Attach chains to the carriage bolts, and then connect the chains to a come-along. If no large tree is available as an anchor for the tensioning, then the towing hitch receiver on a parked large pickup truck will suffice. The attachment point of the truck's hitch must be lined up within an inch or two of the centerline of your new fence, so that tensioned wire can be stapled to a wooden post and then clipped to the T-posts.

CHAPTER 4

SEWING AND LEATHERWORKING TOOLS

There was another thing that the camels carried, and that was various forms of currency. The currency problem was an important one. Through that admirable institution, the Chinese Post Office, I had been able to transfer the bulk of our capital from Peking to points west by simply paying in a cheque at the Peking branch and then drawing the dollars at Lanchow and Sining. But the Mexican silver dollar which they use in China is a big coin, and the country through which we were to pass had a lawless reputation; a suitcase heavy with silver could not be relied upon to remain indefinitely an asset and might indeed prove a major liability. So we carried the minimum of coin—600 or 700 dollars secreted in different places among our gear. With the remainder of our capital—rather more than a thousand dollars—I had bought in Lanchow a 12 oz. bar of gold which, besides being easily concealed, had the advantage of being negotiable anywhere where a file and a pair of scales were available. For the remoter Mongol communities, who often have no use for gold or silver, we took with us eight bricks of tea and a good deal of cheap

coloured cloth, one or the other of which is always legal
tender.

—Peter Fleming, *News from Tartary* (a book about an
overland journey from Peking to Kashmir in 1935)

The ability to cut and join together leather, fiber, and fabric of course dates back to ancient times. These abilities
and the requisite tools are important for any well-
prepared family. And if we ever live through a time of disrupted commerce, then the ability to make our own clothes,
shoes, boots, animal harnesses, pack, slings, and so forth
will become crucial. In the modern context, a heavy-duty
sewing machine will be your key tool for these tasks.

Industrial Sewing Machines

A sturdy sewing machine is an indispensible tool for well-
prepared families. It is important to be able to mend your
clothing and gear when commercial services are not available. Not only will it provide a measure of self-sufficiency,
but it might also provide a crucial home-based business income in the event of a layoff. It is noteworthy that many
modern electric sewing machines can be converted to run
on an antique treadle base. If a machine is powered by an
outwardly visible belt, then it can probably be retrofitted.

A reader who posted under the pen name Lockstitch had this wonderfully detailed information on finding a used commercial sewing machine:

> I have been using industrial sewing machines of various types for over twenty years now. In that time, I have learned much about what machines to look for, and what machines to avoid. Much of this experience has come at significant financial cost, so I hope to help your readers avoid the mistakes I have made over the years. I have not, however, been able to locate an article specific to machine choice, especially regarding industrial machines. I would caution against the old treadle-style machines. Every well-prepared family should have a good *industrial*-grade sewing machine as part of their preparations. As with most good tools, once you've had one, it's hard to see how you ever got by without it.
>
> Over the years I've owned, used, sold, purchased, borrowed, repaired, and modified approximately twenty machines of various makes and models. I've used button-hole machines, computerized bar tackers, double-needle machines, sergers, chain stitchers, straight stitchers—the list is long. Of all the machines I've owned, one is by far the most useful: a compound-feed, walking-foot industrial sewing machine. For those unfamiliar with sewing machines, let me clarify as best I can and give you some suggestions on where and how to purchase one.

WHAT TO LOOK FOR: INDUSTRIAL

Avoid the temptation to buy an off-the-shelf home sewing machine from the local craft mart or that computerized wonder with a million preprogrammed stitches and fancy zipper feet they're selling on the television shopping network. These machines are great for the hobby quilter or craft enthusiast, and as boat anchors in a grid-down situation. Also avoid the old-fashioned treadle machines of the pioneer days. They're okay if you only intend to sew very thin fabric, but they're nearly useless for sewing heavier materials, and finding replacement parts can be dicey. They also take a considerable amount of technique to use effectively. I own a great old (pre-WWII) industrial long-arm Adler with a treadle. It's superbly made and amazingly durable . . . and unfortunately, it's nearly useless for almost all of the sewing I do.

One of the main reasons to go with an industrial machine is the clutch motor. A good industrial machine will be set in a four-foot by two-foot freestanding table with a large electric motor mounted underneath that transfers power to the sewing machine head via a V-belt (like the fan belt in older cars). It does this through a clutch, usually made of very dense cork. Once turned on, the motor is always spinning at full speed; by depressing the sewing machine's pedal, you bring the two cork plates together, engaging the clutch. This transfers the power through the V-belt to the head and you're in business. The clutch lasts for many years. (I have never had to replace a clutch on any of my machines and I sew on them almost daily.) If you're worried, you can perform a quick test. Sit at the machine with it turned off and try to cycle it by hand. It should difficult. If it isn't, the clutch may be worn. Don't give up on the machine just because of this, however, because motors and clutches are not terribly expensive to replace.

If you've found a great sewing machine with a bad motor or clutch, buy it! You can find new motors all day for around a hundred dollars. (Make sure you buy a single-phase motor, though; there are tons of three-phase sewing machine motors out there, but few shops have three-phase power.) If you are in a long-term grid-down situation, it will be relatively easy to replace the constantly spinning motor with another form of spinning motion. For example, I have found that with some simple modifications, I can rig up a stationary bicycle to spin the electric motor. It takes little effort for someone in your group to pedal the bike while you sew. It's best not to remove the motor, because once you get it spinning, its internal weight acts like a flywheel and helps maintain the torque necessary to keep sewing tough thick materials. If you have one of those old-school exercise bikes with the very heavy front wheel, this may not be necessary, but also consider the advantages of leaving the motor intact if power ever does become available again.

Get the necessary parts and modifications tested and working *before* the balloon goes up, and then squirrel them away. It will probably be very difficult to source the V-belts and associated pulleys, etc., you need after an event. This takes some genuine backwoods ingenuity, but I found all the parts I needed easily from McMaster-Carr online. If you have some junk ten-speed bicycles lying around, and some imagination, you could probably source everything you need from them. If you can spin that clutch disc, you can sew. If all else fails, you can cycle the stitches by hand with the machine's hand wheel and it will still be much faster and stronger than sewing anything by hand.

The whiz-bang computerized machines you buy at the craft store are servo operated these days and will be completely useless without electricity. Some of them can't even be cycled by hand without electricity. They also lack the hardy construction necessary to sew heavy materials such as canvas, webbing, and thick leather without blowing the timing and breaking components. Few things will make you say bad words like repeatedly blowing the timing of your sewing machine or breaking needles when you're trying to finish an important project. Think of those little craft machines like those cute little painted hammers they sell in craft stores. They may be great for putting a tack in the wall to hang a picture, but can you imagine trying to frame a house with one?

A couple of last things to consider: The good older industrial machines are completely mechanical except for the drive motor, so they are impervious to EMP attacks. They will last several lifetimes if properly lubricated and can be configured with various attachments to do a surprisingly wide range of specialized sewing tasks. If you look hard enough, you will find them at incredibly low prices.

IMPORTANT FEATURES

Walking Foot

A "walking foot" sewing machine simply means that when the material you are sewing is being pulled to the rear of the machine by the feet, the needle is in the fabric. This prevents bunching and gathering of the fabric and also greatly aids in keeping the top and bottom pieces of fabric indexed correctly. Having been forced to sew on a non–walking foot machine while employed in college, I will never own a straight-stitch machine that doesn't have a walking foot. If you're unsure if the machine has a walking foot, simply cycle the machine slowly by hand, and you will see if the needle is down in the feed plate when it moves to the rear. If the needle is up out of the fabric and only the presser foot pulls the fabric to the rear, don't buy the machine.

Compound Feed

This term is sometimes used interchangeably with "walking foot," but it actually denotes how many feet the machine has. Look for a machine that has two presser feet, not just one. There will be a rear foot and a front foot. This greatly improves the way the machine feeds thick materials as well as how it handles difficult sewing applications. It'll be a godsend if you use a binding attachment or sew heavy zippers into tents, etc.

Top-Loading Bobbin Housing

This is less critical, but a nice feature to have. It just means that you can access the bobbin (the small spool of thread that feeds the bottom stitch) from the top of the machine, rather than from the side or underneath. It makes bobbin changes easier and it makes clearing the dreaded "bird nests" much easier when they occur.

Reverse

This may sound silly, but there are a bunch of industrial machines out there that do not have reverse. It's like buying a jeep with two-wheel drive. Yes, it's a jeep, but you've just lost so much utility and versatility by not holding out for four-wheel drive. You need reverse to backstitch at the beginning and end of seams so they don't unravel. You can't effectively bar-tack without reverse either, and if you're making any sort of tactical gear, you'll be doing a lot of bar-tacking.

Timing Clutch

File this under really nice to have, but not a deal breaker. The timing clutch is a bearing-actuated clutch that theoretically breaks loose before you can blow the machine's timing if you ever jam the machine while sewing. You then simply cycle the machine slowly forward until the bearings reset, and you're good to go. I've only seen a timing clutch on the old Adler 067 model (of which I have two), but it may be on other good-quality machines as well. It's wonderful if you can find a machine that has it. It's difficult to describe how to look for this feature without photos and a long, confusing explanation, so just ask about it when buying a machine. Don't be surprised if you get a blank stare from the man or woman selling the machine, but ask anyway.

Thread Stand and Bobbin Winder

When looking for a machine, make sure it has a good thread stand that holds at least two one-pound spools of thread. Most will hold three, but two is a must. One feeds the machine while the other one winds the bobbin. Also, it should have a bobbin winder. Many are attached to the table under the hand wheel, but some are built right into the machine head. These are neat little contraptions that wind your bobbin for you while you sew. They run off the drive belt and disengage automatically when the bobbin is full. Unless you plan on storing away an endless supply of prewound bobbins, you'll need the bobbin winder. I use prewound bobbins in production for a number of reasons, but I also have an ample supply of reusable metal bobbins that I can wind myself as needed. Prewound bobbins may not always be available, so it's better to go with a long-term solution.

Once you've procured your machine, find out what length of V-belt it uses and write it on the machine somewhere. Now go out and get one or two extra belts. You can buy sewing machine–specific belts for a ridiculous amount of money, or buy automotive V-belts for a fraction of the cost at your local auto parts store. They last a lot longer too. In fact, I've had to replace only two sewing machine belts in my lifetime. Once replaced with automotive belts, they haven't had to be replaced again. If you can locate them, buy a couple of extra sets of feet for the machine. Get a set of zipper feet in right- and left-hand configurations if you can. If you intend to use a binding-tape attachment for your machine, you'll need a set of special feet for that too. They can be sourced online on the various auction sites, or from industrial sewing machine suppliers. While you're at it, get a bunch of extra needles for the machine in various sizes. I keep a large supply of size 140, 150, and 160 needles on hand. These machines are very strong and will shatter a needle quite easily if you happen to tweak the fabric enough to deflect the needle into the feed dogs. They also become dull over time if you sew a lot of dirty canvas. If you can get the operations manual with the machine, grab it! Most of them are available online, but not all. Many are out of print and cost a mint to get reproductions. The Internet has alleviated some of this, but not in all cases. You *need* the operations manual to make sure you can readjust the machine should you blow the timing. It is not an easy task if you're inexperienced at it. If you can't manage to retime the machine, it will be completely useless.

Industrial sewing machines are very heavy. I put all mine on casters so they can be easily moved around my shop. I highly recommend you do this if the machine you buy doesn't have them. These machines are big and take a lot of space in a small garage. It's very nice to be able to just push them out of the way when they're not being used.

BRANDS

If TEOTWAWKI happened tomorrow and I could save only one machine from my factory, and that machine had to last me the rest of my life, I would grab my old Adler 067. It was the first machine I ever bought and I've sewn well over a million stitches on it. I wish I knew how many pounds of thread I've put through it over the years. In my opinion it's the finest straight-stitch machine ever made. It has all of the things I've listed, and old 067s can be found at an outrageous discount if you look around. The Adler 167 is an outstanding machine as well. My second choice would be one of the older Pfaff industrials, like the 145. It is equal in quality and toughness to the Adler, but it lacks the timing clutch. I also own a couple of Juki machines, and they are great. I have a double-needle and a computerized bar tacker made by Juki and I have no complaints. They are a great value, and if you're going to buy new, that's the way I would go. I highly recommend you buy used, old, and German, but if you do buy new, I'd go with Juki. I've used a few Consew machines over the years and they've been hit or miss. I've used a couple that were good, and I've used a couple that were just dogs. The same goes for Chandler (except the ones that were actually made by Adler). I've never used Singer machines, but if you read the forums, they're really hit or miss too. The consensus seems to be to buy the older machines.

WHERE TO BUY

I've purchased machines from dealers, out of the back of a van, and from Internet auction sites, yard sales, estate sales, and defunct businesses. The Internet auction sites are great, but shipping is often as much as or more than the cost of the machine itself. If you do go an auction site, consider just buying the head unit and then sourcing a stand (table) and motor locally. Search the local classifieds for anything that says "industrial" or "commercial" sewing machine. You can find great deals that are close enough to go pick up. Also, research the sewing machine dealers in your area. Most buy and sell used machines. You'll usually pay more, but they may give you a guarantee on a refurbished machine. They are usually good sources for parts too. Keep a sharp eye out for yard sales and estate sales. Be patient and be creative in your search and you'll find some real gems for a few hundred bucks.

CONCLUSION

I really hope you will consider adding an industrial sewing machine to your list of tools. It will serve you so much better than relying on a small home machine to keep your clothing, tents, backpacks, and other gear in good repair for the long haul. If you take the time to really learn how to use it, it can provide a supplemental income for you now and possibly a life-saving means of barter or income after TSHTF.

• CHAPTER 5 •

SHOP TOOLS AND TOOL MAKING

Bryan Prescot: "When all you have is a hammer, every problem looks like a nail."

Agent Alex Marlow: "Conversely, sir, when you have a nail, you can bang at it all day with a screwdriver, a shoe or your hand and get nothing except hurt. Whereas one good blow with the hammer makes the problem go away for good."

—Michael Z. Williamson, *Do Unto Others*

Your home workshop may prove crucial to your survival and your family sustenance in the years to come. So it is important that you set up your workshop(s) logically and with an efficient use of space. And since we envision a period of time when emergency services may be unavailable or severely degraded, workshop safety will be a paramount consideration.

For your primary sets of tools, buy only those that come from quality brand-name companies. Some good brands include Craftsman (early production only), Crescent, Gear-Wrench, Kobalt, Mac, Proto, SK, and Snap-on. Note that many of the Craftsman (the Sears house brand) tools are no longer U.S.-made, so look on the second-hand market for older-generation Craftsman tools that are marked "Made in USA."

If you check with a mechanic at your local car repair shop, he can let you know the next time a tool company sales-man will be visiting. These are often franchised salesmen who typically drive a regular route, visiting auto, truck, and aircraft repair shops. The salesman probably won't mind if you are there to place your own order. After all, most of these men are independent and have an entrepreneurial spirit. You will have a knowledgeable seller, and you will be getting the same discounted price as the mechanics. Best of all, the tools are often delivered free of charge. Tools are heavy to ship, so this is a big advantage. But you may have to wait until the next time the salesman passes through town to take delivery.

Shop Tools You'll Need

SOCKET SETS

Most folks can get by with just one ⅜-inch drive set and one ½-inch drive set. A ¼-inch drive set is necessary only if you do a lot of electronics work, and a ¾-inch drive set is neces-sary only if you do a lot of heavy equipment work. If pos-sible, buy both standard-depth and extra-deep sockets for each size, and both ASE ("inch") and metric sockets.

Spare sockets are not normally needed (quality tools rarely break), although it is possible to strip out sockets that are ¼-inch size or smaller if over-torqued, so take care when using sockets on the smaller end of the spectrum.

WRENCHES

Adjustable Wrench

An adjustable wrench—commonly called a Crescent wrench, in honor of the original brand—is handy for short-duration home projects. These are also often called monkey wrenches or "knuckle bangers," because they tend to slip at unexpected times. Adjustable wrenches are no substitute for a proper socket set, but they are still useful. You can adjust the open end of the wrench by rotating a threaded adjusting thumb-pad screw. These wrenches are available in a wide variety of sizes. My smallest is less than three inches long, and my largest is fourteen inches. Most of mine are the original Crescent brand.

Box and Open-End Wrenches

Buy a full set that ranges from quarter-inch to one-inch, and a set of metric equivalents.

Torque Wrenches

A half-inch torque wrench (click type) is a must if you are going to do any automotive mechanics or will be doing any rifle barrel gunsmithing. With most brands, it is important to store these with the handle cranked down, or they will lose their calibration. However, those made by Precision Instruments do not need to be turned down after use.

Allen Wrenches

Buy plenty of Allen wrenches—both ASE and metric—since these are high-loss, high-wear, and high-breakage tools, particularly in the smaller sizes. You may also have to occasionally shorten a wrench or screwdriver (typically with an abrasive cutoff wheel) to get clearance in very tight spaces, so it is a good idea to buy a spare set of imported "cheapo" wrenches for just this purpose. (In all other cases, my motto is "Cheap tools are for chumps.")

TIP

There are also Allen screws on some machinery that chronically work themselves loose because of vibration. If this is the case for one of your machines, you will want to tape spare wrenches and spare Allen screws to the frames of your equipment. This can be a lifesaver when you are out in the middle of nowhere!

Oil Filter Wrenches

I like the type with a steel handle attached to a heavy cloth belt. Not only are these non-marring, but they are also the most versatile. But if you prefer a metal wrench that is sized for a particular filter, then I recommend the Superb Wrench brand, since they are American made. See superbwrench.com.

SCREWDRIVERS

Every workshop—or toolbox, for that matter—needs to have both Phillips and flat-head (slotted) screwdrivers with a variety of bit sizes for each. There are other types of screwdrivers as well, such as hex and Torx, for more specialized uses. Phillips and flat-head are the most common.

A nut driver works just like a screwdriver, but has a

socket at the end for tightening and removing nuts, as with a socket wrench.

A six-in-one driver is a screwdriver with six interchangeable attachments: small and large flat-head driver bits, small and large Phillips bits, and two sizes of nut-driver bits. I keep one in each of my vehicles. This is the screwdriver that I find myself reaching for the most often. Buy several of them when you find them on sale.

Hollow Ground Screwdrivers

Standard, mass-produced screwdrivers have tapered sides. This means that unless they are individually reground they won't fit screw slots properly and hence they will "cam" out, which can destroy a screw head. Instead, buy what are termed "hollow ground" screwdrivers. These are specially ground to have straight sides for the portion that engages the screw slot. While these screwdrivers cost more, they will save you a lot of aggravation in the long run.

Offset Screwdrivers

These are stubby screwdrivers that have their last inch bent ninety degrees, thus allowing you to work in very tight spaces. Buy two of each, both standard and Phillips.

Magnetic Tip Screwdrivers and a Large Assortment of Bits

Buy plenty of spare bits, since they do wear out. And buy at least one assortment of "high-security" bits with all the strange profiles (triangular, etc.). By the way, the Chapman Manufacturing Company (chapmanmfg.com) makes a fantastic compact ratcheting offset handle that is included with each of its screwdriver sets, so be sure to get one of these sets as a starting point for your collection of screwdriver bits. Chapman's Master Kit 5575 is excellent. It includes standard flat blades and Phillips, Robertson, Torx, as well as both ASE and metric Allen-style bits. Also buy several sets of small precision screwdrivers for small applications such as eyeglasses.

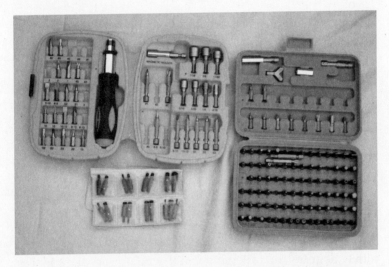

Ratchet screwdriver and assorted screwdriver tips. Buy plenty!

WHEN YOU *DO* WANT CHEAP TOOLS

While I generally shun cheap tools, I do keep a few inexpensive screwdrivers and wrenches on hand to shorten (for working in tight spaces) or to modify for a specific project. This usually involves grinding a different profile on a tool blade or shortening its handle, effectively destroying its usefulness for most other purposes. It would be almost criminal to do this to one of my nice Craftsman tools, but I feel no remorse whatsoever if this surgery is done on a "cheapie" imported tool that I pulled out of some dollar bargain bin at my local NAPA store or that I bought used at a garage sale for fifty cents.

EXTRACTION TOOLS

EASY-OUT SCREW EXTRACTORS

Buy at least a seven-piece set, but if you can afford it, get a thirty-five-piece set made by Irwin Hanson. When you need these, you *really* need these, and there is no good substitute. The short easy-outs are particularly useful, and sometimes the left-hand twist drill bits just by themselves will do the trick.

PLIERS

Buy plenty—preferably two of each. As a minimum: standard, Channellock, vise grips, fencing pliers, and needle-nose.

Also useful: inside and outside circlip (snap-ring) pliers. Buy at least one pair of each.

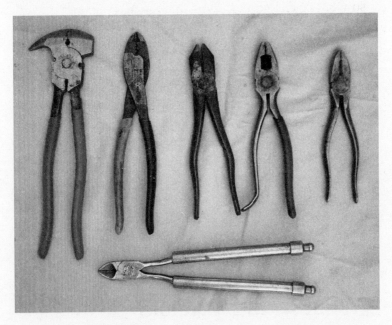

You will need a variety of pliers and wire cutters. Note the modified handles on the wire cutters and on the large pliers, to provide extra leverage.

THREAD REPAIR

The ability to recut threads is essential.

If your budget allows it, buy a thread-repair kit with a wide variety. I like the ones made by Heli-Coil. But even if you are on a tight budget, you can afford a screw-thread-restoring universal sixty-degree angle file. (These are commonly called thread-chasing files.) Silver Seal made the one that I use.

Thread-pitch and feeler gauges are very handy. You will also want a wire strand set of thread checkers. See snipurl. com/27lz9wc.

Cutting Tools

You will of course want a variety of saws, including a hacksaw. For the latter, you will want a large quantity and variety of spare blades.

I would recommend finding good-quality examples of the following handsaws:

- Crosscut saw

- Rip saw

- Plastic pipe saw

- Back saw

- Keyhole saw

- Hacksaw

TIP

When cutting plastic, you will want to cut slowly, so that the friction doesn't melt the plastic.

HARDWARE

Buy fasteners in bulk, whenever and wherever you can find them at bargain prices. Also look for hinges, gate hardware, turnbuckles, timber spikes, springs, lengths of chain (with links of various weights), cotter pins, door latch hardware, spools of wire (various gauges, both insulated and uninsulated), and so forth. There is great value in redundancy, and hardware is a prime example. Even if you don't find everything you need, there is a good chance that you will later be able to barter with what you do have.

Whenever I go to a garage or estate sale, I always ask: "Do you have any kegs or boxes of nails, spools of wire, or any coffee cans full of nuts and bolts for sale?" The answer is often yes, and the price is usually at or below the price of scrap steel. Stock up! As long as this hardware is not rusty, with a light coat of oil to prevent oxidation it will prove more valuable than money in the bank.

BATTERY-POWERED HAND TOOLS

For battery-operated power tools, I decided to standardize with DeWalt 18-volt tools. Of course, there are several other comparable brands, such as Ryobi. I like DeWalt because of their quality and the ready availability of a 12-volt charging adapter to charge their 18-VDC batteries. This makes them ideal for use with an alternative power system. For most of my 12-VDC tools and gadgets, I cut in near the end of the cords and add a pair of Anderson Powerpole connectors.

This allows me to use either the original cigarette lighter plug in a vehicle or an Anderson Powerpole connector with my home, shop, and Bad Boy Buggie 12-VDC power systems.

An assortment of DeWalt 18-VDC battery-powered tools and chargers (both AC and 12-VDC)

I'm fairly confident that following the current offerings of 18- and 20-volt tools, a new generation of 24-VDC battery tools will be developed, and those will eventually dominate the market.

> **TIP**
>
> To determine how much current each of your power
> tools and battery chargers draws, I recommend
> getting an inexpensive Kill A Watt power monitor
> (snipurl.com/286vjh3). These are crucial for "sizing"
> your alternative power system.

Useful References

Pocket Ref, by Thomas J. Glover. This small book has 864 pages
of facts, formulas, tables, constants, and so forth. Be sure to
get the fourth edition (or newer). It is available—along with
many other useful shop references—from Victor Machinery
Exchange. See snipurl.com/27lzahv.

And speaking of references, get a drill-bit-diameter and
resistance-reference-table card for wire gauges. This is a frequently used reference, so I bought a magnetic one and I
leave it inside the top lid of my main tool chest.

Chisels and Punches

As with pry bars, I generally look for these used at garage
sales, estate sales, and farm auctions. Because these are high-
wear impact tools, it is best to find yourself four or five of each
small-diameter punch, two or three of each large-diameter
punch, and perhaps as many as six or seven cold chisels. If
you buy new cold chisels, then I recommend the Mayhew
brand.

Buy lots of punches in all sizes, from tiny pin punches up to three-quarter-inch diameter, and with a variety of head shapes to handle the widest range of work.

The Tops Knives brand pry-probe-punch tool is a handy American-made tool that is a cross between a punch and a nail puller. Its back end is a hardened pointed punch that can also be used to shatter tempered glass.

TIP

If you buy a used punch or chisel, chances are that even if its blade is still sharp, its back end will be deformed into a mushroom shape, from long use. It is important to grind off any overhanging mushroomed lips. Grind them down with a bench grinder until they are flush with the shaft. Failure to do so could be an invitation to eventual failure of the mushroom, turning a piece of it into a projectile when struck.

Next is a six-inch dial micrometer. I may be old-fashioned, but I prefer traditional dial micrometers to the electronic ones. (The latter, of course, require a battery.)

TIP

Buy a one-inch micrometer; keep it stored in your drill register so you can regularly check to make sure that your drills haven't narrowed from their proper outer dimension with use.

Another must is a gear-puller set. For these, I prefer PTC or Snap-on brands.

FILES

Files are the crucial tools for hand-shaping metal. With enough time, and in well-trained hands, a hand file can accomplish an astonishing number of machining tasks. If you work deliberately and check your dimensions frequently, you can make nearly any part out of the requisite piece of bar stock.

File card. A file card is a specialized brush used to maintain hand files.

Dremel tool. Dremel is the brand name of a handheld, very high-speed cutter/grinder/sander/drill. Dremels (and their generic equivalents) are incredibly useful. I highly recommend them.

Abrasives. You will need a large supply of sandpaper, steel wool, stones, and hones.

GENERIC GUNSMITHING SUPPLIES

You will need cotter pins, roll pins, an assortment of coil spring stock (which can be cut to length), a gun screw assortment, and some cold-bluing formula.

PRY BARS AND HEEL BARS

Find pry bars and heel bars of various lengths. It is best to buy these used. A heel bar is a long metal bar with a fat end that looks almost like the head of a railroad spike, which gives it great leverage. It is particularly useful in working on automobile brake assemblies.

SHEET METAL CUTTING SNIPS

You will need a variety of snips for sheet metal. These should include:

- Flat-cutting aviation snips
- Left- and right-curve aviation snips
- Straight-point aviation snips
- Large tin snips

MEASURING AND MARKING

MEASURING TAPES

A thirty-footer will suffice for most projects, but you will need a hundred-foot tape for laying out landscaping or large structures. Stanley makes some of the best.

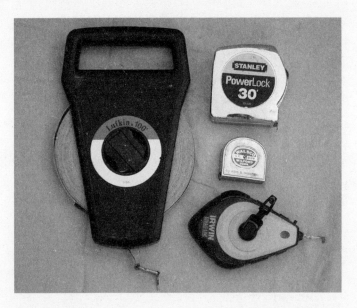

Tape measures and a chalk line box. The latter can double as a plumb bob.

PENCILS

Get both traditional carpenter's pencils (for rough framing) and mechanical pencils for precise work.

CHALK LINE REEL

Most chalk line reels are made in the shape of a plumb bob, so that they can serve dual purposes.

LEVELS

Buy at least one two-foot level and one four-foot level. That set will leave you ready for most jobs.

Shaping and Smoothing Tools

- Drawknife
- Box plane
- Large smoothing plane
- Sanding blocks
- Shingle froe
- Large assortment of sandpaper in various grits

A pair of traditional drawknives

An assortment of wood planes and shaping tools

IMPACT TOOLS

HAMMERS

You will need several hammers of various styles and weights—all the way from light tack hammers to sledgehammers. Be sure to have at least two claw hammers and a gunsmithing hammer with replaceable head pieces.

RUBBER MALLETS

Rubber mallets have many purposes. They are particularly useful for final fitting adjustments in cabinetmaking and other fine woodworking without marring visible surfaces.

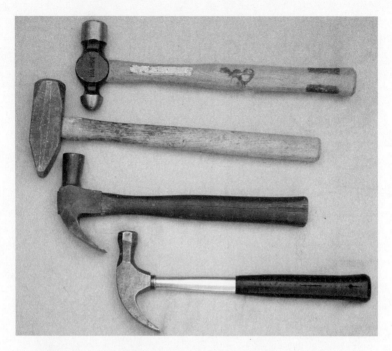

Hammers. A variety of tasks will require a variety of hammers.

WOODEN MALLET AND FROE

Traditional cylindrical wooden mallets might look archaic, but they are surprisingly useful. These are typically used to drive a wood chisel or a shingle froe.

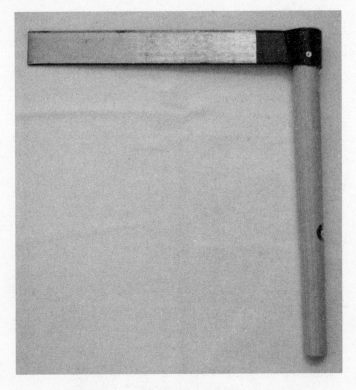

A shingle froe

DRILLS

CORDLESS DRILL

A cordless drill is indispensable for both drilling holes and driving screws. But also find a reversible *corded* drill to use for any large-scale production projects that would otherwise eat up all of your batteries.

HAND DRILL

Have an old-fashioned "eggbeater"-style hand drill for that worst-case situation in which you have neither AC nor DC power. You will also want to be sure to find a traditional bit and brace for larger hole boring.

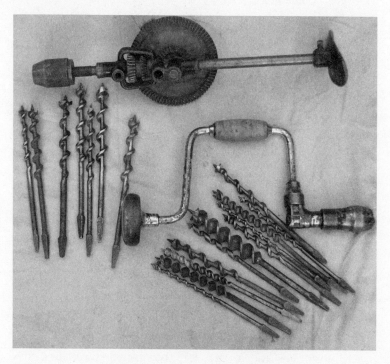

Traditional hand drills and bits

Note that most traditional braces or chest braces use different-style bits with flared shanks; therefore, they are not compatible with modern straight-shank drill bits.

For all of your drills, buy *lots* of drill bits with plenty of spares, especially for the smaller diameters, which are the easiest to break.

A 115-piece drill bit register

PLUMBING TOOLS

Plumbing tools are fairly simple in construction, but difficult to improvise. I recommend stocking up on the following:

- An assortment of pipe wrenches (a pair of ten-inch wrenches and a pair of eighteen-inch wrenches covers most jobs)
- A basin wrench
- A tubing cutter with several spare wheel blades
- A propane torch

- Propane cylinders (buy several—watch for them in summer camping sales in the sporting goods section of department stores)

- A MacCoupler (a cleverly designed adapter that allows you to refill one-pound propane cylinders from twenty- to forty-pound tanks; see maccoupler.com)

- Low-lead solder

- Emery paper

- Steel wool

- Copper brushes

- *Lots* of copper, steel, PVC, and ABS pipe, as well as a generous supply of elbows, caps, tees, reducers, etc., in various diameters

- Teflon pipe tape

- Pipe sealant (white goop)

- PVC purple primer

- PVC adhesive (clear)

- ABS adhesive (black goop)

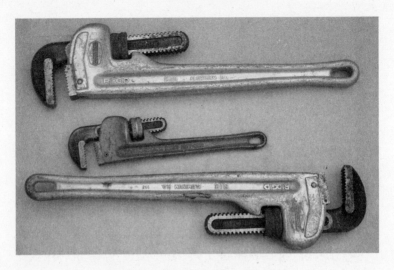

Pipe wrenches. Buy them in pairs.

MISCELLANEOUS HAND TOOLS

You will also need:

- A combination square and a framing square
- Box cutter/linoleum cutter with lots of spare blades
- Cabinet scraper
- Putty knife
- Utility knife
- Electrician's knife
- Large assortment of clamps

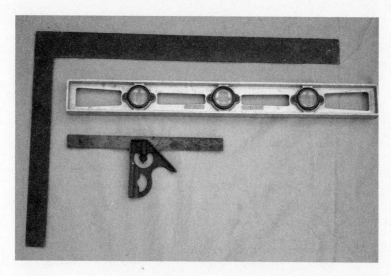

Squares and levels are a must

TOOL MAKING

Detailed instructions on making tools from scratch goes beyond the scope of this book. But I can give you some general guidance:

- Recognize the importance of the tools that can be used to *make* other tools. A lathe and milling machine are priceless assets for tool making.

- A forge, anvil, hammer, tongs, and hand files can be used to make a surprising variety of hand tools. What you lack in precision you can make up for with patience and a hand file. (Hammer out what you need slightly oversize, and then file it to the correct dimensions.)

- Have plenty of raw materials. To make your own tools, you will need lots of steel of all lengths, thicknesses, and profiles.

- There is always a trade-off between dollars and time. Yes, it would be great to own both an Atlas lathe and a Bridgeport milling machine. But not everyone can afford them, nor does everyone have the space to store and operate them. If you lack these tools, you can make up for them with creativity, time, and sweat. Given enough time, a hacksaw, a small assortment of hand files, and *hours* of labor, you can make a huge variety of tools. To illustrate, do a Web search on the phrase "Peshawar gun factory" (without quotes).

· CHAPTER 6 ·

ELECTRICAL AND ELECTRONICS TOOLS

Dr. Watson (Nigel Bruce): "How does the, the thing work?"

Sherlock Holmes (Basil Rathbone): "Electricity: The high priest of false security."

—From the film *The Pearl of Death* (1944)

In an ideal self-reliant world, we would all have simple low-tech alternatives to every electronic and electrical device and system that we've become dependent on in our modern lives. We get a taste of this lifestyle when camping, backpacking, vacationing abroad, or traveling to out-of-the-way places with more primitive services in terms of electrical provisioning and gadgetry. We can make up for a certain amount of technology with well-practiced survival skills that are routinely used and proven. However, this aim of primitive simplicity, while a worthy element in an overall goal of simplification, isn't particularly practical, even in a fully off-grid, back-to-basics, self-sufficient purist lifestyle.

Consider what it takes to both power and maintain all of

your electronic items. When possible, buy 12-VDC-compatible electronics, so that you can power them with your alternative power system or when you are on the road.

Four important criteria for electrical and electronic equipment and tools are: necessity, efficiency, reliability, and cost-effectiveness. Incorporating all of these factors into a home self-sufficiency plan provides an optimum mix and the best use of your time, money, and efforts, for you, your family, and your community.

MAKE A LIST OF ELECTRICAL NECESSITIES

It is helpful (and eye-opening) to make a list of "must-have" electrical and electronic items for actual survival, then add the optional "nice-to-have" semi-essentials and, finally, the luxuries.

With each passing decade, there is a diminishing number of old-timers who can recall an era of simpler technology, let alone a nonelectric or nonelectronic lifestyle. We can learn from history by "turning back the clock" to see how best to use appropriate electrical technology as it has impacted our lives, by looking at modern conveniences such as lighting, refrigeration, water heating, space heating and cooling (including electric fans and air-circulation systems of all sorts), electric (and fossil-fueled) cooking, water pumps (especially well pumps), clothes washers and dryers, dishwashers, microwave ovens, vacuum cleaners, irons, and much more. Turning back the clock means simplifying our lives, reverting to some hand- or treadle-powered tools and appliances, and reducing the amount of electrical current that we use daily. Not only are repairs easier, but lower electricity usage also means that alternative energy systems (such as photovoltaics) can be scaled smaller, reducing cost.

A useful way to prioritize your checklist for electrical self-sufficiency is to think of which conveniences you would find most inconvenient to live without if your current system were to fail, either due to normal wear and tear or power failure or any other issue(s) that might render your current appliance or tool inoperative. For each item, consider how many months, weeks, days, hours, or even minutes you could go without. This exercise will help you to establish your priorities.

Think about the electrical and nonelectrical items in your house. What electrical and nonelectrical tools, equipment, and supplies are needed for maintenance, cleaning, repair, re-placement, or other servicing that maintains the value of each item? For example, carpeting is not an electrical item, but ac-quiring and maintaining a vacuum cleaner that keeps your carpeting serviceable, and the tools that keep your vacuum cleaner serviceable—even if these are only rarely needed—are all part of the system. Bags and belts are often part of the provisions in the nonelectrical department, but what about spare bulbs (if your vacuum uses one) and spare cords (if the current one were to get damaged or frayed)? If you wanted to vacuum something outside your house or outbuildings, do you have long-enough extension cords on hand? How about outlet strips to add to the end of an extension cord that would power both a soldering iron and a mechanic work lamp for a nighttime emergency repair on a car or truck?

Let's back up a bit and consider what constitutes a real need, according to Abraham Maslow's classic hierarchy of needs (snipurl.com/27k81pc is a good reference to keep in mind). The most crucial items in Maslow's list include air, water, food, sleep, excretion, and homeostasis (such as relative stability of light, temperature, humidity, and other atmospheric and environmental parameters). Fortunately most folks don't require CPAP (continuous positive airway pressure) or concentrated oxygen technology to breathe, but dependence on respiratory equipment is a concern for a significant percentage of the population, particularly the elderly. Similarly, medical equipment that uses utility grid power or batteries that are biological necessities must be on the "crucial" list.

If your water supply depends on pumped water from a well, then having even a simple backup like a one- or two-gallon well bucket (snipurl.com/27kepnt) and an appropriate length of rope, plus basic electrical and plumbing tools and supplies, wire, etc., to keep a well pump and domestic water system working might be inexpensive peace-of-mind investments. Even those fortunate enough to have a gravity-fed water system that doesn't depend on any water pumping for domestic water needs might still want to look at their systems for water filtering and purification for potable water and flow controls for garden and orchard irrigation, pets, livestock, etc.

The gadgetry in your kitchen and pantry used for food storage, preparation, and disposal is likely to be one of the largest parts of your electrical appliance and equipment list. Although you might not be able to fully repair and service as many of these items as you'd like, having tools and supplies such as a few spare electrical cords, circuit testers, volt-ohm meters, etc., can afford some of the more basic repairs if you're in a situation in which you need to repair your equipment yourself.

If you use humidifiers, dehumidifiers, or other gadgets to help you get to sleep, sleep well, or wake up, make note of those systems and what is required to keep them functioning. If your waste water/gray water and/or septic/sewer system requires any sort of maintenance, keep in mind the tools and equipment you need to keep those systems working effectively; it doesn't take long for a backed-up septic system to become a high household priority!

That's just a very quick overview of the "crucial need" category. As we progress to the less crucial areas of Maslow's pyramid, we find less urgent needs that are still immediate, such as safety, security, grooming, income/employment, health and property maintenance, etc. Electrical systems in this category can include everything from livestock fence chargers to motion-detecting video surveillance/intrusion/alarm systems, combined photoelectric-ionization smoke alarms, carbon monoxide and ozone detectors, security timers, home automation systems that control vacation lighting, etc.

Of equal importance are any items in the support category that keep your family's income and cash flow in the green, regardless of whether you work at home or commute, in which case the entire automotive sector becomes higher in priority. Don't forget to peruse your garage for items that support your transportation needs, such as battery trickle chargers, tire pumps, road safety flashers, etc.

The grooming and health maintenance category includes items like electric toothbrushes and razors (a watt or two each, but often plugged in 24-7), and hair dryers (these typically use about a kilowatt, but are only on a few minutes a day). Nonelectric backups for these bathroom gadgets are often simple and inexpensive, and replacements and spares don't usually break the bank.

The next level of items in Maslow's need hierarchy are more intangible, such as family, friendship, intimacy, peer respect, career, achievement, and creativity. While these are more long-term, systemic needs, they also should be addressed in any complete plan for sustainable home self-sufficiency. Electronics here would certainly include our personal electronics such as computers, tablets, smartphones, televisions, radios, games, and peripherals. These devices have become more and more important not only to our social lives and home entertainment, but to our livelihood as well.

If your livelihood—or even just basic communication with the rest of the world—depends on your home computer network, consider investing in an uninterruptible power supply (UPS) with enough capacity (rated in volt-amperes, or VA) to safely close files, quit applications, and power down the system including modem, router, powered USB hubs, etc., for each computer workstation in your home. A UPS is cheap insurance, for your data and lost time as well as for minimizing potential hardware damage due to power surges, brownouts, etc. UPS systems are available at all major office supply stores, computer stores, and many large hardware stores. APC is the industry leader and makes some of the best.

If your essential communications equipment also includes a smartphone and/or tablet, consider a portable solar charging system. Modern photovoltaic (PV) technology makes a quick backup battery charge through a sunny window an easy way to provide vital communications backup (for home or remote use) as well as lower your monthly utility charges. Ready Made Resources (readymaderesources.com) is just one company that sells PV battery chargers ranging from five watts on up.

For backing up data, USB thumb drives are now *very* affordable and transportable for vital files. Download and print manuals for all vital electrical and electronic devices for when power systems and/or network connections fail. Spare USB headsets with boom mikes (for Skype, Google+ hangouts, etc.) can keep your communications going. Keep spares, tools, and equipment needed to maintain any ham radio or walkie-talkie gear.

As an addendum, you might want to make another list that includes items that can be used with or without utility grid or even off-grid power. Examples of these hybrid electric and nonelectric items might include grain mills with a hand-crank option, battery or hand-crank flashlights and radios, small solar battery chargers, solar-charged anything that you use routinely, food dehydrators with a nonelectric heat source, etc.

ELECTRICAL SAFETY

Before making any changes, additions, or alterations to your home electrical and electronic systems, routines, practices, and procedures, note all safety warnings on components, maintenance supplies, and tools. For example, having a well-ventilated environment for soldering will minimize lead exposure. Making sure that all your wiring projects meet all applicable building codes and safety standards *and* honor both the spirit and letter of those codes and regulations will reduce fire hazards. When installing or wiring electric components, double-check everything *before* applying power to make sure no components are installed backward (i.e., reversed polarity), which might cause an explosion and/or fire. When opening any high-voltage circuit enclosure, wait a few minutes, then use an insulated wire to discharge electrolytic capacitors. Play it safe, live long!

ELECTRICAL EFFICIENCY

If you're in a situation in which you're going to be rationing electricity, it's imperative that each of your devices be as efficient as possible so that you get the most out of your limited supply.

Look at your list and rank how long you can tolerate going without a particular item. Place the items with the shortest "can't do without" times at the top and start searching for the most electrically efficient candidates for each item. Since efficiency is typically correlated with well-thought-out design, saving kilowatt-hours often translates to saving money on premature replacement costs as well, since electrical components that don't squander their incoming power on waste heat usually outperform their more most wasteful counterparts in terms of life expectancy as well.

RELIABILITY

If you choose equipment and appliances that are well built and designed to last a long time, the need for maintenance, repair, and replacement can often be minimized. In addition to relying on consumer reviews, ratings, and reports, a good rule of thumb to follow is to buy the simplest device you can. A device with one moving part will last longer than one with dozens or hundreds.

Another factor to consider is the stability, likely longevity, and historical track record of the company that manufactures the product, as well as those who make all the various subcomponents, so that when it comes time to replace or repair either part or all of an electrical item you'll be confident the vendor will be around to provide assistance.

Check reviews online as well as recommendations from friends, relatives, and others in your community that might have long-term experience with any tool or gadget on your list for consideration.

COST-EFFECTIVENESS

Buying cost-effective electronics is trickier than it might first appear. As anyone who has ever purchased a cell phone or a computer printer will attest, ongoing costs can quickly surpass initial purchase price, as in the example of monthly usage and data charges for cell phones and printer cartridges for printers. The often-overlooked ongoing cost of the electricity and replacement costs to run a device can also rapidly outstrip the price of the item. A case in point is the incandescent light-bulb, which typically requires replacement ten times as often and costs four times as much in electricity compared with a compact fluorescent bulb.

If you want to measure how much your present 120-VAC appliances are using, devices like the Kill A Watt can help analyze actual electrical use and help you to make informed decisions about what items to upgrade to more efficient and cost-effective alternatives. The win-win-win combination of efficiency, reliability, and long-term cost-effectiveness generally go together, and can often offset slightly higher initial purchase prices.

BACKUPS AND SPARES

Keep in mind that all tools and technologies eventually wear out, some sooner than others. Relying on any one specific device, gadget, or system for crucial needs is just silly. Multiple backups of both the same technology and different technology are recommended for any system in your life that is vital to your well-being and survival, and not just electrical items, of course. For example, if you have (along with a well-stocked drill index) a utility power drill, consider having a cordless drill and perhaps a good old-fashioned brace and bit.

SHARED RETREAT OR NEIGHBORHOOD TOOLS

As for having multiple backups of the same technology, consider how convenient it might be to borrow one from a neighbor by prior arrangement. Imagine what a great backup system you'll have if you make friends with like-minded neighbors and slightly more distant community members (for less frequently needed tools) and plan—in advance!—to collaborate and share equipment as needed.

Several years ago, after looking at our finite resources, we arranged with neighbors to share the cost and maintenance of grading caterpillar tractors, garden tractors, a log splitter, a rototiller, and other gardening equipment by carefully deciding how we would select, purchase, share, store, and maintain this equipment. Now we've all reaped the benefits of these self-sufficiency items for many years without each having to have one that sits dormant most of the year or season in the garage, shed, or whatever. This actually enabled us to have greater rather than fewer resources, both financially and otherwise. With the money we saved, we were able to duplicate the smaller, less expensive tools that it would be a nuisance to have to borrow—a win-win combination. It also allowed us to purchase more reliable, high-performance, cost-effective shared equipment than we would have been able to afford on our own.

Obviously this approach will be less useful if you live on your own private island or are miles from your nearest neighbor, but it's always a good idea to know your neighbors and see where the altruistic spirit might lead in terms of collaboration. Try starting a conversation off with "If you ever need to borrow a . . ." or, if you prefer not to lend out your tools, "If you ever need help with . . ." It's a great way to not only build friendships but also minimize needless expenses. Does every house on the block really need to have its own snowblower?

120-VAC ELECTRICAL PROJECTS: TWO IMPORTANT RULES

Don't be a hero. If you are unfamiliar with electrical wiring, or have the slightest doubt as to your understanding or ability, *always* consult with a licensed electrician *before* beginning a project that could possibly endanger you, your family, your home, or your community. Electrical fires from improper wiring can burn down a home just as easily as matches and gasoline. Also, common household voltages are often lethal if they travel through the heart. Why take chances if you're not sure? Get expert advice and play it safe.

Turn off the circuit breaker! Before doing *any* work on common alternating current (AC) house wiring projects, *always* make sure the circuit breaker to the circuit you are about to work on is off; plug in a lamp and a circuit tester to make doubly sure that all electricity is off. Every member of the family needs to be told that you are working in wiring and to *not touch* the circuit breaker box. Use a piece of masking tape over the applicable breaker switch levers with a "DON'T TOUCH!" warning boldly penned on it. Note that in many jurisdictions, formal "lock-out/tag-out" procedures are required for any commercial electrical project.

HOW-TO VIDEOS AND TUTORIALS ONLINE

It would take another book—or more—to detail even an abbreviated assortment of "how-tos" for the most common wiring projects, including 120-VAC and all the myriad electrical and electronic projects one might consider. Take advantage of the wealth of videos online (Google is your friend here) as well as your public library and whatever other resources you might have. Do you know an electrician? Start there! Be sure to do due diligence. You may discover and explore options you might not have considered. Always ask for help when you're not 100 percent confident about what you've wired, or if you are about to wire something new.

YOUR HOME ELECTRICAL TOOL KIT

An ordinary metal or plastic tool kit can serve as a convenient way to keep common tools and supplies together and handy. Even if you have another tool kit for general construction projects, having a separate kit, kept in an easy-to-access location, just for electrical projects can be quite helpful and convenient. A tool kit like this might include—but not be limited to—the following.

There are some tools and supplies that you will need for making AC home wiring repairs, and to do tests or enhancements. These include:

Circuit tester—for quick checks to see whether an outlet is activated; common indications in addition to correct wiring are open ground, open neutral, open hot, hot-ground reversed, hot-neutral reversed (see snipurl .com/27kdcxy).

Volt-ohm meter (VOM)—for measuring AC or DC voltages, resistance, and DC current (see snipurl.com/27kddfz).

Continuity tester, a.k.a. "beeper"—for checking unpowered circuits for electrical connectivity (see snipurl. com/27kdftv). One that makes an audible tone when the circuit is closed is very handy when testing long runs of wire to save running back and forth when you're the only one working on a project, and it's a good backup for the VOM (and vice versa).

Insulated jumper wires with insulated alligator clips on both ends—you should have a half dozen or more for making deactivated circuit tests and measurements with a "beeper" or VOM (see snipurl.com/27kdsyv).

Small (sixteen- to twenty-five-foot) tape measure—for measuring wire and cable (remember to leave enough for slack and a few start-over recuts, especially if you're new to electrical projects).

Electrical pliers/wire cutter with built-in wire strippers (see snipurl.com/27kdr0z)—for common wire gauges (10, 12, 14, 16, 18, 20); these sometimes include crimping and bolt cutting in the same tool (see snipurl.com/27kdrql).

Utility knife with a retractable blade (see snipurl.com/27kdq7n)—typically with extra blades stored in the handle, for lengthwise scoring of Romex insulation (household wiring such as 14-2, 12-2, or other common insulated multiconductor household wiring).

Scissors—useful for cutting off excess exterior plastic insulation and/or interior paper filler strands from Romex cable.

Wire nuts for joining wires—in various sizes (gray, blue, orange, yellow, red, etc.).

Spare 120-VAC duplex outlets (see snipurl.com/27kdpuw)—remember to use only GFCI outlets (see snipurl.com/27kdpqm) for any exterior, bath, kitchen, or other locations with nearby plumbing. When in doubt, consult with a licensed electrical contractor.

Spare single-pole, single-throw (SPST) wall switches—Morris makes an illuminated version for dark spaces (see snipurl.com/27kds93).

Utility handsaw with tapered blade (see snipurl.com/27kdo97)—for starting, widening, and shaping holes in drywall.

Tools for making low-voltage DC wiring repairs or enhancements include:

Anderson Powerpole connectors and crimping tools—for high current (e.g. alternative-energy home power systems). These connectors, housings, parts, tools, and accessories are vastly superior to and safer than the "cigarette lighter" variety of connector.

Low-wattage soldering iron (see snipurl.com/27kdte7)—such as a twenty-five-watt fine-tip chisel point for fine work, like circuit boards, small wire connections, etc.

Medium-wattage soldering iron (see snipurl.com/27kd-
tie)—for example, forty watts for braid on coaxial cable shield that soaks up more heat before solder will
flow. For some higher-wattage and/or remote purposes, you might consider a cordless rechargeable
and/or butane-powered soldering iron.

Solder—such as 60/40 leaded rosin core.

SOLDERING TIP

If you've never done any soldering, practice on a few
noncritical projects well before you need to do a repair
on a more crucial household item. In addition to basic
safety, the most important goal of each soldered joint is
a nice smooth, shiny connection, rather than a dull ir-
regular one, which usually indicates poor electrical
contact and can even be a fire hazard in some cases. A
well-soldered connection optimizes current flow.

An alternative to soldering for some low-current,
low-voltage applications is to have a crimping tool and
a box of crimp connectors. Get an assortment of both
loop-ended and open-ended prong connectors in a variety of sizes to match various wire gauges. Be sure to
get the proper size connector and the appropriate
crimping tool as specified by the manufacturer.

Flux—usually only needed for heavy-gauge wire projects, if rosin-core solder is used for most other small-
scale soldering tasks.

Sponge—an old one to wipe the soldering iron tip after
each use to keep it clean and shiny.

Desoldering "solder sucker" tool—if you've ever soldered the wrong items or just added too much solder and need to start over, you know that these little vacuum gadgets are invaluable for rework of any kind.

Desoldering copper braid—as a complement to the desoldering tool, a spool of this copper braid can also be invaluable for wicking away mistakes and/or excess solder (see snipurl.com/27ke3rr).

Electrical tape (see snipurl.com/27kdvuk)—usually black vinyl.

TIP

When splicing multiconductor cables, solder and tape one pair of wires at a time, staggering each pair lengthwise so that there's no large bulge in one spot. Distribute the bulges down the length of the splice, then spiral additional electrical tape over the entire collection of splices, covering the exposed wires

Masking tape—for temporarily positioning items while soldering, etc.

A variety of heat-shrink plastic insulating tubing—buy an assortment of diameters and colors. These assortments are available inexpensively via eBay.

Needle-nose pliers (see snipurl.com/27kdw3t)—for making tight, clean bends in wire. Making a closed loop on the end of each wire and linking them together mechanically before soldering saves lots of fumbling.

Diagonal cutters (see snipurl.com/27kdwzw)—commonly called wire cutters or "dikes," these are designed for cutting wire, but are also useful for many other tasks, such as cutting plastic cable ties. Be careful not to exceed their capacity or you will surely break or deform their cutting jaws.

Miniature vise or soldering jig—a fishing fly-tying vise is ideal, but a homemade jig will suffice. Such a jig is usually made with coat-hanger wire and a pair of alligator clips that can be clamped into a machinist's vise. This jig is used for holding wires and components in place while soldering (see snipurl.com/27kdxb4).

Vise-grip pliers—as an alternative or adjunct to the aforementioned jig.

Various lengths of wire—such as scraps of twelve- and fourteen-gauge wire from prior projects, plus other speaker or multiconductor wire, as space in your tool kit allows. If you accumulate too much scrap wire, move some of the larger lengths to a labeled box or storage containers.

Screwdrivers (both Phillips and straight slot in various sizes)—an assortment of small, large, long, and stubby varieties is helpful.

OTHER HELPFUL ITEMS

Nickel–metal hydride (NiMH) battery charger (e.g., this DC-to-DC charging rack: snipurl.com/27keqiu) for AA and AAA batteries and enough batteries of each size to power *all* your household items that use them, plus a few spares. Look for items that use these standard batteries. I recommend that you go through your house,

garage, outbuildings, cupboards, drawers, and vehicles and make a detailed list of how many batteries
you need. It might surprise you how many your collection of gadgets uses!

LED flashlights (small, preferably adjustable, with a
stand for hands-free work)—for working in dark
spaces. Other options for when you're in a pinch: LED
headlamps and key-chain LED lamps temporarily
held on with carefully adjusted vise grips.

Tie wraps and other fasteners such as Romex staples—for
dressing, attaching, and enclosing wire and connections.
If you are working with 120-VAC or alternate energy (e.g.,
24-VDC) home power wiring, be sure to adhere to all applicable building codes and safety standards. Consult a
licensed electrician and/or authorized renewable energy
expert to make sure you're playing it safe, and that you're
getting the best economy for your investment in time,
money, and resources. I generally prefer Anderson Powerpole connectors for all 12-VDC wiring.

Small folding optical magnifier—for inspecting solder
joints, fine wire connections, etc. If you plan to do a lot
of soldering or fine close-up work, consider buying an
inexpensive illuminated magnifying workstation.

Metal coat hanger—pulled apart, ends cut off, then
rolled up into a coil to be used as a "fish wire" to grab
loose ends of wire pushed or pulled through wall
spaces to reach outlets, switches, lamp fixtures, etc.

Telescoping inspection mirror (see snipurl.com/
27ke9na)—for finding and inspecting wires, etc., in
those same wall spaces.

Magnetic stud finder (see snipurl.com/27kdiaa).

Set of jeweler's small screwdrivers—these often seem
to come in handy.

Fold-out set of Allen wrenches

**Indelible markers (fine point), pens, pencils, small note-
pad and/or sticky notes**—these can be handy when labeling connections of multiconductor cables, etc.

Sandpaper (around 120 grit), **an emery (fingernail) board,
a small wire brush**—and other items for cleaning dust,
paint, and debris off connections and terminals.

Support items (e.g., ziplock bags, recycled vitamin bottles)—for batteries, small electronic items, etc.

For those with additional technical expertise, there are lots
of great high-end tools (some of which are expensive), such as
watt meters (see snipurl.com/27keotj), handheld digital scopes
(see snipurl.com/27kemyl), and back to the low-tech realm . . .

Duck Tape—how could we forget this ubiquitous aid to
handy folks?

As you gather your assortment of electrical and electronic repair tools and supplies, consider the full implica-
tions of YOYO time: Are you prepared to live off the grid,
and once you are living in that mode, can you power, repair,
and maintain your electronics for an extended period of
time? Do you have all of the requisite references, in hard
copy? Do you have the batteries you will need, and the
requisite photovoltaic battery chargers? Stock up, and practice maintaining what you own.

· CHAPTER 7 ·

MOBILITY AND COUNTERMOBILITY TOOLS

Thomas Sowell, who is one of our favorite commentators, points out three things that make the collectivists uneasy. These are cars, guns and home schooling, all of which grant to the individual a degree of independence of action which terrifies the champions of the super state.

—Jeff Cooper, *Jeff Cooper's Commentaries*,
September 1998

AUTOMOTIVE MAINTENANCE AND REPAIR TOOLS

A basic set of automotive maintenance and repair tools is a must for any serious prepper. While the under-the-hood complexity of most cars and trucks has risen dramatically since the mid-1970s, there are still many tasks that can be handled by home mechanics without the aid of high-tech diagnostics. At the very minimum, you will need a floor jack, jack stands, tire tools, a full set of socket wrenches, a full set of Torx drivers, a full set of Allen wrenches, an oil filter wrench, pry bars, a volt-ohm meter (VOM), an assortment of screwdrivers, and several sets of pliers. (See Chapter 3 for additional details.)

JACK STANDS

Steel jack stands are available at nearly any auto parts store. You can also purchase a pair by mail order for less than twenty-five dollars from JCWhitney.com. There are special Hi-Lift jack bases—designed to distribute a jack's weight more broadly across soft ground—available from 4WD.com.

A Few Vehicle Hoisting Safety Tips

1. **Never** jack up a car on a slope!

2. **Never work alone** when hoisting a vehicle.

3. **Resist the urge to use four jack stands at once**. The maximum that you can safely use at once is *one pair*. You need to leave at least two of a vehicle's wheels resting on the ground and lift only one end of the vehicle at a time. If the ground is slightly uneven, then lay at least eighteen-by-eighteen-inch scraps of three-quarter-inch (or thicker) plywood under each jack stand.

One extremely important part of using *any* jack safely is to *always* place jack stands under the vehicle before crawling underneath, or you will be placing your life in jeopardy. This rule goes for a Hi-Lift jack as well as for any other type of jack.

Tire Repair Tools

Repairing modern tires is quite labor intensive to do at home or out in the boonies, but not impossible. DIY tire dismounting and repair is becoming a lost art—still practiced primarily by those of us who spend a lot of time in 4WD mode out in remote BLM-managed acreage or in the Australian outback.

My family likes to go rock hounding in a remote region. We are talking about *true* off-roading here, in which getting stranded is more than just an inconvenience. Our tires seem to magically attract very pointy chunks of slate and basalt. A breakdown could mean a twenty-five-mile walk to the nearest paved road. At the very minimum, we always carry one spare tire already on a rim (and sometimes two), a small 12-VDC compressor with pressure tank, and a DC-to-AC inverter. I recommend that you do the same.

Every 4WD and ranch utility truck should have a set of tire tools—including an Aussie Tyrepliers bead breaker, as well as patching materials and goop, a small compressor that can run off a two-hundred-watt inverter, and a good-quality hand pump with an accurate gauge. A tire-plugging kit is a must. By the way, special precautions (including a safety cage or chains) are required when working on tires that are mounted on "split"-style rims. Beware!

Tow Chains and Tow Straps

Every well-equipped retreat will have a variety of tow chains and tow straps. I carry a strap in each light vehicle and a tow chain in each truck, tractor, and ATV. Keep your tow chains clean and well-oiled and your grandchildren will someday use them. But if you fail to do so, you will come upon a rusty, pitted mess in less than a year.

Cold-Weather Essentials

Warm clothing, pile caps, and gloves
Extra pairs of dry socks
Ice creepers (such as Yaktrax, which are widely available)
Snowshoes and spare binding parts (such as the Huron-made snowshoes available from Lehmans.com)
Sleeping bag(s). I prefer the Wiggy's brand FTRSS. We have five of them here at the ranch, and they have served us very well for nearly twenty years.
Fire-starting kit with plenty of tinder

FLASHLIGHTS

I consider flashlights to be key enabling tools for survival. Not only are they crucial for shedding light on mechanical work, for map reading, and for field medicine procedures, but they can also be useful for self-defense as striking weapons. In this role, they are used like palm sticks or kubotans. (Do a Web search on the phrase "palm stick defense" for more information on this.) This is particularly important if you live in a jurisdiction that restricts carrying guns or knives. Carrying a flashlight is *generally* unrestricted, but consult your state and local laws. By the way, large ink pens can be used similarly. They run the gamut from the very inexpensive Cold Steel Pocket Shark to the very expensive Mont Blanc Meisterstück. If you opt for the Pocket Shark (which is what I carry when I take commercial airplane flights), then I recommend scraping off all of the pen's exterior markings.

For nearly all applications I strongly prefer LED flashlights to those with traditional filament bulbs. Not only do they draw far less current (giving your batteries tremendous life), but they are also highly resistant to impacts that would quickly destroy the filaments of traditional bulbs. I've retrofitted a number of my Maglite flashlights with LEDs, which are available from a number of sellers on eBay.

For small flashlights I generally prefer those that use CR123 batteries. These batteries were originally developed for cameras, but they have become ubiquitous with flashlights and weapons-mounted lasers. They have a superior energy density compared with AA batteries. Rechargeable lithium-ion CR123 batteries and chargers hit the market around 2010, making CR123 battery flashlights even more desirable.

I recommend buying only high-quality flashlights. Lights with machined metal body tubes tend to be the sturdiest. Two excellent brands are SureFire and Maglite. One brand that uses a plastic body also deserves particular mention: Gerber's Omnivore series. These lights have a clever battery compartment design that allows them to use size AA *or* AAA *or* CR123 batteries—all with the same flashlight.

For map reading in the field, I recommend red or blue filters to preserve your natural night vision. Note that even when using these filters, reading maps in tactical situations should be done only inside an opaque tent or under a poncho.

Flashlights with one-inch-diameter tubes fit in standard

rifle scope rings. Thus, they can be firmly attached to Picatinny rails, coaxially with the bore of a rifle, pistol, or shotgun. There are momentary on-off switches and tape switches made for many lights. Typically these replace a standard tail cap. In life-or-death situations it is crucial to activate a flashlight only *momentarily*, just before you shoot. Otherwise you will be carrying around a big bright "shoot me" beacon.

Momentary on-off switches can also be useful for signaling with your flashlight, whether you're using Morse code or another code system.

Small flashlights can be carried in headbands, effectively converting them into headlamps. It takes a while to get accustomed to using these, but they can be very useful, since they leave both hands free to work. These headbands are sold under a variety of brand names, such as Nite Ize.

One of my longtime friends mentioned that he has recently been experimentally hiking with an LED Mini Maglite carried in a Nite Ize headband, equipped with a relatively waterproof TacStar pressure tape switch that he can clench between his teeth. For regular trail hiking, the light's head can be cranked down for "continuous on" operation when the standard tail cap is installed. But when operating tactically with the tape-switch tail cap installed, he can activate the light "on demand" by clamping his teeth down on the tape switch. He has even experimented with wire stiffeners, positioning the tape switch and the mouthpiece of his Camelbak hydration pack on either side of his chin. That way he can selectively bite down on one or the other, by just slightly tilting his head. He jokingly calls this the "combat pacifier effect." It's a clever way around the dilemma of how to activate a flashlight on demand and hands-free.

MOBILITY TOOLS

Mobility tools are often ignored outside of fire department and emergency medical services publications. These are tools that help you get from Point A to Point B. Whether the obstacles are natural or man-made, having the right mobility tools with you may make a huge difference in making a successful journey.

When operating a vehicle off-road or on country roads, you should always expect to have to fend for yourself. Service facilities are few and far between. Something as simple as a blown-down tree can impede your progress, and you might be the first traveler to encounter it. So it is wise to carry a set of pioneer tools. These tool sets date back to the days of horse-drawn wagons.

Basic pioneer tools include: ax, round-point shovel, tow chain, Swedish limb saw, digging/pry bar, Hi-Lift jack, and a snow shovel in winter months.

Perhaps the best way to envision the tools and techniques needed for mobility is to anticipate how someone might employ *counter*mobility techniques. If you know how someone or something might impede your progress, then you can identify the tools that you will need to keep you rolling.

Every well-prepared family should have one or more 4WD vehicles with snow tires or chains. For those of you who have an eleventh-hour Get Out of Dodge (GOOD) plan, I trust that you have pre-positioned the vast majority of your food and gear at your intended retreat. Towing a trailer on icy winter roads is a dicey proposition even in the best of times. Piloting an overloaded vehicle with an overloaded trailer when TSHTF is tantamount to suicide. But if you've planned things properly and pre-positioned your gear, there is no need for a trailer. Just one quick trip with fuel cans, bug-out bags, backpacks, web gear, and weapons cases should suffice.

So what do you need to carry in your vehicle? At all times, you should carry a tool kit, flashlights, road flares, engine starting fluid, first aid/trauma kit, chemical light sticks, a CB radio, and your usual bugout bag basics, including food and water. So let's take it a step further and talk specifically about mobility essentials that you should keep stowed in your bug-out vehicle:

SAFETY NOTE

Securing gear carefully in your vehicle is particularly important when you carry pioneer tools. A sudden stop or a jolt on a rough road can turn an ax, shovel, digging bar, or Hi-Lift jack into a formidable projectile, breaking a windshield or much worse. Stow them *low*, and strap them down!

Traction sand. You probably already have a couple of bales of USGI sandbags. Just fill a bag (or two) with coarse sand and tie each of them shut with a pair of plastic cable ties to prevent leakage.

Single-bit ax, at least three-pound (such as Northern Tool + Equipment item #119922)

Shovel. A proper USGI folding entrenching tool (*not* a cheap knockoff) *might* suffice, but I prefer a more substantial forty-inch D-handle round-nose shovel, such as the Kodiak, available from a number of Internet vendors, including HectorsHardware.com.

Hi-Lift jack, a.k.a. sheepherder's jack (such as Northern Tool + Equipment item #14421). See details and important safety warnings on these jacks in Chapter 3.

Choker/tow chain (such as 4WD.com item #26083). These should also be available from JCWhitney.com and most local auto parts stores.

Ratchet hoist, a.k.a. come-along. Make sure you have one of these. Or better yet, carry two. I like the Dayton and Tuf-Tug brands (such as Northern Tool + Equipment item #152911).

Several short lengths of **chain,** *steel* **sleeve-locking carabiners**, and large **grade 8 bolts with large flat washers and nuts** that can be used to connect/secure chains. (Sometimes you need to improvise.)

Tire chains. Yes, even if your vehicle seasonally wears studded snow tires, you may need chains. And if you must depend on a trailer for winter GOOD, then get chains for the trailer too.

Bolt cutters. In addition to lock picks, every well-prepared individual should own a "universal key"—a pair of 36-inch bolt cutters. They can get you through locked gates in a pinch. You never know when someone might misplace a key. They are also useful for cutting rebar and performing other metalworking tasks. The ones that are priced below $50 are nearly all made in China and not very sturdy. Expect to pay between $80 and $140 for an American-made pair of 36-inch bolt cutters. Buy at least a 24-inch length, but I prefer 36-inchers.

Sadly, very few of these are now made in the States, like my trusty old Woodings-Verona brand bolt cutters.

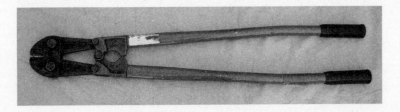

Bolt cutters: the universal key

PSP. Optionally, when traveling in areas with very sandy soil, a couple of six-foot lengths of pierced steel planking (PSP) should be carried. This metal runway mat material provides great traction.

A couple of key points:

- Off-road mobility is usually more difficult than depicted in movies or in television shows. You need to carefully and deliberately think through where you are going, approach and departure angles, and so forth.

- Go *slowly* to prevent damaging running gear. The faster you are rolling, the more damage you will do when your running gear comes to a sudden stop. There is reason why the extreme off-road driving sport is called "rock crawling." If it were "rock racing," then in less than an hour they would have no equipment left. **Go slowly!**

AN IMPORTANT PROVISO

Please don't do anything illegal. Also be advised that in some of the liberal nanny states, carrying bolt cutters or lock picks in your vehicle could be considered "criminal intent." But here in the unnamed western state, folks just call it "a real good idea."

COUNTERMOBILITY

In times of lawlessness, defending your property from looters will become a paramount consideration. Help probably won't be just a phone call way, and the response time for police and sheriff's deputies will stretch to hours. Since help might be slow in coming—if it comes at all—the best thing that you can do to deter looters is to impede their mobility. If you erect barriers to their advance, they will hopefully move on to easier pickings. Or, failing that, the barriers will give you time to organize a defense with your neighbors.

Given his combat experience, I defer to the expertise of SurvivalBlog reader "John Mosby," a multiple tour combat veteran who blogs at mountainguerrilla.wordpress.com. In a SurvivalBlog article, he pointed out some key issues in countermobility:

A substantial stockpile of barbed wire is a must for countermobility. Barriers of any kind are intended only to *delay* and channel aggressors. Only rarely will they stop them outright. Given preparation, planning, time, and determination, *any barrier can be breached*. In a survival situation, however, this adds up to "How badly do you want in here?" Delay and channel designs can force aggressors to choose between paying dearly for entrance and moving on to pick a softer target. And that's what we're looking for.

There are two categories of countermobility: antivehicular and antipersonnel. In the antivehicular category there are two subcategories: above- and belowground. The belowground category consists of obstacles such as ditches, pitfalls, and craters. These are deliberately created, or in some cases simply terrain features that are improved with pick-and-shovel work to prevent vehicles from easily moving across them. For example, a deep ditch with steep walls prevents easy transverse because the vehicle falls in nose first and gets stuck, unable to clear the opposite side. These sorts of obstacles have to be bridged or backfilled in order to be crossed. If you have access to a front-end loader or a large tractor with a bucket, ditches are not too difficult to dig (given the right ground), and when the grass grows over them they don't appear as militant as a chain-link fence. Existing ditches can be modified to achieve a sheer wall on the side facing your main line of resistance (MLR). You can also install obstacles on roads at choke points; for example, at a single point on a road or your driveway where the trees are close to the road. In the West in particular, cattle guards are outstanding. In normal times, the grate stays down, but when it's time to close the road, the grate is removed, leaving a substantial ditch. Unless they've brought a monster truck along, getting across a ditch dug out to four feet deep is going to be an axle-breaking proposition.

There are several drawbacks to belowground obstacles, however. First, if they are permanent and outsiders can't get across, *neither can you*, unless you have your own bridging apparatus planned and on hand or permanent crossing points, such as your driveway culvert. (The classic drawbridge–cattle guard is such an example.) Second, without accompanying antipersonnel obstacles, they make good cover for anyone dismounted, since they are essentially infantry trenches. But if they are far enough away from your MLR, with a good bit of open ground between the ditch and you, belowground obstacles can at least prevent a mounted attack coming in at full speed right to your doorstep.

Then there are the aboveground types of antivehicular obstacle. The concrete barrier is by far the most common type in use here in the U.S. They are permanent and provide cover. There is also the bollard type. These are simply solid posts of various materials ranging from wood to cast iron (or old cannon barrels in some places) that are dug into the ground or set down into receptacles in the ground and locked. Even a strategically planted line of fast-maturing trees will have the desired effect. We see these in use to deny sidewalk parking or restrict access to service roads. Sometimes they are reinforced with heavy rope or chain running between them, especially if they run for any distance. Unlike a solid concrete barrier, they can easily be passed off as a decorative feature. If they happen to be made from something like railroad ties with one-inch cable running between them, they become more formidable, but of course more obvious. Even railroad rails or I-beams, cut to length and placed so that a vehicle cannot squeeze through them, will generally stop anything except a tracked armored vehicle. The real beauty of bollards is that they can be emplaced as needed, usually across choke points, and pulled up and stored out of sight when not needed.

A more permanent type was seen in Britain, where invasion preparations featured concrete cubes or cylinders set like the classic WWII dragon's teeth. There were also the classic I-beam "hedgehogs," in which beams were welded together in a crossing pattern and then secured in some manner to the ground.

Finally, there are good old-fashioned gates. As illustrated in the novel *Patriots*, a gate is only as strong as whatever is locking it closed. They are also generally dependent on hinges. And if the post goes, then so does the gate. Only the most robust structures of this type will stop vehicles.

There is another kind of gate, however, that was employed all over southern Britain in preparation for the expected German landings. Instead of having the opening and closing feature, they were simply two very heavy colonnades of stone and concrete on each side of the road with slots left in them for inserting railroad rails or I-beams when the time came. In the modern "decorative" context, these are usually unobtrusive, which may also be a boon for retreats wishing to avoid the "nutcase survivalist" label. (The slots for the rails simply look like they have been left for the eventual addition of a rail fence.)

Internet searches will give all sorts of good countermobility ideas, as will a copy of the U.S. Army's *Engineer Field Data* manual, FM 5-34.

Lock Picks and Lockout Tools

A set of lock picks can be important for gaining access to buildings and vehicles when keys are forgotten, lost, or separated from their owners in the chaos of a disaster situation. Depending on where you live, these tools might be misconstrued by law enforcement officers. To keep yourself from running afoul of overzealous law enforcement officers, I recommend that you prominently label your lock pick set as an "Emergency Vehicle Lockout Rescue Kit."

Lock picks have many uses, whether around the house or in a GOOD bag. They also weigh next to nothing and take up very little space. I would recommend buying just a small set of five picks and a tension wrench. The big sets are useful for specific applications, but they are overkill for 90 percent of the tasks they will be used for. A set of shortened lock picks and a tension wrench can be carried on a key ring next to your keys, or in your wallet. I carry a set in the liner of my billfold.

Lock picking is a skill anyone can learn, and when you get good at it, a standard five-pin tumbler lock should take less than a minute. These tools allow you to reuse your locks. Instead of drilling a lock out or cutting it off and leaving your property wide open, a lock pick lets you get in, relock the door or gate, and replace the lock at your convenience. A more advanced approach would be taking a locksmithing class and becoming certified.

I'm *not* advocating breaking and entering, and I would only suggest you use lock picks or bump keys in a legal and, more important, ethical manner. But when used legitimately, a set of lock picks is a quite valuable addition to your set of tools.

BUMP KEYS

For cars, the most common tool is a set of bump keys (also called jiggler keys). These resemble ground-down or smoothed car keys. A bump key is one that has all of its shear positions cut to maximum depth. When turned in a lock cylinder with concurrent tapping ("bumping") of a hammer, it will open many locks quickly. Bump key sets are available from BumpkeyAz.com. To use a bump key, you move it rapidly up and down in the lock while simultaneously putting rotational pressure on the lock cylinder. These are effective only on older cars; newer cars have sophisticated systems to prevent theft (so-called chipped keys). While bugging out, losing the keys to your car could cost you your supplies, or even your life. My advice is to keep an extra key hidden somewhere in or on the vehicle. A set of jiggler keys might allow you to get in without breaking a window. If you don't have a key, many old cars can be started with a piece of wire and a screwdriver. For a more permanent solution, the ignition can be bypassed and a starter switch installed.

LOCKOUT KITS

Commercially made vehicle lockout kits are made by a number of companies. I recommend buying a fairly complete set to supplement your set of lock picks. These lockout kits typically include several rods and flat steel lock manipulators. The latter are often referred to as slim jims, after one of the popular brand names. The kits also have a variety of hard plastic wedges that are designed to separate the weather stripping from window glass, allowing you to insert a lock-manipulation tool and give it a useful range of motion. I recommend the Grip brand lockout tool kit. It's priced at less than twenty-five dollars, and it will get you into the majority of cars should you find yourself locked out.

VIBRATION LOCK PICKS

Vibratory lock picks (often called "buzzers" or "power lock guns") use a replaceable pick probe that is vibrated by an eccentric cam on an electric motor shaft.

While quite effective, bump keys and electric vibratory lock picks are both considered illegal to possess in many jurisdictions. Unless you are a bona fide commercial locksmith, you might be able to explain possession of a vehicular lockout set, but *not* a vibratory lock pick or a set of bump keys for residential door locks. Do a lot of research on your state and local laws before buying either of these adjunct tools!

PRACTICE, PRACTICE, PRACTICE

Unlocking car doors requires some practice. If you ever get permission to run around at an automobile wrecking yard, then you can learn how to manipulate the locks on many makes and models. As I often say, "Tools without training are useless." Lock picking requires plenty of practice and is a particularly perishable skill, so it is best to brush up every couple of years. Not surprisingly, YouTube now offers a number of instructional videos on how to use slim jims, lock picks, bump keys, and more.

· CHAPTER 8 ·

WELDING AND BLACKSMITHING TOOLS

> But when oppression would lift its head
> or a tyrant would be lord,
> though we thank him for the plow,
> we shall not forget the sword!
>
> —Charles Mackay, "Tubal Cain" (a poem about
> the world's first blacksmith)

THE HOME FORGE

A home forge is the crucial centerpiece for the shop of anyone who wants to be truly self-sufficient in metal-working. Unlike gas or electric welding, a traditional forge is elegantly low tech. A workable forge can be impro-vised from a barbecue grill and requires no exotic supplies.

Consider some of the likely situations in which welding and fabrication will be needed at a farm, ranch, or retreat: Your vehicles may have their suspension systems damaged and need repair. (In a disaster situation, deteriorating road conditions will mean that suspension damage will be a very common occurrence.) You may also need to repair your home water pumps; an old-fashioned pitcher hand pump can be fitted over the casing of a shallow well. And of course there will be lots of steel cutting and welding needed for hardening your home or retreat against attack by burglars or home invaders. Finally, there will be lots of general household repair, farming implement repair, and tool fabrication. The longer a disaster goes on, the more you will have to provide for yourself.

Welding, shaping, and cutting steel are skills that you need to train for in advance. At the very minimum, investigate the subject on YouTube. The number of videos on practical skills increases daily.

FORGE MATERIALS

You will be able to forge many tools yourself from scrap steel. While I do buy some virgin bar stock, rod stock, channel stock, and sheet metal, much of my material comes out of automobile wrecking yards. There you will find a lifetime supply of steel to repurpose. Axles and leaf springs are particularly useful. Another good source of materials is scrapyards that have salvaged railroad materials. Rail-tie plates (also called sole plates), track chairs, traditional rail spikes, and screw spikes all have multiple fabricating uses in a home metal shop.

One of my friends didn't have the money to buy a heavy anvil, so he used a twenty-eight-inch piece of railroad track as an ersatz anvil for the first few years that he had his home forge. To support it, he simply chain-sawed a twenty-six-inch-long section of a twenty-inch-diameter tree trunk, carefully squaring both ends. He covered the top of it with sheet metal (for fire protection), drilled pilot holes, and then used four railroad spikes to attach the short length of rail to the top. Four inches of rail stuck out over each side of the stump wood. After using it for a few months, he used his cutting torch to cut one of the overhanging rail ends into an anvil-like triangular point—a practical and inexpensive temporary solution.

SurvivalBlog reader Jodier has far more metalworking experience than I do, so I'm deferring to his detailed suggestions on setting up a home forge and tools.

ANVILS

The anvil is one of the most important pieces of the blacksmith's tool set. In the first years of my father's blacksmithing, he used an old, rusty elevator weight as an anvil. A piece of railroad track would work great in a TEOTWAWKI situation. There are many brands of anvils available for purchase. Two of the most renowned anvils were made by Peter Wright and Hay-Budden. You can purchase a brand-new anvil from a farrier supply company for upwards of three hundred dollars. Then again, a Hay-Budden brand anvil can cost seven dollars per pound. At 150 pounds that would be $1,050!

If you insist on having an antique anvil, then look for one with some recoil to it, meaning that when you drop a ball bearing on it the bearing should bounce up and leave the anvil with a ring. An anvil without this quality has either been modified or damaged, or it lacks true quality.

HAMMERS

The blacksmith's second most important tool is the hammer. In a TEOTWAWKI situation a basic claw hammer could be used to push metal around, but a specific blacksmithing hammer would be more beneficial. You can buy a blacksmithing hammer at a farrier supply center. Ball peen hammers also have their place in a blacksmith's arsenal. I mainly use them for shaping ladles and spoons, but they can be used as a general hammer. Most people overlook the importance of how to use the hammer. I use a push-and-pull method, which means I push the metal forward and pull the metal backward, using firm but not overly brutal strikes to the metal.

GLOVES

An item that is just as important as the hammer is a pair of gloves. A good pair of leather roping gloves made of goatskin are often the most comfortable.

FORGES

The third piece of major equipment for the blacksmith is the forge. There are many antique forges on the market, but there are also many do-it-yourself alternatives, such as a brake drum forge, which is an excellent entry-level forge. It is a basic forge design, using a scrapped truck brake drum and some sort of fan to provide oxygen to the nest. I use a small rivet forge for items such as S-hooks, spoons, nails, and knives. One thing to keep in mind when choosing a forge is how hot it gets. My rivet forge will sometimes reach temperatures in excess of 2,800 degrees Fahrenheit.

Another thing to consider is what you are going to burn in your forge—coal or charcoal. You can still find coal today at some farrier supply centers; though it is often low in quality, it will work. I burn a five-gallon bucket in two days of heavy blacksmithing.

BLOWERS

You will need a blower to go with your forge. A blower is a simple piece of equipment that pumps oxygen into the nest of the forge. It is a vital piece of equipment because it raises the temperature in the forge by several hundred degrees. Some of the major blower makers were Royal, Tiger, Champion, and Buffalo. I have seen antique blowers run anywhere from forty dollars to three hundred dollars at flea markets. As far as home brews go, men have converted squirrel cage fans into blowers as well as car heater fans.

VISE

A vise is an invaluable tool. It works as a strong second set of hands and a rock solid anchor point for grinding and welding. If there is a piece of vintage equipment that I recommend you buy, it is a blacksmith's vise. The blacksmith's vise is designed to be open and closed quickly, so that you spend more time working the metal and less time letting it cool. The vises vary in size and price, usually starting at fifty dollars and going up into the hundreds of dollars.

I would add one other crucial item of my own to Jodier's list of essentials.

TONGS

A well-made pair of blacksmithing tongs should last you decades if you don't abuse them. You will need several contours for even simple hobby blacksmithing (flat-nose, round-nose, riveting, and so forth). And eventually you will find that you also need variants with larger jaws or specifically contoured handles for comfortably handling different thicknesses of stock. Real blacksmiths, of course, *make* their own tongs. But it takes a tool to make a tool, so you'll probably end up buying your first pair. The folks at Hammersource.com are a good source of American-made hammers and tongs. Click on their "Blacksmithing Hammers and Tongs" page. Their tongs labeled "300mm Mandrel Blacksmith Tong for 13–15mm material" should get you started. If you are on a tight budget, then you can just use an old pair of large channel locks or vise grips to hold the stock to make your first pair of proper blacksmithing tongs. Let the adventure begin!

WELDING

While describing how to weld in detail goes beyond the scope of this book, I will begin with some basics. But before anything else, you need to understand the nature of iron and steel. To quote my friend G. M., "If you can't tell the difference between regular steel, stainless steel, aluminum, and cast iron, then you shouldn't be welding."

In essence, you have to know what welding process to use and which filler metal to use for various metals. The selection of the right filler metal is very important. If the wrong filler metal is selected, the weld can have major defects and not be fit for service. Shielding gas selection is also very important. Preheat and post-heat are important on cast iron and high-strength alloy steel. Preheating is required whenever the metal to be welded is below 70 degrees Fahrenheit because the cold metal quenches the weld. When large welds are needed, it is better to make more small welds than a few large ones. Low-carbon steel, also called mild steel, is easily welded by all common welding processes. However, long arcing of the weld will allow air to enter the shielding envelope, so proper welding technique is needed to avoid inducing air, which will cause porosity and other bad effects.

ELECTRIC WELDERS

If you still have access to electric power, then wire or stick welding would be the preferred method. This also holds true if you have a generator available. If not, then you are left with oxy-fuel welding. Wire welding is the preferred method for any novice. It is much more intuitive for a novice to get the feel of it, but setting the machine can be intimidating. Let's start with the machine. If you are going to invest in any machine, consider one of the new smaller, more portable inverter welding machines that can do four major welding processes: wire with cover gas, flux cored gasless wire, stick, and TIG. Older machines that are strictly constant current or constant voltage are larger and heavier and can basically do only one dedicated type of process, with the exception of TIG. If you are going to spend your money on a new welding machine, why not buy the most versatile one?

It is also important to have a ninety-degree grinder, wire brushes, clamps, and cleaning tools available when you are welding. Grinders are great for both prepping and cleaning up after you weld. Wire brushes are good for quickly cleaning the welding cup and tips and for removing scale and spatter from your workpiece. Aside from specialized tongs, vise grip–type pliers are the preferred clamping tools, because with them you can quickly set up, adjust position, and unclamp your workpiece. One other useful but not crucial tool is a scale hammer, which can be used to quickly knock off the spatter or scale from your workpiece.

SAFETY

Safety in cutting and welding cannot be overstressed. Some things will injure or even kill you if you try to cut or weld them. *Never*, under any circumstances, weld on a gas tank, or on any container with unknown contents.

Welding is hot work, so you need to know if there is anything around that can catch fire. Remove all flammables, or cover them so they don't cause a problem. Be sure what you're welding on is adequately restrained or supported so it won't injure you or someone else.

All welding involves heat; there is always the possibility of burns. Your safety is your own responsibility and you must address it yourself. Many burns are caused by contact with hot metal or slag. I have seen students try to reach out and grab something they just welded—you can get burned even though you are wearing welding gloves. Be careful of hot weldments and sparks and splatter from your own welds and those of others. Ultraviolet light from welding will cause flash burns to your retinas. Wear shade 5 lenses for cutting and oxy-fuel welding, a minimum of shade 8 for MIG weld-ing, and shade 10 or greater in your welding hood for stick welding, TIG, thermite, or any other welding.

Always wear safety glasses when doing any work and ear protection when it's necessary. A good respirator that will fit inside your welding helmet is also good to have. You can buy a standard welding helmet with fixed glass or an electronic welding helmet that activates when the sensor de-tects a weld. The standard helmet has a replaceable fixed shaded glass and requires a jerking motion with your neck to close it after you position the welder and are ready to weld. The electronic helmet has an adjustable shade setting that darkens when you're welding. This allows you to per-form multiple welds without lifting the helmet and saves your neck from the constant jerking motion.

Both cutting and welding processes should be well ven-tilated. Fume sources that are bad for your health include paint, oil, grease, and coatings on metals such as zinc and cadmium. Older machinery and farm equipment may still have lead-based paint. Do no welding or cutting on refriger-ation or air conditioner pipes.

Wear the appropriate welder clothing: a long-sleeve shirt, long pants, leather shoes, a welder's cap or beanie to protect your head. A special welding jacket of leather or flame-proof canvas and leather welding gloves should be worn.

Oxygen and acetylene cylinders should be chained se-curely in separate areas at least twenty feet apart unless they are in a bottle cart and chained to it. Never lift a bottle by the cap or by its safety valve. When in use, oxygen bottles and cover gas bottles should be opened all the way to the back seat position after the regulators are properly screwed on. Open the valve on a full cylinder just briefly to blow out any dust, then attach the regulator. Acetylene bottles that have been laid on their side should be stored upright for at least four hours before being used. After attaching the regulator, open the acetylene bottle enough just to get full pressure on the gauges.

Again, welding is considered "hot work," so you are responsible for fires. Keep a fire extinguisher handy. A five-gallon bucket of water or sand would also be wise. Welding can cause electrical shock, so keep your leads and other equipment in good shape. Use the right type of regulator for the process you are setting up. Acetylene and fuel gases use left-hand connections with a notched nut. After you turn on gas cylinder main valves, back off the adjusting screw of all regulators after use so as not to distort the diaphragm. If possible, take a welding course. You'll have a skill that will stand you in good stead and be very valuable, especially in a TEOTWAWKI situation.

Here at the Rawles Ranch, we have several levels of welding preparedness that extend from nineteenth- to twenty-first-century technology. Wire welding is the easiest to learn, but it requires both shielding gas and electricity. For the home handyman, I recommend a Miller 110-watt wire welder with either a 20-pound tank of CO_2 or 75/25 mix (75 percent argon and 25 percent CO_2). If you have a generator with enough amperage, you should be able to run this little work-horse for odd jobs around your retreat. And if you have a *large* photovoltaically charged battery bank, then it too can power this welder. This welder is great for body and fender work and can apply a fairly large bead to quarter-inch-thick material for short lengths of weld.

You will also want a small oxy-acetylene cutting torch

rig. Fabrication is one half of welding work; the other half usually involves cutting steel. (A lot of people miss this point.) The other essential piece of equipment for basic fabrication is a good handheld ninety-degree grinder with an assortment of grinding and cutting disks, along with wire wheels and sanding pads. In addition to standard 120-VAC corded models, there are cordless versions, made by DeWalt and Ryobi, that use eighteen-volt rechargeable batteries. If and when you ever run out of oxygen or acetylene, you can probably cut most metal projects with a hand grinder.

Reader G. M. notes:

Arc welding is the best for a survival situation, but it has a steep learning curve. This is where welding is truly an art. You have to have your machine set between being too hot and too cold. This can be compensated by the amount of stick you feed into the weld puddle. If it is set a little hot you will be feeding the rod in at a fast rate to keep the weld puddle from dropping out. (Dropping out is when the puddle liquefies too much and the molten metal drips down the face of your material.) If it is set too cold, then the welding rod will have a tendency to stick to your parent material and no weld puddle will form.

The best way to look at welding is to stop thinking of welding rod or wire as a solid. It is not. Your arc rod or MIG wire is a *fluid*, similar to water but more like runny mud. You are trying to control a fluid and where it wants to flow. This is analogous to a cake decorator who is decorating a cake with a bag full of icing. It is the same principle. The trick is having a steady, patient hand while the liquid metal forms a bead and solidifies. The most common mistake made by new welders—other than not wearing the proper protective equipment—is not being patient with their puddle to let it form and solidify.

ESSENTIAL WELDING MATERIALS

The following are some essential materials and tools for welding:

You'll need a 120-volt welder with CO_2 tank and roll of 70s wire or gasless wire with extra welding tips.

All serious fabrication needs C-clamps, vise grips, and furniture clamps to hold metal pieces together when you weld them.

The problem with welding equipment is that it is consumable. That is, it has to be replaced on a regular basis. For a grid-down scenario, there are certain pieces of equipment and consumables you should stock up on: grinding disks, cutting disks, drill bits, welding rod, gouging rod, and welding lenses. And, of course, plenty of cylinders of oxygen and acetylene. You will use roughly twice as much oxygen as you will acetylene. And you will need roughly twenty cubic feet of capacity for each hour of welding.

YOUR WELDING ROD ASSORTMENT

The following is a list of the primary welding rods people should consider having. You should have a small can (usually a can is ten pounds) of each rod in two sizes: ³⁄₃₂ rod and ⅛ rod. Professionals would just use ⅛, but they are using big machines with lots of amperage. (The home shop setup will probably be able to do ⅛ but might have problems with insufficient amperage.):

- 7018 for MS (mild steel)

- 6011 or 6013 for welding rusty, dirty steel (called "farmer's rod" in the industry)

- 6010 or 5P+ for welding pipe

- 308L stainless steel ³⁄₃₂ rod for welding very thin steel (A little trick I learned over the years: It "ignites" without you having to strike the rod on the part. This is very handy for delicate projects. Use only ³⁄₃₂ size rod.)

- Inconel rod for welding steel to cast iron (You have to preheat the part before welding, then let it cool slowly in a pile of sand.)

- 11018 for HS (hard steel)

- Surfacing rod for plows, tool edges

- Carbon gouging rod ¼, ³⁄₃₂, ⅜

Some useful Web sites on welding products include:

Vehicle Welders

- snipurl.com/27sknm0

- snipurl.com/27sknp0

- snipurl.com/27sknsb

- snipurl.com/27sknvg

- snipurl.com/27sko6r

Punch and Chisel Sets

- snipurl.com/27skoap

C-Clamps and Vise Grips

- snipurl.com/27skoey

Handheld Grinders

- DeWalt: snipurl.com/27skol1
- Makita: snipurl.com/27skonz

Grinding Disks

- snipurl.com/27skoqo

Sanding Disks

- snipurl.com/27skovc

Die Grinder

- snipurl.com/27skp04

Welding Hood

- snipurl.com/27skp7c (This version allows you to use your hood as a face shield for grinding by using the sliding lens mechanism.)

Welding Cover Lens

- snipurl.com/27skp98

Shaded Cutting Torch Lens for Welding Hood

- snipurl.com/27skpcz

Normal Shaded Welding Lens

- #11 shade, #10 shade, #12 shade (available from *many* vendors)

WELDING WITHOUT GRID POWER

Keeping farm and other machinery operating in a long-term TEOTWAWKI will be a challenge. Obviously arc welding is out, unless someone has a huge solar battery bank. And gas welding will not be an option once the available welding gas supplies run out.

One alternative is welding with thermite. (The formerly patented trade name was Thermit.) Thermite welding is a simple process that just employs a mixture of iron oxide and aluminum powders to create what my high school teacher Mr. Dibari called "a vigorous exothermic reaction."

Thermite is most commonly used to join railroad tracks, using specialized molds and tooling. (Thermited rails don't make that traditional *clickety-clack* sound.) The only fairly exotic material needed is magnesium ribbon to ignite the mixture.

An aside: My number-one son found that BlastMatch and Sparkie fire starters both work just fine as thermite igniters.

The iron oxide and aluminum powders needed for thermite welding can even be produced locally, albeit laboriously, with materials from your local automobile wrecking yard (hint: look for aluminum mag wheels).

Welding with thermite can be tricky: If you use too little or if you don't contain the puddle properly, then you don't get a good weld. If you use too much, then you destroy the parent metal. (It will punch right through the parent metal.) Practice *a lot* with thermite now with scrap metal so that you don't make costly mistakes later.

WARNING!

All the usual safety provisos for welding apply, and then some! Thermite burns at 2,500 degrees, and looking directly at the reaction can cause permanently blinding retinal burns. Since a thermite reaction creates its own oxygen, unless you have a class D fire extinguisher, there is basically *no* effective way to fight a thermite fire. Without a class D extinguisher, you have to just wait until it burns out. Also, keep in mind that if burning thermite contacts water or even mud, it can cause an instantaneous steam explosion that will throw globs of burning thermite in all directions. Using finely ground thermite powder or containing the expanding gases in any way can also cause an explosion, **so use extreme caution**. If you aren't wearing welding clothes and dark welding goggles when igniting thermite, then you are foolish. After mixing or otherwise handling thermite powder, be sure to wash your hands thoroughly before using it.

Thermite has many other clever uses, some of which are described in my novels. Reprints of two old thermite welding references are now in the public domain and are available from Amazon.com: *Thermit Welding Process 1914*, by Richard N. Hart, and *Thermit Welding*, by Ethan Vial. Thermite welding is also briefly described in the free Kindle e-book *Oxy-Acetylene Welding and Cutting Electric, Forge and Thermit Welding Together with Related Methods and Materials Used in Metal Working and the Oxygen Process*, by Harold Phillips Manly.

An inexpensive source for iron oxide powder, aluminum powder, and magnesium ribbon is AlphaChemicals.com. They have been a SurvivalBlog advertiser since early 2011, and I must mention that I have had zero complaints about the company. They have excellent customer service, and have had thousands of happy SurvivalBlog-reader customers. Most of AlphaChem's iron oxide powder and aluminum powder is now packaged in resealable heavy-duty Mylar pouches. This keeps everything neat and dry. It's double-packaged and discreetly shipped via UPS in boxes that just have one small blue "ORM-D" safety label. (You mix the component powders yourself.)

Because of its weight, any casting equipment (molds, crucibles, refiner's sand, etc.) is best found locally, from an industrial supply company or, perhaps better yet, used, via Craigslist. And of course terra-cotta clay pots are available at garage sales or your local garden supply store. Lastly, keep in mind that if you are planning to cast metal with thermite, then wet sand or damp clay processes cannot be used. (See my previous warning about instantaneous steam explosions.) Your molds must be quite dry!

A Few Final Words on Forging and Welding

Before you get started on setting up your own forging and welding supplies, keep these tips in mind:

- Always wear the appropriate safety gear when working metal. (Our motto is ATGATT: "All the gear, all the time.")

- Goggles or at least safety glasses with side guards are a must for *all* metalwork, and the appropriate shade of welding goggles (#5 or #10) must be worn when welding.

- Sturdy boots and a welding apron are musts.

- Never work around fire alone.

- *Always* keep a big fire extinguisher handy!

SAFETY NOTE

Used motor oil has long been utilized for quenching in small forge operations, but since it has been found to be carcinogenic, this is no longer advised.

Additional References

You can never have too many references. Look for blacksmithing books in used bookstores and on Amazon.com or eBay. When shopping for used shop manuals, you may find that the books that have the grungiest covers are often the best—the grunge shows that they were used as actual workshop references. The Boy Scouts merit badge book on blacksmithing is a surprisingly complete starter book.

Another great book is the slender volume *The Book of Blacksmithing*, by Michael Cardiff.

The standard reference on anvils is *Anvils in America*, by Richard A. Postman.

The Complete Modern Blacksmith, by Alexander G. Weygers, is a great resource. It is *the* book to buy if you want to get serious about blacksmithing. Weygers really knows his stuff.

• CHAPTER 9 •

FIRE PREVENTION AND FIREFIGHTING TOOLS

Firefighting skills and tools are important today, but they will become crucial during YOYO time, since there may not be working telephones or even a functioning fire department available to respond. As firefighters like to say, if you become involved in a crisis situation, you will not rise to the occasion; rather, you will default to your level of training.

We need to address preventing fires and reducing fire risk at your home or retreat.

Follow all of the normal guidelines on sources of ignition within your home (electrical and open flame) and outbuildings. Also pay particular attention to the risk of spontaneous combustion. Oily rags or rags that have contacted oil-based stain or paints should be stored in a galvanized steel container with a lid and positioned away from walls and anything combustible.

Needless to say, every home should be equipped with both smoke detectors and carbon monoxide (CO) detectors, and their batteries changed annually.

MAKING YOUR PROPERTY DEFENSIBLE AGAINST WILDFIRES

There are two concerns: The first is the roof material of your buildings; the second is the defensible space you have around your buildings.

Metal roofs are best, and tile roofs are a close second. Less desirable but still marginally adequate are class C or better rated building materials. Be sure to build or retrofit your house and outbuildings with "boxed" eaves so that embers from a fire do not flow into your eaves and start a fire underneath your roof.

Situate your buildings away from the tallest trees at your site. Having a metal roof doesn't help much if a burning tree crashes down on it.

Immediately near the structures, there should be *no* combustibles. (Think sand, gravel, and bare earth.) As you get farther away from your house/building, you'll need to minimize burnable material. Keep grass watered and mowed. Trim your shrubbery. Keep your woodpiles and fuel storage tanks at least fifty feet away from your structures.

My friend J.T.F. offered this sage advice on firefighting tools:

> Suddenly, you smell smoke. If you've bugged in, the house or apartment next door is on fire. Or the vegetation

upwind from you is on fire—grass, brush, woods, whatever.

If you've bugged out or are living at your retreat, the vegetation upwind from you is on fire—grass, brush, or woods.

Have you prepared for firefighting? Is your area fire defensible?

For a bug-out or bug-in location, I'm a big fan of pressurized water extinguishers for most class A at-home firefighting. You can fill them yourself and use a hand air pump to pressurize them. I also have an abundance of BC and ABC dry chemical extinguishers handy.

Here is a review of the classes of fires and the common agents/extinguishers used to fight them:

A: Ordinary combustibles—wood, fibers, plastic—can be easily extinguished by applying an appropriate stream of water to the base of the fire *or* droplets of water into the superheated area and gases above the fire. The latter method causes the water droplets to flash to steam, smothering the fire. The former cools the fuel below the point at which it will burn. ABC extinguishers (generally monoammonium phosphate) can be used on class A fires.

B: Flammable liquids/gases—gasoline, diesel, propane, natural gas. Foam systems will smother the fire. Dry chemical extinguishers work by interfering chemically with the fire. BC (sodium bicarbonate), potassium bicarbonate (purple K), or ABC extinguishers can be used. Foam and carbon dioxide extinguishers can also be used.

C: Fires in electrical equipment—electric motors, stereos, DVD/CD players, computers. Once the electricity is shut off, the fire can be fought as a class A fire. If you're not sure about whether the electricity is off, attack it with a BC or ABC extinguisher.

There are two other types of fires using American standards, class D and class K.

D: Combustible metal—titanium, magnesium, potassium, steel, uranium, lithium, etc. These fires require special and sometimes specific extinguishing agents. Water reacts with such metals by splitting into hydrogen and oxygen, which can cause an explosion. Explosions around fires are not good things!

K: Cooking oil or deep fryers. You can use class ABC extinguishers on them. But you do have to be careful not to splatter burning grease with the pressure of the extinguisher. You'll have the same issue with most class B foam extinguishers. There are specific class K extinguishers designed to fight cooking grease fires. As I understand it, the "specially formulated aqueous solution of organic salts" reacts with the hot grease to form grease-saponified foam.

Active defense. Active defense is a somewhat new idea. I've heard great reports about how effective it is.

There is a fire prevention gel called Thermo-Gel, which you can spray on your house to defend against an active wildfire that is bearing down on you. A wet gel on any combustible surface, including sidewalls, will keep embers, sparks, and radiant heat from starting a fire.

Inside the house. You should have at least one medium to large ABC extinguisher (at least a 4A rating, which always has a 60+BC rating). I also have four pressurized water extinguishers. I always take one or two with me when I car camp.

It does work. An example: Twenty years ago, a friend asked me how he could make his place less likely to burn down from grass fires.

He implemented my suggestions:

A. Clear out all brush at least a hundred feet from home fence line and all buildings.

B. Do controlled burns around the area to help keep grass fires from house and outbuildings.

C. Permanently plumb in some impact-type lawn sprinklers. Make sure the sprinkler coverage will include the ground around the house and outbuildings and/or the sides of the house and outbuildings.

D. Spend the money to purchase a pump and water-storage system that will enable all of the sprinklers to run for 45 minutes *and* accommodate all ¾-inch x 100-foot garden hose stands. (Tips are the straight bore type with a shutoff). A local volunteer fire department had just put a 750 gallons per minute (GPM) fire truck up for sale—he bought it and put it up on blocks, built a concrete tank that took overflow from an existing windmill-supplied water tank, and plumbed them all in.

His home and outbuildings all had metal roofs. Most of his outbuildings are all metal. His big barn is hundred-year-old wood with a tin roof.

Several years ago a county in Texas had a wildfire that burned more than thirty thousand acres of land (that's more than forty-eight square miles). After that happened my friend called me and said what I had suggested had kept his home and barn from burning down. The fire burned up to and around his home and outbuildings. He said he started the sprinklers when the fire was about five hundred yards away. He and his wife and two sons manned the garden hose sections and used them to put out spot fires while his daughter ran the pump station. He said the water supply ran out about ten minutes after the fire had burned past. He and his family sustained no injuries and lost nothing in the home area to the fire.

Mr. F. offered this primer on the science of fire:

To understand firefighting tools, it is important to understand the dynamics of a fire. Some of you may recall learning about the "fire triangle" in school. The theory is that combustion occurs when all three components (oxygen, fuel, and heat) are present, and removing one or more will extinguish the fire. While this is a simplistic approach, it makes an appropriate foundation to start with. First off, this means that the fuel and oxygen components must attain proper geometric distribution, or fuel-to-oxygen mixing. This usually requires the fuel, whether in a liquid or solid form, to be heated until it vaporizes. This is where heat comes into play. "Flammable" means that it will vaporize at temperatures below 105 degrees Fahrenheit and generally includes liquids such as gasoline, alcohol, propane, etc. "Combustible" refers to fuels that vaporize at temperatures greater than 105 degrees, thus requiring more heat input for the combustion process to occur. This is also why it is harder to start a campfire in the dead of a Canadian winter than in summer in West Texas. As a fire burns, the combustion reaction produces large amounts of energy in the form of heat. This in turn becomes the heat necessary to sustain and/or grow the fire. The hotter the fire, the more fuel that becomes available and the more rapid the fire's growth. The only limitation now is the available air. It is important to note, however, that not all fuels need to be in vapor form. Fine dust particles, when airborne in high-enough quantity, can attain the proper mixing with oxygen to burn quite rapidly. This is important for anyone with bulk storage of grains, coal, sawdust, and even dusty hay.

The oxygen, or oxidizing agent, in the context we are concerned with comes from "standard" atmospheric air—roughly 20 percent oxygen and 79 percent nitrogen. As the fire burns, hot combustion gases expand and rise in a superheated plume. As these gases rise, fresh air is drawn into the fire at the base, heated, consumed in the fire, and again released upward. This is what is referred to as a convection current and one reason why you aim a fire extinguisher at the *base* of the fire. Also note, however, that in some instances, such as with gunpowder, no outside oxygen is required for combustion. Some chemicals, such as nitrates, contain sufficient quantities of oxygen within the molecules and are easily released during the combustion process. These burn rapidly and are difficult to control.

The risk of chimney fires can creep up unwittingly. Unburned volatiles called "creosote" are given off primarily due to green/wet wood, low-temperature fires, and insufficient airflow. This creosote builds up until it either blocks the flue or is ignited by a hot fire. If a fire occurs, immediately close all inlet vents on the stove to smother the fire. If it is an open fireplace, extinguish the fire below, then carefully try to close the damper if you can. Do not attempt to cover the chimney, but do try to water down the roof if possible. There is otherwise very little that can be done for a chimney fire. Water sprayed into the flue will likely crack the flue liner. Even the extreme temperature generated is likely to cause damage to the chimney. Damaged flues and chimneys drastically increase the likelihood of a structure fire. It is best to take every precaution to avoid a chimney fire. (Woodstove chimneys should be cleaned *at least* once per year!)

Get Away!

It is important to keep your distance, as explosion or eruption is possible. Any type of fire is a bad situation and there is little you're going to be able to do. A pressurized hose could be used to cool surfaces but at the risk of overflowing the tank or can, thus spreading the fire. In the event of a leaking propane line that catches fire, shut off the gas at the source if it can be done safely. It is unlikely that anything else you try will be successful, and even if it is, you'll be releasing raw fuel that is likely to reignite.

One of the most common and dangerous household fires is the grease fire. This generally occurs from superheating animal fats or vegetable oil and also applies to paraffin. Again, do not use water. Find something to cover it with, such as a pot lid if you are cooking. The next step is to do nothing. That's right, don't touch it. Let me repeat that. *Do not touch it.* Don't even think about it. You see, as oil, grease, and paraffin burn, the autoignition temperature decreases. That means that if any air is introduced, it *will* flash over again, unless it has cooled sufficiently.

FIREFIGHTING TOOL SOURCES

Several of my readers have mentioned HomeFirefighting Systems.com in Pollock Pines, California. They sell pumps, foam, gel, tanks, and equipment that would be appropriate for retreats.

The Ben Meadows catalog is a great place for all kinds of outdoor equipment. The print catalog is a few hundred pages long, with everything from soil testers to firefighting gear and arborist supplies. Their Web site has a "Wildland Fire Management" page; see snipurl.com/27lzb6i.

In conclusion, here are some of my own firefighting suggestions: If you are building a retreat from scratch or if you are replacing an existing water system, I recommend that you spend a little bit more and put in a large cistern, preferably with gravity feed with a substantial head, and put in a two-inch-diameter schedule 40 service line to the house. Just outside of the house install a "T" in the two-inch line with a 2-inch gate valve. (Downstream of that "T" is where you can reduce to one-inch or smaller lines for your house pipes.) Those 2-inch gate valves are outrageously expensive—currently more than $150 each—so shop around; perhaps buy them used. At the big gate valve, you can attach a proper high-volume firefighting hose rig. Effective firefighting is all about dispensing a large volume of water, *fast*. Anything smaller than a 2,000-gallon cistern and a two-inch-diameter line will *not* suffice! (Okay, perhaps a one-and-a-half-inch line if you are on a tight budget and you feel lucky.)

CHAPTER 10

TIMBER, FIREWOOD, AND LUMBER TOOLS

Free wood is puppy dogs and sunsets! Free wood is money in the bank, fuel for the furnace, and landscaping all in one! It's miraculous in its absence of liquidity. Ever seen a lawyer come and steal half your firewood? Had a politician skim 10% of the top of the cord? Had it vanish in a hard drive crash? I think not. Free wood is peace and joy. . . .

—The Adaptive Curmudgeon's Blog

Turning standing trees into a pile of firewood or a stack of lumber is both a science and an art form. The basic tools you will need are a chain saw (with lots of spare chains and at least one spare bar), a full complement of chain saw safety gear, several axes of various types, a splitting maul, a sledgehammer, and several wedges. The more advanced tools—for those who own substantial stands of timber—can include log-milling machines (commonly called a chain saw mill or Alaskan mill).

I have been cutting and splitting my own firewood since the 1980s, but I recognize that there are others with far more experience. Here is some advice from SurvivalBlog reader Sam D.

CUTTING WOOD

One of my first investments was a Stihl chain saw with a 20-inch bar. Starting with little experience, about ten chains, one sprocket and two replacement bars later I'm finally getting pretty good at felling trees. A 20-inch inch bar is a good size for using with a sawmill, as it can fell trees up to 2 to 3 feet in diameter. Having a smaller, 12- to 16-inch backup saw will be a lifesaver the first few times your bar gets stuck in a tree. It's also much lighter and easier on your back for small jobs.

A pair of chain saws, combination tool, chain file, and a combination safety helmet (with integral mask and earmuffs)

One thing to consider is the cost of chains. I get my 20-inch pro chains locally for about $15 each, but most places charge more than $22. At this point, accessories and replacement parts have cost me as much as the chain saw, so plan accordingly.

CHAIN SAW CARE AND MAINTENANCE

I struggled with sharpening chains early on. There are some great YouTube videos that teach the basics. The overview by Wranglerstar is very thorough. I use a large C-clamp in the woods to hold the bar steady, and I tighten the chain first to prevent wobbling. A sharp chain will cut straighter and faster, run cooler, stretch out less, and last longer. Watch the wood chips coming off the saw. When they go from little squares (chips) to more of a sawdust consistency, stop and sharpen. It may seem like a pain, but a sharp chain will save you a lot of headache in the long run.

If your chain saw is cutting sideways, it's because the chain is dull, the teeth were not sharpened evenly all the way around, or the rakers need to be filed down. Keeping your chain out of the dirt is also extremely important. Sand will stretch out your chain faster than anything.

Mistakes can happen in an instant, so work carefully and *always* wear a full set of safety gear!

The Crosscut Saw Company (crosscutsaw.com) sells traditional one-man and two-man saws for those who are chain saw adverse, purists, the fuel deprived, and for those who value quiet. (In a societal collapse, there may be a huge advantage in being able to work quietly.)

A Home Sawmill

While considering the resources available living on a tree farm, and the lumber required for my earthbag dwelling, I decided to purchase a sawmill. The two manufacturers that have the best reputation are Wood-Mizer and TimberKing. A basic manual sawmill will run about $3,000 to $5,000 used. Adding hydraulics for log loading, turning, and cutter-head movement bumps that up to about $10,000 to $15,000. A computer-controlled mill starts at around $30,000, and the mechanically inclined can build one for about $2,000.

I decided on a used TimberKing 1220, their basic manual 15-horsepower band sawmill with a 28-inch capacity. I paid about $5,000 and it came with two cant hooks (a must), a $900 blade setter/sharpener kit (strongly recommended), a trailer kit, and a track extension that cuts lumber up to 24 feet in length.

Anyone living on a large plot of land with trees should seriously consider buying or building a sawmill. Every year we get dead trees from the summer drought, lightning strikes, and blowdowns from the storms. For folks on small plots in the country with lots of trees available, a sawmill can make sense. I've cut down large cedar trees for neighbors who wanted more grass growing for their cattle. I've even picked up logs cut by the power companies to prevent downed power lines. I've had requests to mill lumber from a small timber company and supply wood to a man who makes furniture.

I run the mill by myself 90 percent of the time using either the cant hooks or my backhoe with a set of skidding and lifting tongs to move logs around. Skidding tongs are for dragging logs; lifting tongs are heavier duty and rated for overhead lifting. Forks can be added to the backhoe as well, but it will make an already twenty-foot machine even longer. A skid steer is the ideal companion for a sawmill, but I get by with my backhoe using the tongs. The downside is tongs only work on one log at a time, and moving logs or leftover slabs in bulk requires forks.

Most logging operations won't touch anything under ten acres because of equipment moving and setup costs, and this leaves a lot of good timber available for small mill operators. Another option is to offer a portable sawmill service or have people bring logs and pay you to cut them or give you a portion of the cut timber (usually up to a 50 percent share).

We used to pay someone to cut, stack, and burn our dead trees that fell into our hay pastures. Now they produce a very basic building material that in a TEOTWAWKI or natural disaster scenario would prove invaluable. This is especially true for the lower-end sawmill designed for manual operation.

SAWMILL CONSIDERATIONS IN A POST-COLLAPSE ENVIRONMENT

With the higher-end models, what happens if something in the hydraulic system breaks down and you can't fix it? Can it be run manually? How will you get a twelve-hundred-pound log four feet off the ground without the hydraulic loader? There's also the extra fuel consumption to consider, as some models have a separate engine to run the hydraulics.

I've spent several hundred dollars stocking extra parts and new blades and doing repairs on my mill. The setup is fairly simple, and the engine is a Kohler Command Pro, which is commonly found on riding lawn mowers, so replacement parts or complete replacement engines are easily sourced.

I've cut large 24-foot, 6-by-6-inch and 9-by-9-inch pine beams to support a living roof on my earthbag home. I've used the slabs (a waste product) to build a rustic heavy-duty chicken coop. A sawmill really opens up a lot of creative possibilities for woodworking projects. I also have a huge pile of leftover slabs that I can sell for $50 on Craigslist or bury to create a hugelkultur bed. Hardwood slabs can be burned for charcoal, which is added to soil or used in filters. I scoop up the sawdust and use it in natural building and spread it in the gardens.

THE HARDEST PART OF RUNNING A SAWMILL

Working big logs stands out as the toughest job on a manual mill. Two men using cant hooks makes this easier. A long heavy crowbar is also useful for moving and straightening logs. The longer and bigger the lumber you're cutting, the heaver it gets and the more difficult it will be to move. The toughest job is lining up a big log to cut the maximum length your mill can handle. You have only an inch or two of clearance on the ends, and manually sliding a big log from the end is hard. Using a backhoe can/will snag on the frame and drag the whole setup off level footings, and you will find yourself spending the next hour re-leveling.

Cutting is simply setting the blade height with a crank and then turning a second crank to move it forward. A rough-cut 2-inch by 12-inch by 20-foot pine is around 80 pounds if fairly green, and this must be moved and stickered (stacked with small stakes in between each board to let them evenly dry). So the bigger the log, the more likely help or tractors are needed. Anything less than 10 inches is hardly worth cutting up, and anything more than 18 inches is much easier with help.

WHAT TENDS TO GO WRONG

Just like with the chain saw, having a sharp, properly tensioned blade is important to avoid wavy cuts and other problems. New blades tend to stretch after their first use. Not observing the tension loss and running into dense knots has led to wavy boards several times. I've run a blade so dull that it stopped in the middle of a log. It won't back out because the band will slip off the wheels, and getting it out is a real pain. The trick is to pay attention and change the band as soon as it starts to dull.

It also can be tricky to square up the cut side against the log stops while locking it down for the next cut. It can twist a bit and I hence end up with trapezoids instead of square boards. A bit of close observation and practice can minimize this. Putting the lumber through a planer or "turning the cant" (squared-up log) back and making a second pass can fix this.

I spend about 30 minutes setting and sharpening each blade, which can be done anywhere from four to eight times, depending on the steel's hardness. Two men running a mill all day will go through three to five blades, which cost about $28 each, with shipping.

GETTING TO A FINISHED PRODUCT

Fresh-cut lumber will need to be stickered and dried out either naturally or in a kiln. I dry lumber on cinder blocks to raise it off the ground, and cover it with large tarps from billboards. Used billboard tarps can be found at flea markets, trade days, or on Craigslist for less than fifty dollars. They are heavy duty compared to hardware store tarps.

If you want to produce and sell dimensional lumber, you will want to consider building a kiln. It's basically a shed with a heater. In an off-grid situation, it should be possible to use a rocket mass heater to dry out lumber by burning the leftover slabs every few days to heat the shed. It would certainly require a commitment over several weeks.

Beyond that, you will want to consider a robust thickness planer and shaper if you plan to make wood flooring or other finely finished wood products. All that's left is to figure out what to do with all the inexpensive lumber that you'll have sitting around.

A FEW CLOSING THOUGHTS

Putting a roof over a stationary mill is a good idea. A large span is ideal to move logs in, which for me means thirty-plus feet. Used chicken-house trusses are ideal. They typically have a forty-foot span and room at the sides to stack lumber, and they can be purchased for about a hundred dollars each.

One final note: Having worked with axes and handsaws, I can't overstate the importance of storing fuel to run your equipment. In my case this is in a plastic fifty-five-gallon HDPE drum, treated with PRI-G fuel stabilizer annually (for up to twelve years of storage), a hand-operated transfer pump, and a bung wrench. It's important to seal the bungs tightly so that moisture doesn't intrude or so that the lighter fractions in gas don't evaporate, making it difficult or impossible to start an engine.

None of us know what the future holds, but the ability to produce usable lumber for your local community is an invaluable asset for you and your neighbors. In a post-collapse situation, it could prove to be a worthy bartering resource.

• CHAPTER 11 •

RIFLES, SHOTGUNS, AND HANDGUNS

Guns only have two enemies: Rust and Politicians.

—Derry Brownfield

A FIREARM IS A PARTICULARLY VALUABLE AND USEFUL TOOL

A recurring theme in Western journalism, academia, and collectivist politics is the quaint notion that firearms are intrinsically evil. That is, that they have a will of their own, which somehow incites their owners to murder and mayhem. I liken this nonsensical belief to voodoo.

Cartridge firearms are compact vehicles for change that have shaped modern history. The righteousness of their use is entirely up to their users, since, like any other tool, they can be used either for good or for ill. A rifle is no different from a claw hammer. To wit: A hammer can be used to build a house, or it can be used to bash in someone's skull—the choice of uses is entirely up to the owner. A bulldozer can be used to build roads, or to destroy houses. A rifle can be used to drill holes in paper targets, or to dispatch a marauding bear, or to murder your fellow man. Again, the choice of uses is entirely up to the user.

If a criminal or psychopath with evil intentions uses a firearm, then it is a tool for evil. But if it is used for good (to defend life and property), then it is a tool for good. A firearm by itself has no sentience, no volition, no moral force, and no politics. The proper term for this is "adiaphorous"—neither good nor evil. A firearm is simply a cleverly designed construction of metal, wood, and plastic in the form of a precision tool.

Ever since the invention of accurate rifled firearms, the men who've wielded them have set the course of human history. For someone to exclude himself or to seek to disenfranchise others from owning or carrying them is absurdly illogical. Because they are such useful tools, our founding fathers recognized the great importance of safeguarding our ownership and freedom to carry arms at all times and in all places. Arms of all descriptions are specifically protected by the Bill of Rights. These enumerated rights should be taken at face value and not misconstrued. The Second Amendment is about protecting your right to go deer hunting the same way that the First Amendment is about protecting your right to publish poetry.

SURVIVAL GUNS

I am often asked, "What is the best gun for survival?" The answer is, in short, the best gun that you and your friends can afford. Sure, you might get by with a well-worn SKS or even a lever-action .30-30, but your chances of survival are significantly better with a .308 battle rifle.

Please note that I mention you *and your friends* because commonality of magazines, common training, and commonality of spare parts might prove crucial.

SURVIVAL GUN SELECTION

Just how many guns will you need? If you are on a budget, you might get by with a good-quality bolt-action rifle chambered in .308 or .30-06, a 12-gauge pump shotgun with a spare riot-gun barrel, a .22 LR rifle, and a .45 automatic pistol. However, in order to have the versatility required for the many shooting tasks at most farms and ranches, you will likely need at least twice as many guns. For a more complete discussion of guns suitable to a self-sufficient and self-reliant lifestyle, the late Mel Tappan's book *Survival Guns* (Rogue River, OR: Janus Press) is generally recognized as the best general reference in print. And for a more complete discussion of guns suitable for self-defense, I highly recommend *Boston's Gun Bible*, by Boston T. Party.

Acquiring a battery of guns for use at your farm or ranch should be considered a necessity, just like buying a Hi-Lift jack or a chain saw. Purchases should be made systematically and dispassionately. As with buying any other tool, you shouldn't skimp on quality. A well-made gun can deliver decades or even generations of reliable service.

A BASIC FIREARMS BATTERY

There are two schools of thought regarding establishing a firearms battery for use in the event of societal breakdown:

1. Maintaining a broad range of firearm types and cali-
    bers, but in a shallow depth of supply. This allows
    for the flexibility of moving to another system or cal-
    iber if something should break or a logistics stream
    should dry up. It also allows different styles of tools
    to be available to meet the needs of differing sizes
    and physiques among the team members.

2. Maintaining a narrow range of firearm types and
    calibers, but in greater depth of supply. The idea here
    is to maintain familiarity with the given system and
    to simplify the logistical stream.

I am definitely in the "narrow but deep" logistics camp.
Commonality of calibers, magazines, spare parts, and weapons familiarity has its advantages. In general, I recommend
buying duplicate modern firearms chambered in common
calibers such as .308, .30-06, .223, 7.62x39, .50 BMG, 12-gauge,
.22 long rifle (rimfire), .45 ACP, .40 S&W, and 9mm Parabellum.

Here at the Rawles Ranch, for many years we standardized with M1A (semiauto M14) rifles, but after M14 magazines
and spare parts became prohibitively expensive, we transitioned to L1A1 rifles. Even more recently, we transitioned
again, to AR-10 rifles. Our decision to switch to AR-10s was
partly for training compatibility, since my kids had all done
their transitional training to high-power shooting with
M4geries, and some of them might end up serving in the
U.S. military. It was also because the supply of L1A1 (and
FAL) parts is definitely drying up. A nice British L1A1 parts
set (sans receiver) now sells for six hundred dollars or more.

As of 2005, military rifle parts sets could no longer be imported with barrels because of an ATF dictate. Meanwhile, AR-10 parts are getting more and more common, and falling in price, since there are now more than fifteen AR-10 makers in the States. Another issue was magazine commonality with HK91s, since we have a couple of those here at the ranch. Lastly, AR-10s weigh more than a pound less than a FAL, L1A1, BM59, HK91, or M1A. So for the same weight as an iron-sighted L1A1, we can carry an AR-10 with a Trijicon ACOG scope. Another strong inducement to make the change was magazine availability. I like to have a dozen spare magazines on hand for each rifle. L1A1 magazines are now selling for more than thirty dollars each, new in the wrapper. Metric FAL magazines cost just a bit less, but HK G3 alloy magazines are still less than three dollars each in like-new condition, and can often be found used for under two dollars each. For anyone considering buying an AR-10, I strongly recommend buying a Rock River LAR-8. This gun can accept FN/FAL magazines and L1A1 (inch pattern FAL) magazines.

My generic guidance for North America is as follows, but your mileage may vary, depending on your locale and your preferences:

Main Battle Rifles: M1A, AR-10, or FAL variants (including the L1A1)

Secondary (Intermediate Cartridge) Carbines: AR-15, M4gery, or AK-47

Shotguns: Remington 870 or Mossberg 500 series, 12-gauge

Long-Range Countersniper/Hunting Rifles: Remington Model 700 or 770 or Savage Model 10 series .308

Winchester (or possibly .30-06 in Canada—see note on page 158 on M1 Garands)

I've heard a lot about the new Remington Model 770 rifles, as a low-cost alternative to the Model 700. These use 6-groove button-rifled barrels. These rifles can be found new, and factory equipped with a 3-9x40 variable scope for less than $375, or less than $500 in the more weather-resistant stainless steel variant with camouflage stock. The scopes are already bore sighted at the factory. One of these rifles, along with a few spare 4-round detachable magazines, is effectively an "off the shelf" countersniper rifle capable of shots of more than 500 yards on man-sized targets. For caliber commonality and a manageable recoil, most folks will want to buy one chambered in .308 Winchester with a 22-inch barrel. But if you live in elk, moose, or caribou country, or if you desire a very long-range counter-sniper rifle, then experienced shooters might consider the variant of the Model 770 chambered in .300 Winchester Magnum, with a 24-inch barrel. That rifle would be capable of 700-plus yards, in the right hands.

Ultra–Long-Range Countersniper/Hunting Rifles: Windrunner .50 BMG. Alternatively a Spider Firearms Ferret .50 if you are on a tight budget.

Primary Defensive Handguns: Colt, Springfield XD, SIG, or Glock chambered in .45 ACP or possibly .40 S&W

Secondary/Concealment Defensive Handguns: Smaller-capacity Colt, Springfield XD, SIG, or Glock, with cartridge and magazine commonality with your primary handguns. Good choices include the Colt Officer's Model, the XD Compact, and Glock Model 30.

Note: If you buy a later SF-variant Glock, in most cases you cannot use the older-generation magazines. But the more recent-production magazines (recognizable by the shiny notch in the front) will fit and function in both early- and late-generation guns. Those are the magazines to buy for all of your spares! Note that Gen 4 Glocks are reportedly able to use older-generation magazines and incorporate the SF-variant features.

For all of the aforementioned, buy ammunition, spare magazines, spare parts, spare optics, and cleaning equipment and supplies *in depth*. That means a *bare minimum* of six spare magazines per handgun, and eight magazines per rifle. Also, be sure to acquire a full set of load-carrying web gear for each long gun. And for the sake of longevity, if you have the option to buy stainless steel for any particular model, then I advise you to buy it. Someday your great-grandchildren may thank you for doing so.

Furthermore, I suggest that you be wary of the "cool" factor. Just because a gun looks sexy doesn't make it more capable or more practical. Sure, *outwardly*, the SIG 550/551 series is mechanically and ergonomically "the best" 5.56mm battle rifle ever made. But that doesn't mean you'll be able to find magazines or spare parts for them once the world falls apart (unless, perhaps, you live in Switzerland). You are far better off buying a ubiquitous M4gery or AK, just for the sake of availability of magazines and spare parts.

The only exceptions to the preceding general guidance would be for specialized firearms that are added to a battery because of (A) regional peculiarities, (B) legal loopholes, or (C) exceptional logistical circumstances.

Regional Peculiarities Could Include:

1. Proximity to a national border. If you live close to Canada, for example, then it might be wise to own L1A1 rifles, which have parts and magazine commonality with the obsolete but still warehoused Canadian C1 service rifles. Other possibilities include Lee-Metford or SMLE rifles chambered in .303 British. And the Mexican army (*ejército*) still uses HK G3s, so there is also a potential future source of spare parts and magazines.

    In Mexico, the .38 Super cartridge is still popular among civilian shooters (because of the ban on civilian ownership on guns in military chamberings), so it might be useful to have one pistol chambered in .38 Super if you live close to the Mexican border.

2. Plentiful big game such as elk, moose, and caribou, which would necessitate adding a belted magnum caliber. If this is true of your locale, then make inquiries to determine which caliber is the most popular, regionally.

3. The presence of dangerous predators, particularly brown bears and grizzly bears. This might mean adding a handgun in a potent caliber such as .44 Magnum, .454 Casull, .45 Winchester Magnum, or perhaps .500 S&W.

4. Caliber commonality with the local gendarmes. If the local police or sheriff's department issues an unusual caliber such as 10mm or .357 SIG, then it might behoove you to add a couple of pistols and plenty of

spare magazines and ammo to match. Or, if you are a dyed-in-the-wool .45 shooter, but your local police or sheriff's department issues (or mandates the purchase of) .40 S&Ws, then it might be wise to add a couple of the same model to your battery, funds permitting. If nothing else, having the extra ammo and magazines on hand might earn you a few brownie points when the balloon goes up.

5.   Especially draconian gun laws or strong local social stigma on open carry that might push you toward purchasing very compact or more concealable handguns. If this is the case, then who knows? Perhaps an AMT Backup .45 ACP or even a Kel-Tec .380 ACP might be a better handgun for you to buy.

Legal Loopholes Could Include:

1.   Owning an oddball caliber in a state where a particular caliber is banned. For example, California banned .50 BMG rifles, but wildcat .49-caliber cartridges based on the same cartridge case are legal. (At least, they are for now. Just give those nanny-staters time. They'll eventually try to ban everything except butter knives.)

2.   Some countries such as France and Mexico restrict ownership firearms in "military" chamberings such as .223/5.56mm NATO, or .308/7.62mm NATO. So in those locales it would be illegal to own a Mini-14 chambered in .223 Remington, but it might still be legal to own one in .222 Remington. And likewise you can't own an M1A or AR-10 chambered in 7.62mm NATO, but it might be legal to have one chambered in

.243 Winchester. In Mexico, you can't own a .45 ACP, but you *can* own a .38 Super or a 10mm. (Consult your local laws through an attorney.)

3. Pre-1899 guns in the U.S. (and pre-1898 guns in Canada) provide a special opportunity to acquire some guns without a paper trail. Laws on antique guns vary widely between countries. (See the FAQ that I coauthored on the subject: snipurl.com/27sngnv.) Antique guns are available from a number of vendors and auction sites, including:

- 1898Colts.com

- Antique Arms Inc. (antiquearmsinc.com)

- 1898andB-4.com

- Empire Arms (empirearms.com)

- GunsAmerica (snipurl.com/27p0j1l)

- Auction Arms (snipurl.com/27p0j72)

- Fine Old Guns (snipurl.com/27p0jjj)

(See Appendix C for further details on pre-1899 guns.)

4. In Canada, nearly all center-fire semiauto rifles have magazine restrictions, limiting them to five-round magazines. But there is a specific exception made for M1 Garands, which use an eight-round en bloc clip. So Canadian preppers might consider making the M1 Garand their main battle rifle, and buying bolt-action countersniper rifles chambered in the same cartridge (.30-06), for the sake of commonality.

5. In Australia, nearly all semiautomatic rifles are re-
    stricted, but bolt-actions can still be purchased (albeit
    with registration). This makes SMLE bolt-actions—
    including the Ishapore 7.62mm NATO variant—
    particularly attractive.

Exceptional Logistical Circumstances:

1. The importation of large quantities of military sur-
    plus ammunition in an unusual caliber. For example,
    in the 1990s, military surplus 8x57 Mauser was inex-
    pensive and plentiful. And more recently, large quan-
    tities of 7.62x54R (the Mosin-Nagant and Dragunov
    high-power ammo) have been imported into the U.S.,
    at prices far below the prevailing prices for most
    modern center-fire-caliber ammunition. This makes
    it advantageous to buy a rifle in one of these calibers—
    particularly a pre-1899 specimen—to take advantage
    of inexpensive, plentiful ammo, for target practice.
    Similar opportunities might arise in the future. For
    example, if a boatload of 7.5x55 Swiss ever comes to
    our shores, I can assure you that I will buy a lot of it,
    and a couple more Schmidt-Rubin straight-pull rifles
    or carbines to match.

2. Acute shortages of particular calibers might necessi-
    tate buying alternate arms, or in exceptional circum-
    stances perhaps even re-barreling some of the guns
    in your battery. Military adventures overseas and
    political firestorms domestically have created some
    ammo shortages of varying durations. Only time
    will tell whether or not these will turn into chronic

shortages. During WWII, virtually all of America's gunmakers transitioned to almost exclusively filing military contract orders. During the war, civilian hunters were eager to buy almost any gun in almost any caliber that they could lay their hands on. There were plenty of buyers, but precious few willing sellers, and new guns were very scarce.

Rawles's Recommended Firearms

BATTLE RIFLES

Selecting a battle rifle for self-defense is a highly subjective topic. I recommend that you carefully weigh these factors: ergonomics, parts and magazine availability, reliability, and accuracy.

Here are some possible battle rifle selections, including some pros and cons:

AK family—These are ubiquitous and unquestionably very reliable. The Cadillacs of the AK family are the Valmet M76 and the Galil (chambered in .223 or .308). But they are expensive and have quite expensive, proprietary magazines. It is also difficult to mount optics on them.

Galil .223—Difficult-to-mount optics and fairly expensive magazines

HK93 .223—Scarce and expensive rifle and magazines, but the clone rifles are less expensive than the originals

SIG556—Uses very common AR-15/M16 magazines. Has easy-to-mount optics.

Mini-14 .223—Not as accurate as an AR at long range. But with a wood stock, it looks fairly low-key and decidedly unmilitary, which, depending on where you live, might be an advantage with a five- or ten-round magazine inserted.

SIG716 Patrol—A bit spendy at $1,725, and so new that it has no established track record

FAL and ParaFAL clones—Magazines are getting more expensive.

AR-10—This is a rifle that looks like an AR-15, but it is chambered in the more powerful 7.62mm NATO/.308 Winchester. Of these, the Rock River Arms (RRA) LAR-8 is probably the best .308 semiauto on the market. One key advantage is that the LAR-8 uses FAL magazines, which are more widely available than AR-10 magazines.

AR-15—With millions in circulation and more than eight hundred thousand produced just in 2013, the AR-15 (and M4gery variants) is the most popular semiauto center-fire rifle in the United States. Spare parts, magazines, and accessories are all available in profusion. The cartridge that these guns shoot (5.56mm NATO) is underpowered for self-defense.

I previously recommended buying the AR-10 variants that use the inexpensive HK G3 magazines. But unfortunately, the two makers, CMMG and SI Defense, both dropped them from their product lines. If you can find one of these discontinued rifles, jump on it. Then do yourself a favor: Buy fifty spare magazines per rifle. That will ensure a multigenerational supply of magazines for your family. I hope other AR-10 makers will begin producing rifles that can accept the ubiquitous G3 magazine.

SPARE PARTS FOR AR-15 AND AR-10 RIFLES

Ideally, it would be best to a have a complete spare carrier assembly, to provide a quick "in the heat of battle" replacement in case you break a firing pin or extractor, or you gall an ejector. (Ninety-nine percent of AR bolts are "automatic headspacing," so the assembly is a drop-in replacement.) If you are on a tight budget, get just one each of these critical high-breakage/high-loss subcomponents from the bolt carrier group: firing pin, firing pin retaining pin, ejector, ejector spring, ejector retaining pin, extractor, extractor retaining pin, and extractor spring (with nylon insert). The only other parts that I've seen break (or get lost) are ejection port cover springs and buffer retainers. However, both of those are noncritical to the function of the rifle. Buttstocks and handguards also break, albeit less frequently. If you have a generous budget, get spares of all of those in addition to a complete spare bolt-carrier assembly.

HKs AND CLONES

While original German Heckler & Koch–made rifles (identified by an HK prefix) are now very expensive and rare collector's items, there are a number of good clones on the market that are built with military surplus parts kits supplemented with a few U.S.-made parts to meet the requisite U.S. Section 922(r) parts count. These include PTR Industries (PTR prefix), Century Arms (C prefix), Special Weapons (SW prefix), and Vector Arms (V prefix).

While HK93/33 magazines are fairly expensive, the 7.62mm NATO HK 91/G3magazines are *very* inexpensive. Used, HK German army contract, 20-round aluminum G3 magazines can be found for as little as $2 each in good functional condition, and brand-new ones are often less than $4. When you compare that with $30 FAL magazines or $35 M14 magazines, they are a definite bargain.

Spare parts and accessories for HKs are available from HKParts.net, HK Specialist, and RTG Parts. RTG has both original HK and POF (Pakistani Ordnance Factories—not to be confused with POF-USA) G3 parts.

I prefer Heckler & Koch 93s with 1:7-inch twist barrels, so that they can stabilize the now popular 62-grain bullets. If it has a 1:7-inch twist barrel, it will be marked "178" on the bottom of the barrel near the trunnion. Many of the original HKs with this barrel had "II" date codes. A few 93 clones using these barrels can be found, but that might take some hunting. A quick way to spot these at gun shows is that they often have a longer flash hider than the standard HK93 or HK33 flash hider.

Optics mounting for HKs and HK clones is a bit more tricky than for AR-15s and AR-10s. The original HK claw mounts are still available, and they work well on the PTR series with either STANAG rings or with a Picatinny rail adapter. You can also still find original Hensoldt (Bundeswehr contract) scopes with claw mount for less than $400.

PTRs also now come with an aluminum forend, which Picatinny rails are easily screwed onto.

THE SPRINGFIELD ARMORY M1A

The Springfield Armory M1A is a 7.62x51 NATO semiauto-only version of the venerable M14 rifle. The M1A is a very rugged rifle. It is basically a clone of the M14, but capable of only semiauto fire.

The M1A would be an excellent addition to any survival battery. There aren't many spare parts you need to keep on hand to keep it going. Perhaps buy a recoil spring, firing pin, extractor, and extractor spring/plunger unit. However, don't attempt to replace the firing pin or extractor without the proper bolt disassembly tool and the training to do so.

THE BULLPUPS

Most nations are in the process of transitioning to bullpup designs for their infantry rifles. These are carbines that have their magazines positioned behind their pistol grips. While they don't offer many weight advantages, they are much shorter and handier to use, without sacrificing barrel length. This makes them particularly handy for use when inside vehicles.

Steyr AUG-SA. The "SA" stands for "semiauto." With the original full-auto military models, pulling the trigger partway back results in semiautomatic fire, while a pull all the way to the rear results in fully automatic

fire. The AUG-SA can be converted to left-hand shoul-
dering, with a substitute bolt. The earlier (pre-ban)
models have limited sighting options, but the later
models have a Picatinny rail, providing umpteen sighting options. Most AUGs use proprietary magazines
that cost twenty-five to forty-five dollars each. However, a factory replacement NATO stock allows the use
of standard M16 magazines.

Microtech STG-556 (a Steyr AUG look-alike). These are
often mistakenly called a clone of the AUG, but they
really aren't clones. Very few parts interchange, nor do
their magazines. I do not recommend them, since they
are no longer in production, and therefore the availability of spare parts and magazines in the long term is
doubtful.

IMI Tavor. These were developed in Israel and just recently introduced into the American market. They use
standard M16 magazines. Now available for less than
seventeen hundred dollars, these are highly recommended if you prefer a 5.56mm NATO bullpup.

FN FS2000 bullpup. These use standard AR-15 magazines and are fairly lefty-friendly.

Kel-Tec RFB. As this book goes to press, the RFB is the
only semiauto .308 bullpup in regular production. It's
not very lefty-friendly, but it's ideal if you want a .308
bullpup. It uses FAL magazines. If they made a variant
that accepted the plentiful HK G3 magazines, then the
RFB would be a huge success.

SurvivalBlog editor Michael Z. Williamson had this to
say about the LAR-8:

I recently got my hands on an LAR-8, which is Rock River Arms' entry into the AR-10 clone market. This model is the LAR-8 16-inch barrel flattop, with a suggested retail price of $1,100. It's a heavy rifle compared with the AR15, at 8.1 pounds (for a carbine, remember), but it's quite reasonable for a .308. From the rear: The buttstock is a standard 6 position, and aftermarket stocks will fit; likewise for the Hogue grip. The internals are proprietary, but it appears that standard AR fire control parts will fit. The trigger felt really odd, almost like a hair trigger, until we weighed it at about 6 pounds. It is just exceptionally crisp with a very sweet let-off. The fire control switch is right-handed only, which is a little odd, since the magazine release is ambidextrous (button on each side), and the bottom-mounted bolt release is, too. It appears that standard handguards will also fit. The controls are easy to reach. I do like the bolt release. Insert a magazine, brush downward with your thumb, and it clacks into battery. Operation was flawless for the full day. This is on the rifle as delivered, with no oil, teardown, anything. It chambered and fired every time, and there were no hitches. Here's one of the prime selling points: The rifle accepts metric and inch FAL magazines. I had a little more trouble with inch mags, but I suspect they were older. I bought ten at a gun show for $50. That's enough magazines for 210 rounds of ammunition (nine 20-round, one 30-round). That's about the price for *just one* of the competitor's magazines. Feed and function was fine with both, assuming the magazine was good. At that price, though, one can buy a case and keep the tight ones for spare parts. The weapon is tight, well made, with excellent fit and finish. It is well balanced and comfortable. It felt very robust and durable, though because it was a loaner, I didn't do an all-out abuse test. If you are familiar with the AR-15, the only relevant differences for handling are the weight and the location of the bolt release, which is lower than one is trained for, but easily managed. Since most of us slap the paddle as the hand goes down anyway, there's no problem adapting to carrying the motion to the base of the magazine well. Other minor differences are the *much* heavier recoil spring, and the previously mentioned excellent if unusual trigger. The rifle came without iron sights on this model (other models have M16A2-style sights). This was a minor problem. I have excellent scopes, but no riser to bring them high enough above the receiver, and no mountable front sight. I managed by attaching one of my EOTechs. The EOTech is a combat sight, not intended for long-range precision, but it seemed to work well enough. I was within 8 inches of center with the first shot (before zeroing). That's good enough for combat shooting at 100 yards. Weather was 64 degrees Fahrenheit, 62 percent relative humidity, barometric pressure 29.87 and falling, and elevation was 630 feet above sea level. Using South African surplus R1M1, I was able to keep 4-inch groups of 20 rounds. This is 4 MOA, with 30-year-old ammo, a short barrel, and a combat sight with a red dot shooting at a red target. I find this acceptable. With U.S. military surplus Lot 1-80, three shot groups ranged from 2.125 inches to 2.375 inches, very consistently. Using U.S. military match grade XM118 LR PD (2002, Lake City), our groups ranged from 1.125 inches to 1.6 inches, median 1.375 inches. This is well within the 1.5 MOA accuracy promised, using an inadequate sight.

For anyone wanting .308 power and range with the AR's handling, welcome home. For those wanting a reasonably priced precision rifle for target shooting, hunting, or when TSHTF, you'll be hard-pressed to do better than a Rock River LAR-8. The availability of AR-platform accessories and mods is a significant point in favor of both, as are the very inexpensive military surplus FAL magazines. One can buy the rifle and included case; customize stocks, grips, handguards, and mechanicals; load two hundred and more rounds in magazines, and still be money ahead of a competing AR-10 clone. Add in the exceptional accuracy and strength, and it tops my list.

I have had a personal preference for AR-10s, L1A1s, FALs, and HK91s, but I hardly rule out functionally equivalent rifles such as M1As. I particularly recommend AR-10s for readers who are prior U.S., Canadian, or Israeli military service—those who already have a lot of muscle memory invested in the AR platform, namely the U.S. M16 series and the Canadian C7 series. (The sights and controls will seem quite familiar and "right" to them.) I also appreciate the low weight of AR-10s. (They weigh more than a pound less than most other .308 semiauto battle rifles.) The only major drawback is that the AR-10 has the same dirty gas tube action as an AR-15. Just be sure to clean your rifles frequently and scrupulously.

I strongly prefer the varieties of AR-10s that can use standard FN-FAL magazines. Specifically, I recommend the Bushmaster AR-10 FAL magazine variant (now out of production) and the RRA LAR-8. Standard metric FAL magazines can be found for as little as fifteen dollars each (used), versus up to fifty dollars each for some of the proprietary AR-10 magazines. The cost of spare magazines may not be much of an issue to casual shooters, but it is a big issue for well-prepared folks who want to salt away twenty-five or more spare magazines for a "lifetime supply." At forty dollars each, a supply of twenty-five magazines would cost nearly as much as the rifle itself! If properly cared for, rifles using noncorrosive ammunition may last for three generations of regular use. But magazines are the most fragile part of most guns, and cannot be expected to put up with the rigors of regular field use. They are also easily lost when in the field. They are, after all, very vulnerable when you drop to a prone position. Another factor to consider is the prospect of another federal magazine ban. Based on the experience of the ill-conceived 1994 to 2004 bans, I anticipate that any new ban will probably bump the prices of FAL magazines to more than $60 each, and AR-10 magazines to $120 each, or more. If the anticipated new law is permanent (with no sunset clause), then magazine prices might reach even more absurd heights.

I generally prefer gas piston designs, since the Stoner gas tube design is notoriously prone to fouling. But if you are scrupulous and consistent about firearms cleaning, then an AR-10 should serve you well.

FALs and L1A1s

If you don't mind a paper trail, some of the best bargains are some of the "builds" done by individual members at the FAL Files forums (see snipurl.com/27skqqs). With sales often prompted by circumstances (such as car repairs, job loss, and divorce), these are sometimes sold below cost. It is even possible to get lucky and find a FAL or L1A1 listed at the FAL Files Marketplace board that is being sold in your own state by a private party. Of course, any transfers across state lines would have to be processed through a federal firearms license (FFL) holder. State laws on firearms also vary widely. Research them before you make a purchase.

If avoiding a paper trail is a high priority, then I recommend that you make all of your gun purchases at gun shows from private parties, or through GunBroker.com (online auctions) or GunsAmerica.com (fixed-price sales—usually more expensive). Both of these Web sites have search features that allow you to search by state. Again, that way you won't run afoul of the federal law that prohibits the transfer of a modern (post-1898) gun across state lines except through an FFL dealer.

TELLING "INCH" FROM "METRIC" FAL MAGAZINES

Metric magazines have a small (quarter-inch wide) front locking lug that is merely punched out of the body of the magazine. Metric magazines also have a slim floorplate that is the same width as the body of the magazine. In contrast, inch pattern (British Commonwealth) L1A1 magazines have a relatively large and beefy (half-inch wide) front locking lug that is brazed onto the front of the magazine. They can also be distinguished by their floor plates, which are wider than the magazine body, and have a "button" floor plate release on the bottom.

MAGAZINE DUPLEXING

I've always considered dual- or triple-magazine systems a bit gadgety. It's something that the Tommy Tactical/armchair commando crowd often consider a necessity. But in my humble opinion, if you can't solve your immediate tactical problem with *one* magazine without a lightning-fast reload, then you are severely outnumbered. You should have been working as part of a fire team! But, in fairness, I suppose that they might make sense for a GOOD or escape-and-evasion situation in which you are on your own and you need to lay down suppressive fire to break contact.

I should also mention that one problem with duplexed or triplexed magazines is that you typically carry just *one* of these duplexing devices, with the remainder of your ammo in standard magazine pouches. So where do you put the duplexed magazine once it is empty? It doesn't fit in an ammo pouch. You can always use a dump pouch. And I surmise that you could put a parachute cord loop on it and clip it to a carabiner on your web gear once it's empty. But again, aside from some specialized situations, the whole duplex and triplex magazine concept seems like more of a mall ninja fashion statement than something that is truly practical.

Semiauto Belt-Feds

One subject that is rarely discussed in TEOTWAWKI disaster planning is the role of belt-fed semiauto rifles. For those who already have their basic battery of guns and who have squared away all of the other crucial aspects of preparedness (food storage, water sources, communications, first aid, nuclear, biological, chemical [NBC], etc.), it might be time to move up to a belt-fed semiauto rifle. In this section, I'm going to briefly discuss four of them, three of which can be fired from both a bipod and a tripod, and one that can be fired only from a tripod or a heavy pedestal mount.

The first is the Ares Shrike (snipurl.com/27skquq). This is a .223 replacement "upper" for an AR-15 or M4 that uses M27 SAW disintegrating links. I've owned one of these for several years. It is the only belt-fed that is light enough that I would consider taking it on a retreat security reconnaissance patrol.

Slightly larger is the D.S. Arms RPD carbine chambered in either the original 7.62x39mm or in 6.8mm SPC. This uses a non-disintegrating link belt. I haven't fired one of these, but I hear that it's a quite robust design. This would be a good choice for any group that has standardized with the 7.62x39mm Russian (AK) cartridge.

The Shrike costs much more than the RPD, but it is in a more common caliber, has far better spare parts availability and a huge range of accessories, and with a bit of plastic grinding it can also be equipped with a Slide Fire stock, to allow *fairly* accurate bump firing at a high cyclic rate. (A two hundred-round belt going through one of these in bump-fired bursts via a Slide Fire stock is a sight to behold!)

If you have a big budget, then you might even consider an Ohio Ordnance Works semiauto M240-SLR or a TNW M2 or M3 Browning .50 BMG. These weigh twenty-eight pounds and eighty-five pounds respectively—and that is without any ammunition or a tripod! Fully equipped, with several cans of linked ammo, spare barrel, tripod, T&E mechanism, and their specialized tools, these are *quite* heavy and can only be considered crew-served weapons, with very specialized functions—such as protection for vehicular convoys or defending the perimeter of a large fixed retreat in plains country (from a tripod mount).

GAS PISTON AR-15s AND M4s

As this book goes to press, the jury is still out on gas piston uppers for ARs. I consider this a situation roughly analogous to the Betamax versus VHS "war," back in the 1970s. For a while, nobody knew which format would prevail.

One legitimate fear is that if you buy a piston AR-15/M4 upper from a maker that drops out of the running, then eventually you'll be stuck with an upper with poor (or perhaps no) availability of spare parts. Other than one HK MR556 upper that I bought to test, I am not yet jumping on the gas piston AR bandwagon.

I'm often asked about Ruger Mini-14 rifles. Because the factory-made Mini-14 thirty-round magazines cost three times as much as AR magazines (and the aftermarket magazines are junk—so don't be tempted to buy those), your total cost on a rifle with ten or twelve spare magazines is less when buying a typical AR-15 or M4 with a dozen spare magazines. Further, because of the profusion of spare parts available for the AR and its modular design, I prefer it. I only recommend Mini-14s for folks who live in localities with stringent gun control laws, where AR-15s are banned because of their looks.

HANDGUNS

The choice of a handgun is even more subjective than the choice of a rifle. My general advice is to buy a reliable semi-automatic pistol from a reputable manufacturer, in a common caliber that starts with the number 4 (namely .40 S&W

and .45ACP). Beyond that, I recommend that you test-drive a lot of handguns to find one that is comfortable in your hand, with a natural point of aim, and that fits your budget. Many indoor shooting ranges offer handgun rentals. This provides a way to shoot a lot of different models before you make a purchase. Those rentals will be money well spent!

My particular favorite is a Glock 30S. This is the narrow slide variant of the compact Glock .45 ACP with a ten-round magazine. (Although it will also accept the thirteen-round magazines made for the Glock Model 21.)

Remember: A handgun that is too heavy to carry comfortably will eventually get left at home or in your vehicle on the wrong day. That could prove disastrous. Better to buy a lighter handgun that you'll be able and willing to carry at all times.

FIREARMS STANDARDIZATION

Standardization of defensive weapons is a worthy goal. It results in commonality of training, of magazines, of stored ammunition, and of spare parts. This is a win-win in many ways!

For defending a fixed location, you should standardize with .308 Winchester for your rifles. The only advantage of .223 is that the rifles weigh less and you can carry more ammunition. These are meaningful factors only for long-distance patrols. If weight is not an issue, why not standardize with a full-power cartridge? Since a CETME can be purchased for less than the cost of an AR-15 clone or about the same as a Ruger Mini-14, and magazines for CETMEs are far less expensive (less than three dollars each), I would forgo buying any .223s and buy *all* .308 CETMEs. I don't consider it a serious man-stopping rifle. I think that you should get .223s only for any of your family members who are under sixteen or who are too frail to handle the weight and recoil of a .308.

I think the following "group standard" should make sense: CETME .308 rifles (one per adult), Mossberg 590s (one for each two or three adults), and Glock or S&W (M&P) .45s (one per adult) will make a fully adequate no-frills battery.

ONE COMMON CALIBER FOR RETREAT RIFLES AND HANDGUNS?

Using one common caliber *sounds* like a great idea, but it just doesn't work in today's world—at least not for primary defensive firearms. Let me explain my reasoning, starting with a little historical background.

Much of the recurring "cartridge commonality" thinking stems from America's pioneer Old West experience. In the late 1800s it was popular to carry a Winchester lever action .44-40 rifle or carbine, and a Colt or S&W revolver chambered in the same cartridge. This is just what my great-grandfather Robert Henry Rawles did in the 1880s and 1890s. He came out west by covered wagon in 1857, at age twelve. From the late 1870s until his death in 1911, he habitually carried a Colt Single Action Army (SAA), and, when on horseback or while hunting, he supplemented the revolver with a Winchester Model 1873 rifle. Both guns were chambered in .44-40. One of his cousins did essentially the same thing, but instead carried a Smith & Wesson .44-40 top-break revolver and a fairly uncommon but highly sought-after Colt Lightning pump-action .44-40 rifle. Doing so had a big advantage in cartridge commonality. But that was back in the days of black-powder cartridges, which all had high-arcing trajectories. Today, if you were carrying a carbine chambered in a pistol caliber, and your opponents had a detachable magazine 7.62x39 or .308 battle rifle—with high velocity and flat trajectory—then you'd be badly outmatched.

Typical pistol chamberings (such as 9mm Parabellum and .40 S&W) are not sure and quick man stoppers at two to seven yards (typical combat pistol shooting distance), and they are absolutely pitiful stoppers at two hundred to three hundred yards. They just don't have the requisite oomph at long range to penetrate and put Mr. Badguy out of the fight. Furthermore, at long range they have a "rainbow" trajectory, which is difficult to compensate for under the stress of combat. For your primary defensive rifle, you are much better off with a flat-shooting high-velocity cartridge like .308 Winchester. There is some utility in owning a pistol caliber carbine, but in my opinion that is limited to small-game hunting, pest shooting, and training youngsters. But do not make the mistake of thinking that they are adequate for self-defense in the twenty-first century.

The other possible "one cartridge for carbine and pistol" compromises that I can envision might include:

1. Selecting a quite powerful handgun cartridge like .44 Magnum, .45 Colt, or perhaps a .45 Winchester Magnum. As political pundit (and gun enthusiast) Kim du Toit so aptly puts it: "To put it in perspective, a 250 gr. bullet in .44 Remington Magnum arrives with 775 ft.-lbs. of energy; [but] the 260 gr. bullet in .45 Win

Mag arrives with 1,300 ft.-lbs. Ouch." In my opinion, both of these cartridges are slightly overpowered for a combat handgun, but still underpowered and not flat shooting enough for use in a carbine or long-range self-defense. Because .44 Magnum is a traditional rimmed cartridge, nearly all of the carbines that are available (such as those from Marlin, Puma, and Winchester) are lever-actions with tubular magazines. Ruger does make a semiauto .44 Magnum carbine (a complete redesign of their .44 carbine from the 1960s) and a lever-action (the Model 96/.44), but unfortunately both use a fairly fragile four-round rotary magazine (hardly suitable for self-defense). For handguns there are a lot of great .44 Magnum revolvers (including the S&W Model 629), and of course the .44 Desert Eagle pistol. But given its clunky ergonomics, I consider the Desert Eagle strictly a choice for advanced shooters. (It would take a lot of training to learn how to shoot fast and accurately.)

The .45 Winchester Magnum is a rimless cartridge, which makes it compatible with a wider range of magazine designs. Three years ago, I read that Collectors Firearms was doing .45 Winchester Magnum conversions for M1 carbines. But unfortunately their Web site no longer mentions those, so I suspect that they are out of production. (Perhaps they still have a few pieces of old inventory.) But I'm sure that some enterprising individual will soon come up with one on an AR-15 platform. Nor would I be surprised if both Ruger and Marlin expanded their semiauto carbine

offerings to do likewise. (Carbines in .45 Winchester
Magnum would be a good market niche.) Pistol options for .45 Winchester Magnum include the Wildey
and the LAR Grizzly, but given the heavy recoil of the
cartridge, I presume that even more training would
be required than for mastering the Desert Eagle. As
for .45 Colt, I don't consider it a serious self-defense
cartridge, for two reasons: First, nearly all of the factory loads are extra-mild, for liability reasons—since
ammo makers fear that they might be loaded in an
early iron-framed Colt SAA. Second, the exposed rim
width of .45 Colt brass is considerably smaller than
that of the .44 Magnum. In my experience it is not unusual for a fired piece of brass to slip past a .45 Colt
revolver's extractor "star" on the ejection stroke and
get jammed underneath. This would be a very bad
thing to have happen in the middle of a gunfight.

2. Buying both a pistol and a registered (Class 3) submachine gun chambered for the same cartridge,
preferably .45 ACP. If you substitute a submachine
gun (SMG) for the carbine, three-shot-burst capabil-
ity and 30-round-magazine capacity could make up
for a pistol cartridge's lack of power at moderate
ranges. (Although the practical accuracy of a three-
shot burst from an SMG at more than 100 yards is
dubious.) And of course you would have to weigh
the risk/reward ratio of making yourself "high profile" by getting a registered Class 3 SMG. (In the U.S.:
fingerprinting, a federal transfer tax of $200, a back-
ground check, and the consent of your local sheriff

or chief of police.) Other possibilities with the same magazine capacity (but a lower social profile) might be semiauto SMG clones. These include the HK USC semiauto carbine in .45 ACP (the semiauto variant of HK's UMP SMG), the Rock River Arms or Olympic Arms AR-15s chambered in .45 ACP, or the semiauto versions of the venerable Thompson SMG. But with any of these guns, you are still limited to the relatively low power and rainbow long-range trajectory of .45 ACP.

The two preceding approaches *might* work if you live in a heavily wooded eastern state (or perhaps a western rain forest such as on Washington's Olympic Peninsula) and all of your anticipated combat shooting will be at less than 120 yards. But I don't think that if I were in that circumstance I would be willing to put my life on the line, all for the sake of being able to say that I had achieved absolute cartridge commonality nirvana. And as for anyone living in open country, like in the Plains states and most of the western states, limiting oneself to only a pistol cartridge—even the whomping .454 Casull—would be absurd.

3. Someone of very small stature (weighing, say, ninety-five pounds or less) might be justified in buying an FN PS90 carbine and an FN Five-Seven pistol as a companion gun. Both shoot the FN 5.7x28mm cartridge. This, again, would be a considerable compromise.

One other consideration is that even if you get a pistol and a semiauto carbine chambered in the same cartridge, odds are that their magazines will not be interchangeable. Hence, if you needed to rob Peter to pay Paul, then you would have to unload one type of magazine and reload it into another magazine. This doesn't sound like much fun to do in a hurry, when the air is thick with lead.

In my estimation, the best that you can hope for in terms of maximizing cartridge commonality while still being able to "reach out and touch someone" is to have all of your handguns chambered in one cartridge and all of your rifles chambered in another. For example, here at the Rawles Ranch, nearly all of our handguns are .45 ACPs, and nearly all of our rifles—both bolt-actions and semiautos—are .308s. (We do have a couple of .30-06 rifles, but only because we are in elk and moose country.) We also have a few AR-15s and Tavors, but we consider them transitional trainers for teenagers and preteens who will eventually grow up to shoot .308s.

ADVICE ON 5.56MM VERSUS 6.8MM VERSUS 7.62MM RIFLES

There has been some conjecture that the U.S. military might someday switch from the 5.56mm NATO cartridge to 6.8mm Remington for the standard service rifle. So, should American preppers switch to 6.8mm Remington, in anticipation? The short answer is no.

If the economy were to hold together, and *if* the new 6.8mm round were to eventually gain long-term civilian-market popularity, then it someday might be a viable option. Otherwise, I do not recommend it, since supporting your firearms battery logistics could be troublesome at best, or perhaps even a complete showstopper at worst. If you have a huge budget, you might want to buy both 5.56mm and 6.8mm upper receiver/barrel assemblies to mate with your AR lower, and several thousand rounds of each type of ammo. Otherwise, I would skip the small calibers altogether and get a battle rifle that is chambered in a true stopping and versatile caliber: .308 Winchester. (Parenthetically, I'm amazed how many letters I get from readers who say that they wouldn't trust a .223 for hunting 150-pound deer, but they are willing to trust their lives to a .233 for hunting 200-pound armed men. I fail to see the logic there.)

SAFETY NOTE

You can shoot soft-nose commercial ammo in .223 Remington bolt-actions and in an M4 or other AR-15. But the 5.56 military ammo can be shot in *only* in the M4, because of a mismatch in chamber dimensions, which can cause pressure problems in commercial bolt-actions. *Just the opposite* is true in .308s: You can shoot 7.62mm NATO in a .308 Winchester, but you cannot shoot .308 Winchester in 7.62mm NATO-chambered military rifles.

GUNS ON A TIGHT BUDGET

My advice to my readers is to always have an effective means of self-defense close at hand. For someone on a tight budget, I recommend buying a reliable military surplus bolt-action and plenty of ammunition. Mausers, Enfields, and Mosin-Nagants are all good "budget" rifle choices.

With time, as your budget increases, you can then upgrade your battery to include a reliable semiauto 7.62mm NATO rifle for each adult in your family. The low-end choice in this category would be a CETME clone. The medium-price choices would be FN/FAL or L1A1 "parts kit" clones built on IMBEL receivers, HK91 clones (such as a PTR 91, Vector Arms, or Century Arms, or low-end M1As from makers like Norinco. Eventually, with disciplined savings, you should be able to afford more expensive MBRs from "name" makers such as original Belgian FALs, original H&K-made HK91s, or M1As from Springfield Armory or Fulton Armory. If at all possible, retain your earlier rifle purchases. These are great guns to keep on hand for barter and charity.

Depending on your state and local concealed-carry restrictions, an inexpensive bolt-action rifle is perfect for use as a "trunk gun"—a gun that you keep handy in the trunk of your car at all times. If your car gets broken into or stolen, or if it's destroyed in a fire, then you will surely regret losing your old "beater" $150 Mauser, but it would be a severe financial blow and the cause of more substantial mental anguish to lose a $2,500 top-of-the-line ACOG-scoped AR.

Most important: Upgrading to the crème de la crème of rifles is something that should be done only *after* you have your key logistics squared away. By this, I mean after you own a water filtration system, an honest one-year food supply, communications gear, non-hybrid seeds and gardening supplies, traps and snares, and plenty of first aid gear. Far too many survivalists slip into the "armchair commando" mind-set and overemphasize firearms purchases.

DEER RIFLE AS BATTLE RIFLE?

I've had several readers ask me about using a semiauto hunting rifle such as the Remington M742 or Model 7400 as a makeshift battle rifle. That might seem like a great idea for someone who is budget conscious or who lives in a restrictive state, but I *do not* recommend it.

I consider owning a full-power .30-caliber center-fire rifle essential for both hunting and self-defense. But keep in mind that civilian hunting semiautos and pumps are not designed to withstand the sustained high rate of fire that might occur in a full-scale post-TEOTWAWKI firefight. Their internal tolerances are so precisely machined that they are likely to bind up when the action gets hot. Also be aware that they are more tightly chambered than military arms, which have intentionally loose dimensions. You cannot depend on something like a Remington 740 or 760 series to keep shooting reliably after two hundred rounds of rapid fire. Nor can you expect them to keep shooting reliably with muddy or gritty cartridges. A civilian pump-action or semiauto hunting rifle might suffice in a pinch for a gunfight, but *not* in an extended large-scale firefight!

Don't expect a civilian semiauto hunting rifle to do the same job as a military rifle. It won't be up to the task.

For anyone in states like California, New York, and New Jersey, which have so-called assault weapons bans, I recommend that you buy an early-generation military-issue semiauto rifle such as the M1 Garand (.30-06, fed from an 8-round en bloc clip), the FN-49 in

.30-06 (10-round semi-detachable magazine, stripper clip–fed), or perhaps if your state law will allow it, the Argentine contract FN-49 in .308 (10- or 20-round detachable magazine). A poor second choice might be a Russian or Chinese SKS (7.62x39mm, stripper clip–fed, with a fixed 10-round magazine). By the way, I do not recommend the French MAS series semiautos of the same era, because they have demonstrated reliability issues. Nor do I recommend the U.S. M1 carbine, because it shoots an underpowered pistol-class cartridge (the .30 M1 carbine cartridge).

And in locales where all semiautos are banned, consider a Steyr, Ruger, or Savage Scout chambered in .308 Winchester. All of these bolt-action rifles look very low key, which is an advantage for those living in restrictive states.

HOW MUCH AMMO?

I'm often asked by both my blog readers and consulting clients how much ammo to store. I recommend stocking the following as *minimum quantities* for self-defense and hunting: 4,000 rounds for your primary rifle (preferably .308), 3,000 for .22s, 1,000 for shotguns (20 percent buckshot, 5 percent slugs, and 75 percent bird shot), 3,000 for your pistols, and 500 rounds per secondary or nonstandard-caliber guns (such as a .38 Super, .44-40, or .25-20).

For each muzzle-loader, store enough lead, powder, and percussion caps to provide 500 shots.

AK-47s as Survival Rifles

SurvivalBlog reader Z. M. made the following observations about AK-47s and their merits as survival rifles:

> The AK-47 is known for its ability to function under incredibly challenging circumstances. While some rifles may require regular and frequent care to keep them running properly, the AK requires only ammunition and a clear chamber to function reliably. Of course, the rifle will perform better and will be far more durable if properly cared for, but if engaged in a protracted struggle and without the room, tools, or time to safely maintain the weapon, the owner of an AK variant is going to find himself very satisfied with its performance even if several days, weeks, or months pass without cleaning or lubricant application. While I will regularly strip, clean, and lubricate my rifle, it should not be picky or prone to jam should I fail to do so for a longer period of time. The Kalashnikov family of weapons has absolutely proven itself in this arena for several decades.
>
> Where else can one find a massive stock of .30-caliber rifles in a military configuration for less than six hundred dollars each? Certainly not in an AR variant platform. While I heartily endorse the rough-and-ready nature of the ROMAK WASR-10, the only alternative for a shooter who wants a full-power cartridge in a semiautomatic, magazine-fed rifle is the Saiga line, where you can affordably find .223, .308 Winchester, and 7.62x39 rifles. However, I always recommend a WASR on the grounds

of parts commonality. The Saiga line of rifles uses a different magazine well, requiring modification to use military surplus and commercial 30-round magazines—and their proprietary magazines are expensive.

My number one reason for recommending a WASR over a Saiga is the availability of replacement parts and aftermarket accessories. The AK parts market is a leviathan in our country, with numerous small shops dedicated to crafting excellent-quality parts for Kalashnikov rifles. Most gunsmiths will have an easy time modifying just about any part of the rifle or adding any part you might come across.

A shooter who doesn't have the $1,200 to $2,000 required for a high-quality full-bore rifle and glass may just find that an AK and good scope will fit better into a smaller budget, and it will offer comparable battlefield performance to a trained marksman. Above every other consideration, the quality of the shooter's *training* is paramount. In most cases, the AK offers an opportunity to acquire rifle, glass, ammunition, and ample training for the price you'd pay to get a rifle and glass in some of the AR-15 or M1A designs.

As with all things in life, we take the good with the bad. The AK platform does, clearly, have some of the latter. If not, then wouldn't nearly everyone be an AK shooter?

First, an out-of-the-box AK will not have tack-driver accuracy. Nor would we want it if it did. A "new" AK rifle, fed the most economical Wolf-brand commercial ammunition, will generally deliver a two-to-four MOA (MOA = roughly one inch at one hundred yards) performance. For most AK owners, the knowledge that they can hit a circle averaging three inches in diameter at one hundred yards is adequate. These shooters always aim center-of-mass, and rely on the power of the 7.62x39 cartridge, which is fully capable of taking down combatants.

There are a few AKs out there that have better-than-typical accuracy, which in the hands of a good shooter can produce one-to-two-MOA groups. However, the vast majority of AK owners will never tune their rifles to the extent to get this tight, because the steps needed to wring this performance out of the rifle will also have a deleterious effect on the reliability of the firearm. Imagine that you have a two-ended spectrum; on the left, you have "looseness" or reliability, and on the right, you have "tightness" or accuracy. The AK-47 may be tuned for either purpose, though the platform has a natural affinity for the reliability side of the spectrum.

FIVE SEVEN?

The 5.7x28 caliber (commonly called Five Seven) is growing in popularity, but it is a pipsqueak. Mostly for purposes of experimentation, I bought both rifle and pistol AR uppers in the 5.7x28 caliber. (I own just one "pistol" marked AR lower, sans buttstock, and also have a spare 10-inch 5.56 barrel for it.) In toto, I have put nearly a thousand rounds through my two 5.7 uppers. I found that the pistol upper chambered in 5.7 functions quite well, but the rifle upper in 5.7 jams frequently for some reason that has been difficult to trace. These jams smash the loaded cartridges. These are slow to clear, since they necessitate removing the magazine. That was disappointing. The top-mounted magazine allows very low prone shooting, but I found that it was almost a three-handed operation to swap magazines. I can't imagine it ever being as quick and convenient as traditional magazine changes. That would take *a lot* of practice.

Most important, since it is still essentially an oddball caliber and underpowered, I consider the 5.7x28 cartridge a substantial step down from the 5.56mm NATO in power and range. So I plan to continue to use my 5.7 uppers mostly as transitional trainers for my younger children, and perhaps for some varmint shooting, but nothing more. In essence, the AR-57 has good looks, but it simply doesn't have a lot else going for it, at least in the context of disaster preparedness. My recommendation is to skip buying a spare 5.7 upper for your AR *unless* you are small of stature and plan to carry an FN Five Seven as your primary sidearm. Again, since it is an unusual chambering, that approach would necessitate laying in a lifetime supply of ammunition. Buying guns in oddball calibers goes against the conventional wisdom of common standardized calibers for survivalists.

A FEW FINAL WORDS ON GUNS

You can buy the best guns in the world, but unless you practice with them often, you are *not* prepared. Getting training at a firearms school like Gunsite Academy or Thunder Ranch is money well spent. Gunsite was founded by the late Jeff Cooper. It is still run in harmony with his training philosophy.

I'll end this chapter on guns with a ground truth reminder: Guns are like parachutes—if you don't have one when you need it, then chances are you won't ever be in need of one again.

CHAPTER 12

ARCHERY

The people of the various provinces are strictly forbidden to have in their possession any swords, short swords, bows, spears, firearms, or other types of arms. The possession of unnecessary implements makes difficult the collection of taxes and dues and tends to foment uprisings.

—Toyotomi Hideyoshi, Lord Chancellor of Japan, August 1588, from the order that instituted the Great Sword Hunt

There is a place for archery in survival preparations. It is a nearly silent method of taking game. There may come a day when you won't dare risk the sound of gunfire, which might attract either looters or authorities, so the silence of archery can contribute to the privacy and security of your farmstead.

I've had several readers and one consulting client in the U.S. who mentioned that they've bought archery equipment, but no guns. This is a foolhardy approach. Even the most highly skilled archer with many years of training is no match for a man armed with a high-power rifle and only rudimentary skills. By intentionally under-arming themselves, they will be making themselves the equivalent of aboriginal tribes in the late nineteenth century—and we all know how well they fared. You should acquire and train thoroughly with the best weapons available. Archery is an alternative best suited to folks who live in gun-deprived jurisdictions. If you under-equip yourself, then you are, to paraphrase popular parlance, merely bringing a bow to a gunfight.

Because I have only limited experience with archery, I defer to the expertise of a couple of SurvivalBlog contributors. First, from Muscadine Hunter:

Instinctive Shooting

As with all things, modern technology has made archery a precision shooting experience. But in a true TEOT-WAWKI, how many of the archers using those fancy compound bows will be able to maintain them for more than a year or two before they do not have either the tools or the expertise to properly tune the bow for maximum performance? I don't use any mounted sighting aids, meaning I use the "instinctive" method of aiming. If you practice and learn to use this method, it has several advantages in a survival situation. First, you are not dependent on a sight that can easily get damaged or knocked out of alignment. Second, you can get on target faster shooting instinctively than you ever could trying to line up your target in the peep sight. Third, anything added to your bow equals more weight and often more noise when you shoot. Not learning how to shoot instinctively at the beginning, I believe, will handicap you later. You become too dependent on the use of sights, which as I mentioned earlier can get knocked out of alignment or damaged.

I know many will say the advantages of the compound bow outweigh the disadvantages. I am not here

to debate the pros and cons of compounds over re-
curves or longbows, but here is the biggest reason to
learn to shoot instinctively with a recurve or longbow:
low maintenance. You never have to tune a recurve or
longbow, and in a pinch you can literally make a new
bowstring in less than ten minutes from the inner
strands of 550 parachute cord. You cannot do that with
any compound bow that I am familiar with!

Archery is something the entire family can enjoy, and
although I have harped on the use of traditional archery
equipment in a TEOTWAWKI, to get the wife and kids
started and to make sure they enjoy their initial experience, investing in a compound bow may be a better choice.
Compounds require less strength by the shooter to pull
the bow to full draw. They also deliver more power.

Repair and Maintenance

I always have at least three or four extra bowstrings in
my preps. A supply of beeswax is really about the only
thing you need to keep the recurve or longbow operating at optimal performance. Every time I take my bow
out, I run the beeswax up and down the bowstring
once I have strung the bow. This preserves and protects
the bowstring and maximizes its useful life. Using a
bow and arrow takes a bit more skill because you have
to be much closer to your target, but for OPSEC and
stealth it's hard to beat.

Besides bending or breaking an arrow, the most
common problem you'll encounter is with the fletching,
or feathers. If you shoot frequently, as I do, the fletching
will get damaged or come completely off the shaft.
When this happens, the arrow is useless until it is repaired. For less than fifty dollars you can get everything

you need, including extra fletching, to repair dozens of arrows. A simple fletching jig can be had for about twenty dollars and is a one-time investment. I still have and use the first fletching jig I bought when I was fifteen. In addition, a tube of glue or fletching cement and the feathers are all that is needed. Add some nocks (the nylon or plastic tips on the arrow that the bowstring is placed into) and, depending on the type of shaft you are using, either some epoxy or a resin glue stick and some field points or broadheads and you're ready to repair or even make your own arrows. While store-bought fletching is much easier to use, in a TEOTWAWKI a single common bird feather can make at least two fletching feathers.

While re-fletching arrows is a common necessity with both traditional and compound bows, the advantage of traditional is that arrows are much easier to make, if you have to, to shoot in a recurve or longbow. Due to the tremendous thrust a compound bow initially creates when the string is released, wooden shaft arrows will sometimes splinter, making them unsatisfactory for compound bows. In a TEOTWAWKI, aluminum or graphite shafts will be hard if not impossible to find. Even though I use a recurve bow, I prefer aluminum shafts. They are more accurate and last longer than wood. But if I had to make my own wooden arrow shafts, my recurve bow would shoot them, whereas a compound bow would just splinter them.

A Backyard Range

Another advantage of archery is that you can build a backyard range even if you live in the city (in most cases, but check your local ordinances first). The least expensive route is to get four bales of hay from the local feed store or co-op. Ask to select the bales yourself, or tell whoever is going to select them at the store that you need only ones that are tightly and evenly baled, since you are going to use them for archery targets. I lay two of them down lengthwise, then place the other two upright behind them. The two bales' thickness will stop any arrow you can shoot, except maybe from some more powerful crossbows. Having the two stacks turned opposite ways prevents the arrow from slipping through the crack between the two bales should it hit exactly at that point. As with any type of shooting, always be mindful of what is downrange behind the target, especially if you live in a subdivision and put in a backyard archery range.

ARCHERY FOR SELF-DEFENSE

And from A. T., this guidance on archery for self-defense:

Bows can be swift, silent, accurate, and deadly, and in the right circumstances, they may be preferable to firearms.

Let me state at the very beginning that shooting wooden arrows out of most modern compound bows *should not be done* and usually will result in the splitting and shattering of the arrow, hopefully not directly into your arm and hand. If the bow has a cam on it, it is possible to match a much higher draw weight than you think you are capable of. As the bow is drawn, the draw weight increases to a peak and then "lets off." The cam allows for a much greater let-off in the muscle and force needed to keep the bowstring fully drawn. The let-off is usually between 65 percent and 80 percent of the peak weight. This results in the equivalent of eliminating two-thirds to three-quarters of the force needed to draw a bow at a certain point, so that it becomes easier on the muscles and bones of the archer. More technically, the cam system maximizes the energy storage throughout the draw cycle, provides let-off at the end of the cycle, and has less holding weight at full draw. A traditional type of bow has a linear draw force curve—meaning that as you draw the bow back, the draw force becomes increasingly heavier with each inch of draw. So it's easier at the beginning and harder at the end. You store very little energy in the first half of the draw stroke and much more energy at the end of the draw stroke, where the resistance is heavier. The compound bow may reach its peak weight within the first few inches of the draw stroke, and the weight remains flat and constant until the end of the cycle, where the cams let off and allow a reduced holding weight. This manipulation of the peak weight throughout the draw stroke due to the elliptical shape of the cams is why compound bows store more energy and shoot faster. The design of the cams directly controls the acceleration of the arrow. Bows can be had with a variety of cams, in a full spectrum from soft to hard (harder gives you more speed).

Overall, a modern cam results in using a larger draw weight, a faster arrow, more accuracy, and a flatter trajectory, with more penetration. High-draw-weight bows require a heavier, stiffer arrow shaft—so while they will generate more energy at the target, they may not generate much faster arrow speeds. Lower-draw-weight bows can use lighter, more limber arrow shafts. International

Bowhunting Organization (IBO) standards allow 5 grains of arrow weight per pound of draw weight. So a 70-pound bow can shoot an arrow as light as 350 grains. A bow set for 60 pounds must have at least 300 grains, and so forth. Surprisingly, when set for IBO minimum standards, many bows are only marginally faster in the 70-pound version versus the 60-pound version. Since a 70-pound bow must shoot a heavier arrow, the savings in arrow weight offsets the loss of energy storage during the draw stroke. A properly set up 60-pound version of most bows will perform within 10 feet per second (fps) of the 70-pound version.

The average bow of fifteen to twenty years ago was barely able to reach 230 fps, and even at that speed many bowhunters got clean pass-throughs on large game like whitetail deer. Today the average bow is shooting over 300 fps at 70-pound draw weight. This means that even bows in shorter draw lengths and lower draw weights will provide plenty of velocity to penetrate the rib cage of a whitetail deer and other large game. A modern single-cam bow with a 50-pound peak draw weight will still send arrows out at well over 220 fps. If you plan to hunt larger game such as elk or moose, or if you plan to take shots from longer distances, you will need additional kinetic energy for complete penetration. A 40- to 50-pound draw weight should provide sufficient energy to harvest deer, and a 50- to 60-pound bow weight will provide sufficient energy to harvest larger, elk-size species. Unless you're planning to hunt huge animals, a 70-pound or greater bow really isn't necessary. Penetration is most often expressed as kinetic energy (KE) and this number should be available with purchase of the bow or by calculating it. The measurable "power" of your bow is its total kinetic energy output. This depends upon just two variables: the mass and the speed of the arrow. Kinetic energy of an arrow can be found by using the formula $KE = (mv^2)/450{,}240$, where m is the mass of the arrow in grains and v is the velocity of the arrow in fps. As a provided example, if your bow shoots a 400-grain arrow at a respectable 250 fps, your actual kinetic energy or power will be roughly equal to 55.5 foot-pounds. That is more than enough to take out a man.

Kinetic Energy Recommendation Chart (as often quoted by Easton and other bow manufacturer catalogs)

<25 ft lbs: small game (rabbit, groundhog, etc.)
25–41 ft lbs: medium game (deer, antelope, etc.)
42–65 ft lbs: large game (elk, black bear, wild boar, etc.)
>65 ft lbs: toughest game (cape buffalo, grizzly bear, musk ox, etc.)

Bleed-out is dependent on the cutting diameter of the blades on a broadhead. With an arrow, more vital organs, arteries, and tissue are cut on the way through the flesh, which usually results in a faster bleed-out of the target than with a bullet. Typically when a bullet goes through the human body, the wound channel closes back up. With a broadhead arrow, the cutting action has left a much larger wound channel that cannot close back up as efficiently, and thus more blood escapes the body at a faster rate. Arrows do not have even remotely the same shattering effect on bone that bullets do, but they can, through blood loss, put a man down as efficiently as a bullet. This appears to be true in my own personal experience with deer, but it is tempered with the fact that I have also knocked deer off their feet with a deer slug, which is not going to happen with an arrow.

Every time that arrow is moved, it causes pain and severe internal damage and creates confusion and hesitancy in the mind of the target. Many who are shot with a bullet often don't realize that they have been wounded until later. If a thirty-inch-long piece of aluminum or carbon fiber is sticking out of someone, then he will realize it, even if it's just a hindrance to his natural body movement.

A bow is not a close-range weapon (it should have a range of at least a hundred yards), because your enemy can usually close with you faster than you can load, draw, and aim. If he is shooting at you, you will need some solid cover. It is possible to get accurate shots from the kneeling position, but too often the knee interferes with the bow limbs and tracking a target. Chances are you are going to have to stand and present a full standing side silhouette to your opponent. A bow is great for shooting a target from ambush (even within your darkened house) and for keeping your location a relative mystery. After your initial shot(s), as your opponent is closing in on you from yards or so, throw the bow down and draw your pistol. You are going to need it.

Thus it is possible for a bow to give power out of all proportion to the individual shooting it (just like a firearm), and you can be confident in taking out the target as surely as people have done for the past several thousand years.

ARCHERY EQUIPMENT FOR THOSE
LIVING IN GUN-DEPRIVED LOCALES

If you live in an area where procuring a gun is difficult or nearly impossible, my general advice is to buy a medium draw-weight compound bow rather than a crossbow. This is because compound bows are much faster to fire repetitively than crossbows.

If you can afford it, there might be some utility in getting a compound bow for yourself, and medium-power crossbows for your wife and children. The latter require less practice, but can be kept "cocked" for brief periods. The key question for determining the maximum draw weight of a crossbow is whether they can handle the task of reloading with a crutch (a crossbow-reloading tool, also known as a cocking lever). Join a local hobby archery club, and choose the right equipment for your particular circumstances. Then be sure to practice, practice, practice.

ARROWS

Most modern arrows are essentially modular. The current trend is toward carbon fiber shafts. You can screw on plain target points for practice, bird points for garden defense, and various broadheads for big-game hunting or self-defense. Some broadheads even have individually replaceable blades. Buy plenty of carbon fiber arrow shafts, spare heads, and spare fletchings. Any arrows or components that are in excess of your needs might someday be valuable barter goods.

Arrows can also be used with some slingshots. So if there is no paperwork required to own a slingshot and arrows, then that might be an even better option than a bow and arrows for anyone who strives to maintain a low profile.

OTHER WEAPONS

Check on the local legality of owning and/or carrying edged weapons, impact weapons, slingshots, flammables, Tasers, stun guns, and chemical irritant sprays. If you opt for a sword, then a wakizashi (Japanese short sword) is the best length for home defense. (Longer swords are too unwieldy in tight confines.)

Laws vary widely from country to country, province to province, and even city to city. Do your homework and stay legal. If all else fails, in almost all locales there is recourse for the humble cane or walking stick, which has been discussed at length in SurvivalBlog (search the blog archives).

CROSSBOWS

Bill H. has some specific advice on crossbows:

> Often romanticized by movies, the crossbow seldom performs the way the purchaser hoped. The nature of the short prod or bow offers a very powerful but short-lived energy source. It does not have the accurate range of a bow, yet has the benefit of being able to be left cocked and fired from a prone position. The crossbow is capable of taking large game and has the additional benefit of being able to reuse its ammo. However, it is clearly recognized by any observer and as such if seen garners the same attention as a firearm. It is, however,

quiet compared with a firearm and therefore can be a good choice for survival hunting.

There are three basic types of crossbows available: standard, compound, and pistol. Of these three, I find that the pistol crossbow is most commonly a novelty item with very little practical use. Arguments have been made that at up to a 75-pound prod it's capable of taking small game and has the benefit of being highly portable. I disagree with this reasoning but encourage readers to make up their own minds.

The compound crossbow looks quite impressive, and the mechanical advantage of the wheels does make the bolt travel faster. The cost of these tools, however, tends to be quite a bit greater than that of a standard crossbow, and the decision of whether the extra cost is worth it depends on your budget. A compound crossbow has the disadvantage of being more difficult to repair than a standard crossbow and has more failure points.

The standard crossbow comes in a variety of designs both modern and archaic. The average draw weight is about 150 pounds, which is more than enough to hunt medium-sized game. Heavier prods, or bows, are available and can increase its capabilities. Repairs to the mechanical aspects are fairly simple and strings can be made just like making a bowstring. If the prod is damaged another can be fabricated using T6 aluminum, fiberglass, or even a leaf spring from a small car.

Crossbow Repairs

Regardless of the design and strength you choose, make sure that you purchase additional strings and a cocking lever to use with it. The cocking lever uses the mechanical advantage of a lever to make cocking the crossbow easier. It also has the added advantage of applying pressure to the prod evenly on both arms. This is important for increasing the accuracy of the tool. Practice with it and know its limitations. If you work within its limits, the crossbow can be a useful addition to your survival tools.

NOTE

If you plan to buy a crossbow, do plenty of research beforehand. Many models have inferior designs that exert excessive friction on their bowstrings, leading to early failure. Some have been known to fully "eat" their bowstrings in as little as two hundred shots!

In conclusion, remember that archery, edged, and less-than-lethal weapons should be integrated into your retreat tools planning, but not at the expense of more modern and capable weapons if they are available in your jurisdiction. Don't leave yourself at a disadvantage for YOYO time.

CHAPTER 13

MEDICAL AND SANITATION TOOLS AND SUPPLIES

Be careful about reading health books. You may die of a misprint.

—Mark Twain

Any well-stocked retreat will have more than just a basic first aid kit on hand. For folks with retreats in remote areas and for *anyone* who anticipates and extended period of YOYO time, it is important to be able to handle a wide range of medical situations, including both acute and chronic care. This takes both equipment *and* the skills to go with it.

FIRST AID

Kory Mikesell, of FrostCPR.com (a SurvivalBlog guest writer), has the following advice on what to stock in a first aid kit:

Most of the commercially available first aid kits are little more than "boo-boo" kits, to fix life's little cuts and
scrapes. An example of this type of kit is available from
CVS Pharmacy and manufactured by Johnson & Johnson; its self-described purpose is for the treatment of
cuts, scrapes, minor burns, pain, swelling, and itching.
This 170-piece kit has 138 Band-Aids, a few ointments,
pads, wipes, and little else. If you were counting on this
kit to save someone's life in an emergency, then both
you and the victim are in deep kimchi!

Preparedness and survival are our ultimate goals,
so we need a larger variety of supplies that will actually be useful in a real life-or-death emergency. If
you've taken a first aid course in the past five years
(and if you haven't, shame on you), your instructor
should have told you that after you've taken care of the
victim's primary needs (ABCs—airway, breathing, and
circulation), you need to look after secondary needs
(serious bleeding, shock, and spinal injuries). Your first
aid instructor should have prepared you for the worst-
case scenario: when advanced emergency care is either
delayed or unavailable and you are the one who must
provide extended care to the victim.

In addition to acknowledging what you know,
consider where you live and what you do for recre-
ational and vocational activities when gathering your
supplies—a well-stocked first aid kit should reflect your
geographic region, activities, and how many people you
may need to treat. Of course, there is a basic minimum
for every occasion, but if it's a kit you are building for a
boat that sails off the coast of Florida, do you really need
a snakebite kit or a tick kit? If you live in the desert south-
west, do you really need vinegar for jellyfish stings? You

wouldn't take an eight-pound megatrauma kit while backpacking, but you would certainly want a comprehensive kit at a survival retreat. Just as there is no single gun to fit all needs, there is no one kit that will fill all medical necessities. Let's explore what a generally appropriate starter kit looks like.

Note: With few exceptions, quantities are excluded because they will vary with the size of the kit and the number of people served.

A Basic First Aid Kit

Your kit should generally include most of these items.

A durable case—preferably with compartments for storage and ease of access

A good first aid reference manual—as a reminder of practices and protocols

A card with emergency numbers (poison control, out-of-state contacts, etc.)

Gloves (latex or nitrile)—at least two pairs, to protect against contamination and pathogens. (Nitrile gloves are preferable in case of unsuspected latex allergy in the patient or even caregiver.)

CPR barrier—to protect against disease transmission

Large absorbent dressings/AB pads (5-by-9-inch or larger)—to stop or control bleeding

Sterile gauze pads, various sizes—to stop bleeding and dress wounds

Roll bandages, various sizes—to dress wounds

Ace-type roll compression bandage—for sprains and strains

Self-adhesive bandages (Band-Aids), various types and sizes—to dress minor wounds

Steri-Strips (butterfly bandages)—for closing wounds

Adhesive tape—to dress wounds

Non-adherent pads, various sizes—for burn wounds

Triangular bandages—for immobilization of dislocations and fractures

Cotton-tipped swabs—for cleaning wounds and applying salves and ointments. (Note that cotton-tipped swabs can leave behind fibers, or even the entire tip. You may also want to include tongue depressors for applying ointment to gauze dressing.)

Bandage shears/EMT shears—cutting bandages or victims' clothing

Tongue depressors—for checking throat issues and as small splinting applications

Tweezers—for splinter removal

Sewing needle—to assist in removing foreign material

Penlight—for emergency lighting and for examination

Oral thermometer (non-glass)—to check vital signs

Syringe or squeeze bottle—for irrigation of wounds

Splinting material—for dislocations and fractures

Emergency blanket—for warmth and treatment of shock

Instant cold pack—for treatment of hyperthermia, sprains, dislocations, and fractures

Instant hot pack—for treatment of hypothermia and some stings and muscle strains

Bio bags—for disposal of gloves and medical waste

Eye cup—for aid in removal of foreign matter in the eye

Eye solution—for eye contamination and aid in removing foreign matter from the eye (Johnson's baby shampoo can be diluted for an easy low-cost eyewash, and used for wound irrigation as well.)

Antibacterial soap—for cleaning wounds and hands after treatment

Antiseptic solution or wipes—to clean wounds

Antibiotic ointment—for wound treatment. (Bacitracin is the preferred topical antibiotic. The commonly sold triple-antibiotic ointment is more likely to cause allergic reactions, which can be confused with worsening infection.)

Hydrocortisone cream—for stings and irritations

Burn gels and ointments

Burn pads—for treating larger burns

Ibuprofen—to reduce swelling of inflamed joints, muscles, and ligaments, and for patient comfort (Ibuprofen will not help swelling of the legs and in fact can cause it, particularly in the elderly.)

Antihistamine tablets—for allergic reactions

Blood-stopper powder—for stopping severe bleeding (QuikClot, TraumaDEX, and Celox are quite effective.)

Pen and index cards—for annotating victims' vital signs

Hand sanitizer—when you can't wash your hands with soap and water

Moleskin—for treatment of blisters and abrasions

Additional Items

In addition to the aforementioned items, there is a list of add-ons that could be included in your first aid kit. These can vary greatly depending on your needs, location, and activities. Some of these may require additional cost, training, or certification:

Separate complete burn kit—for treating multiple or very serious burns

Snakebite kit

Israeli battle dressing—one of the best on the market for serious trauma

Stethoscope—for listening to breathing and heartbeats

Cervical collar—to immobilize the neck from possible further harm

Foldable stretcher—for carrying victims unable to walk on their own

Blood pressure cuff

Sutures—to close serious wounds. (You will also need a needle holder and iris scissors or other small scissors.)

Hemostats/forceps—for closing major bleeding vessels and for aid in suturing

Automated external defibrillator (AED)—for treating ventricular fibrillation that can lead to cardiac arrest. (If the heart has already stopped, the AED won't be effective.)

Scalpel—for removing tissue and for minor surgery

Blood-borne pathogen kit—to assist in cleaning up

Surgical masks—to prevent disease contamination and blood-borne pathogens

Eye shields/goggles

There are also items and medications your victim may need (some of these may require a doctor's prescription):

Asthma inhalers—for the treatment of asthma, COPD, and serious allergic anaphylactic reactions

Nitroglycerin—for the treatment of heart patients

Aspirin—for treating heart patients

Sugar pills—for diabetic stabilization (for low blood sugar)

Electrolyte solution powder—for treatment of dehydration. (Salt and sugar can be mixed with water for an oral rehydration solution. To one liter of water add six teaspoons of sugar and a half teaspoon of salt. These can be dry-mixed in advance in incremental packaging and clearly marked with instructions for mixing with each liter of water.)

Imodium—for treatment of simple diarrhea (Note that Imodium is contraindicated with certain causes of diarrhea such as *C. difficile*.)

Tums—for gas and heartburn

EpiPen—for treatment of severe allergic reactions

Eyedrops—for tired or irritated eyes/contacts

There are also nonmedical items that can work well in a first aid kit:

Headlamp—for clearly seeing your work area

Instant glue (superglue)—to close wounds

Tampons—for penetration or gunshots wounds as well as their primary function

Glasses repair kit

Multi-tool/Swiss Army knife

Insect repellant wipes

Sun block

Lip balm

Hand lotion—for dry and chapped hands and feet

Talcum powder—for treatment of rashes and for foot care

Desitin ointment—for treatment of rashes and sore areas

Hair comb—for removing items from victims' hair and for personal hygiene

Disposable razor—for cleaning treatment site and for personal hygiene

Duck Tape—Who couldn't find a use for it?

Paracord (10 feet)—same as Duck Tape

Now that we have everything and the kitchen sink, what items would I consider to be essential to any kit no matter what size?

Triangle bandage—has so many uses that it is a must-have: sling, bandage wrap, splinting wrap, bandanna, hat, baby diaper, water filter, sarong, halter top, face shield, shade covering, blindfold, dust mask, CAT tourniquet, pressure bandage, ankle wrap, foot covering, gloves, handkerchief, washcloth, personal cooler (wet and tied around the neck), belt, ponytail tie, basket, cold compress . . . Why do you think every cowboy wore a bandanna?

Self-adhesive bandages (Band-Aids) in multiple sizes—There really are no good substitutes.

Antibiotic ointment—Secondary infection of a wound can be fatal.

Sterile gauze pads (various sizes)—Many things can be improvised to slow or stop bleeding, but to properly dress a wound, a sterile covering is vital.

Containers

Now that you have gathered every conceivable medical essential, you will need a place to put it all. Your choice of container is almost as important as what goes into the kit. The size of the kit will be determined by several factors. Is it stationary, or will it be carried? Where will it be going? Where will it be stored? How much room do you have for the kit? Will its environment be wet or hot, or will it be jostled about? Here is a list of possible nonstandard containers for your first aid kit.

- Fishing tackle box
- Tool kit
- School lunch box
- Electronics box
- Ziplock bag
- River rafting "dry bag"
- Pelican-type waterproof container
- Rubbermaid-type storage container
- Plastic office drawers
- Zippered nylon pouch or bag
- Army surplus bag
- Ammo can (painted with a big white cross so you don't take the wrong can to the range)
- Tupperware-type containers
- Cigar box
- Fanny pack
- Small nylon or canvas backpack

A few final thoughts: Rotate, rotate, rotate! Just like food in your pantry, some of your first aid supplies have a limited storage life. With frequently changing and expanding information on expiration dates, I will not advise you when to discard your out-of-date ointments, creams, and medicines. But what I would like to address are those items that people don't often realize have a limited life span. Nitrile and latex gloves are notoriously short-lived, especially in hot environments like a car, RV, or boat. Check them at least once a year and replace when necessary. It is very frustrating to be halfway through putting on a glove when it tears, and if you've done this a couple of times, the cut on your victim's arm may be the least of his worries! Another item with a frustratingly short lifetime is the self-adhesive bandage. As Band-Aids get older, heat and age tend to break down the adhesive and it loses its cohesive strength. If a self-adhesive bandage can't "stick," it really serves no purpose.

Kory's recommendations are excellent, but remember that a first aid kit—just like any tool kit—is only as good as your training. Take a CPR/first aid course. If you already have done so, but it has been a few years, then take a refresher course.

I follow the adage that "It's better to have it and not need it than it is to need it and not have it." That time-proven wisdom applies to guns, first aid kits, pocketknives, and many other tools. In essence, it means that you should carry a first aid kit in your car *at all times*, and a smaller kit whenever you venture afield.

Also make it your practice to back up your supplies with redundant reserves. It is important to be able to restock. (In just one trauma incident, you can use up an alarming number of bandages and rolls of gauze.)

The most expensive item on Kory's list is the automated external defibrillator (AED). We have one, a Philips HeartStart, that we carry in our primary vehicle at all times. Since it is a fifty-five-minute drive (in good weather) to the nearest small hospital and a three-hour drive to the nearest major hospital, having that AED gives us considerable peace of mind.

BEYOND FIRST AID

If you can afford it, buy a full set of minor surgery instruments, even if you don't know how to use them all yet. You may have to learn, or you will have the opportunity to put them in the hands of someone experienced who needs them in the midst of a disaster. This is going to be a big list. I recommend that you buy relatively inexpensive stainless steel instruments made in Pakistan.

DISASTER DENTISTRY

Don't overlook do-it-yourself dentistry tools! Your home dentistry kit should include oil of cloves (a toothache pain killer), a temporary filling kit, tooth-extraction tools, gauze, etc.

SANITATION

Human waste is a problem in times when municipal water supplies are disrupted and toilets won't flush. Modern Americans are no longer accustomed to dealing with personal bodily waste. In urban areas, a grid-down collapse could become a public health nightmare, within just a few days. The average person produces one pound of feces and two to three pints of urine per day. If you multiply those numbers by the number of people in your group for a week or a month, then the problem is self-evident. If your city sewer or septic system is working, then you can still use your toilet by pouring water directly into the bowl to flush the waste.

If a septic system is not working or your water supply is limited, then you will need to construct an improvised outhouse. Plan on a twenty-inch-diameter hole that is at least four feet deep. Once it has been filled with waste to within one foot of the surface, cover it with soil, move to an adjacent location, and dig a fresh hole.

You will need:

- Round-point shovel
- Pick and digging bar (for digging in rocky soil, if needed)
- Several 6-gallon HDPE buckets (just the right height for an improvised privy)
- Two toilet seats with lids (these fit standard 4- to 6-gallon HDPE buckets)
- Materials to construct privacy screens
- Fifty pounds of powdered lime (or fireplace ashes)
- Toilet paper (in quantity)
- Hand soap
- Hand sanitizer

SANITATION IN APARTMENT BUILDINGS

Without water for flushing toilets, odds are that people in neighboring apartments will dump raw sewage out their windows, causing a public health nightmare on the ground floor. Since you will not want to alert others to your presence by opening your window, and no doubt the apartment building's septic system stack will be clogged in short order, you will need to make plans to store your waste in your apartment. I suggest five-gallon buckets. A bucket-type camping toilet seat (one that attaches to a standard five- or six-gallon plastic pail) would be ideal. You should also get a large supply of powdered lime to cut down on the stench before each bucket is sealed. You must also consider the sheer number of storage containers required for a week or more of accumulated human waste. (If they are occasionally emptied, a dozen five-gallon buckets with tight-fitting O-ring seal lids should be sufficient for a family of four, indefinitely.) Since you won't have water available for washing, you should also lay in a supply of diaper wipes.

You will need sacks of powdered slaked lime (calcium carbonate) for the outhouse. Buy plenty! (Fireplace ashes will also suffice.) You will also need toilet paper in quantity. (This stores well if kept dry and away from vermin. It's lightweight but very bulky, so it's a good item to store in the attic. See my novel *Patriots* about stocking up on used phone books for use as toilet paper.) You will of course need soap in quantity (hand soap, dish soap, laundry soap, cleansers, etc.), as well as bottled lye for soap making.

SOAP

Providing details on soapmaking is outside the scope of this book. (There are some outstanding resources on soapmaking available online, most notably in the SurvivalBlog archives.) I also recommend these two books:

The Soapmakers Companion, by Susan Miller Cavitch
Soap Maker's Workshop: The Art and Craft of Natural Homemade Soap, by Robert S. McDaniel and Katherine J. McDaniel

I would be remiss if I didn't warn that it is important to have the right tools and safety equipment for soapmaking. (Lye can cause nasty chemical burns, so you will need rubber gloves, goggles, aprons, and so forth.)

Remember that even if you and your family exercise good sanitation practices in the midst of a disaster, you will very likely be surrounded by neighbors who don't. Therefore, plan on local water supplies being fouled. It is vital that you lay in a supply of plain hypochlorite bleach and have a good-quality water filter (such as a Katadyn or a Big Berkey). A water filter may turn out to be one of your most important tools for survival in that dreaded worst-case scenario.

CHAPTER 14

KNIVES AND TRADITIONAL HAND TOOLS

Each man of the three companies bore a rifle-barreled gun, a tomahawk, or small axe, and a long knife, usually called a "scalping knife", which served for all purposes, in the woods.

—John Joseph Henry, *An Accurate and Interesting Account of the Hardships and Sufferings of That Band of Heroes, Who Traversed the Wilderness in the Campaign Against Quebec in 1775*

THE EVERYDAY CARRY (EDC) KNIFE

Your daily carry knife is one of your most important survival tools. Not only is it available for daily utility tasks, but it can be useful for hunting, outdoor survival, and self-defense when you are in gun-deprived jurisdictions. Most people carry a sheath knife, a folding pocketknife, or a multi-tool.

SHEATH KNIVES

Sheath knifes are stronger than folding knives, but they have a few disadvantages:

1. They are bulkier, and therefore tend to get left at home when you need them most.

2. They are more conspicuous.

3. They are restricted in some locales. In many cities and states, a blade length that is perfectly legal in a pocket-knife is a misdemeanor to carry in a fixed-blade equivalent. Yes, this flies in the face of logic, since sheath knives are generally carried unconcealed, while pocketknives are generally carried concealed. But the law is the law, and we can't do much about it.

One other option is what is commonly called a neck knife—a small fixed-blade sheath knife that is designed to be carried on a cord around your neck, concealed beneath your shirt. The cord is attached to the tip end of the sheath, so the knife hangs with the handle pointing down. It's normally drawn by reaching under your shirt and tugging the knife free from the sheath. Many folks find these uncomfortable, but others love them. (If you like wearing loose-fitting shirts that are not tucked in, then this might be a good choice for you. Your mileage may vary.) One neck knife model that is currently popular is CRKT's Crawford N.E.C.K. This knife was designed by Pat and Wes Crawford. It is a compact recurve tanto.

Note: Be advised that state and local laws vary widely, so a neck knife might be considered a concealed weapon in some jurisdictions.

POCKETKNIVES

There is a dizzying array of folding knives available. I generally prefer half-serrated tanto-style blades, but choose what suits you. For what it's worth, I often carry a Cold Steel brand Voyager model.

My general advice is to carry the longest-blade knife that you can and *will* carry every day, without fail. The knife that gets left at home because it is too bulky or heavy is almost worthless.

Yes, you can buy a great big Rambo-esque dedicated "survival" knife, but will you have it with you when you really need it? In my estimation, the EDC knife concept is much more workable.

MULTI-TOOLS

The Swiss Army knife, which was the original multi-tool, has morphed from the original four-blade pocketknife into a dizzying number of varieties with dozens of tool varieties.

While they are still quite useful, Swiss Army knives have been eclipsed by the Leatherman. This was the first multi-tool that was built around a folding pair of needle-nose pliers rather than just a variation of a penknife. It is *much* more versatile and inherently stronger than a Swiss Army knife. As of this writing, the Leatherman Wave, Rebar, and Charge Al models represent the current state of the art for multi-tools. Their closest competitor is the Gerber Multi-Plier.

ATGATT CONCEPT

Reader J.D.C. in Mississippi noticed a trend on motorcycle blogs regarding ATGATT (pronounced "at-gat"). This acronym stands for All the Gear, All the Time. He sums up the ATGATT mind-set as follows:

> If you believe a helmet or leather jacket or good sturdy boots are a good idea at any time, you should wear them *all the time*.
>
> Personally, I wear a helmet, leather jacket, good boots, gloves, etc. whenever I'm on the bike. I usually wear them when I'm not on the bike as well, out of habit. But I also carry a decent medical kit on the bike or in the truck, whichever I'm using at the time. I'm an EMT and like to be prepared for incidents that occur when I'm not on the clock. Add a bullet- and stab-proof vest whenever feasible, a sidearm (when allowed, which in my case means not at work), materials for making fire, a knife, and some other goodies, and I think I have ATGATT.
>
> The ATGATT term has replaced EDC in my vocabulary: Your "everyday carry" should be "all the gear, all the time." It doesn't take much space or weigh much if you go minimalist, and it really could save your life, or someone else's. I also have a GOOD bag, and one each for my wife and daughter, but if necessary I'd be fine with the things I carry and wear every day. I'm not saying I carry an ax, adze, and flock of chickens with me. Difficult, that would be. But I could go into the boonies now and stay there for a week or perhaps a month without suffering much, partially due to experience and partially due to equipment.

And it bears mentioning that a large portion of life-threatening trauma (from both combat and accidents) is head trauma. Kevlar helmets (including the later-generation ACH and MICH) are sold by several mail-order firms, like BulletProofMe.com. Proper sizing is important for helmets, so don't just buy any Kevlar helmet on eBay. (Many of these same companies also sell Kevlar body armor vests. There again, sizing is crucial.)

It is important to wear a full set of safety gear whenever you fire up a chain saw, even if it's just to make a couple of quick cuts. (Kevlar safety chaps, boots, combination helmet/earmuffs with face screen, etc.) Murphy's Law implies that the one time you omit the safety gear will be the time that your foot slips. Remember: All the Gear, All the Time.

Quality American Knife Makers

Knife making is one of the few industries in which there is still a large number of American makers. We can maintain this presence by only buying from these makers:

- Bear & Son Cutlery (made in Alabama)
- Becker Knife and Tool (Washington)
- Blind Horse Knives (Idaho)
- Calico Forge Knife Co. (Idaho)
- Case (Pennsylvania)
- Continental Divide Knives (Arizona)
- Dogwood Custom Knives (Pennsylvania)

- Fiddleback Forge (Georgia; they also make a fantastic machete.)

- Fletcher Knives (Georgia; for now, this is still a small, "made in batches" maker with a small line; you get on a dibs list to order.)

- Knives of Alaska

- Montie Gear (North Carolina)

- Ontario Knives (Because of its name it is often mistakenly thought of as a Canadian company. It is actually *south* of the Canadian border, in upstate New York.)

- Randall Made Knives (Florida; the original product line of this legendary maker is quite expensive [$500+] and there is a multiyear order backlog, but the ESEE Knives line is more affordable and more readily available.)

- Shadow Tech Knives (Ohio)

- Tops Knives (Idaho)

- Zero Tolerance Knives (This a subsidiary product line of Kershaw, but not all of the parent company's knives are American made.)

Note: There are thousands of smaller custom knife makers in the United States—too many to list here. (See the Official KnifeMakers Database on SurvivalBlog.com for a detailed list, with links. Most of these are home-based businesses that do custom work.)

FORMERLY MADE IN USA

Many knife and multi-tool makers have moved part or all of their manufacturing offshore. Gerber is typical of this trend. Not only is Gerber owned by a foreign company (Fiskars, of Finland), but more than half of its knives are now made in China. On a similar note, I still have readers recommend Marble's brand knives. They were all made in Gladstone, Michigan, until a few years ago. But the company has started importing them from China. If in doubt about the origin of a product, then refer to MadeInUSA.org, AmericansWorking.com, or USAb2c.com.

IMPROVISED AND HANDCRAFTED TOOLS

One category of tools that is particularly important to sur- vivalists is what I term improvisational tools. I've already mentioned the importance of the ability to adapt to austere environments. Part of this is being able to *make* tools (with a home forge, metal lathe, and milling machine), but there are also some other quite simple tools and semifinished materi- als that allow you to improvise, adapt, or combine *other* ma- terials. These include:

- Hardened-steel wire draw plates, for resizing wire (see snipurl.com/27mib0e). These are also made with square, triangular, and half-round holes—which is mainly of interest to jewelers, but useful also for some hobbyists, like model train builders.

- Stronghold Haywire Klampers (specialized wire-wrapping tools—buy several of them, and *lots* of compatible-gauge wire; see snipurl.com/27lzbye)

- C-clamps (umpteen uses!)

- Plastic cable ties (commonly called zip ties). These are much less expensive if you buy them in the mega-assortment plastic canisters.

- Pierced metal pipe strapping tape. You can find this in the plumbing section of your hardware store. Buy several rolls.

- Pipe clamps (various sizes)

- Pierced steel box bar stock (particularly important if you don't own a welder)

- Pentagonal and hexagonal starplates (for making geodesic structures)

- Electrical tape

- Duck Tape. Buy plenty of it. High in the Himalayas, a wise old man once told me, "Duck Tape is like the Force: It has a light side and it has a dark side, and it holds the universe together."

AN ASIDE

Duck Tape is often mistakenly called duct tape. Duck is the brand name of a company headquartered in Avon, Ohio (see DuckBrand.com). But duct tape is something a bit different. It is a special metallicized tape, made specifically for joining metal HVAC ducts. The two types of tape are made in different ways and have different uses. My advice: Stock up heavily on Duck Tape. But buy only a couple of rolls of silver duct tape.

Traditional Cutting Tools

I put an emphasis on nineteenth-century technology tools, such as shingle froes, scythes, adzes, draw knives, gimlets, bark spuds, axes, crosscut saws, splitting mauls, and so forth. Many of these and other old-fashioned tools are available from Lehman's.

I recommend a great YouTube video on using traditional wood-felling and bucking tools, "Getting Back to Basics—Wranglerstar." His other videos are also quite educational.

For best use in most small woodworking, a drawknife requires the use of a shaving horse. A shaving horse has a foot treadle to operate its clamp. This speeds up the work tremendously and leaves both hands free to work.

You will also need a broadax and adze to shape beams.

Find several splitting mauls and sledges of various weights. For particularly knotty wood, or if you live in country where there are large trees (sixteen-inch-diameter or larger), then you will also need a variety of steel splitting wedges.

SAFETY NOTE

Never use steel wedges when felling trees! Use only hardwood or plastic wedges. Steel wedges are used only for splitting wood, and never around any chain saw work.

BARK SPUD

A bark spud is used to peel the bark from logs. Few folks recognize the importance of a bark spud. (In fact, most wouldn't even be able to name this tool if they were handed one.) It's expensive to buy new, so look for used ones, via Craigslist. Or watch for garage sales or estate sales where "logging tools" are mentioned.

FROE

A froe to rive boards and shingles is important. I recommend CrosscutSaw.com. Although I haven't personally done business with them, the folks at Crosscut Saw Company have a good reputation. It is noteworthy that most of their products are American made.

And speaking of using traditional hand tools, I'd encourage you to watch a YouTube video that was suggested by SurvivalBlog reader Ron S. back in 2009, "Cherry Log to Country Chair," showing a gent making furniture with hand tools. Every self-sufficient carpenter should own a shingle froe, a hardwood mallet (maul), a shaving horse, an adze, and a drawknife.

TRADITIONAL PULLING AND LIFTING TOOLS

One often-overlooked category of tools is traditional pulling and lifting tools that use mechanical advantage. These include things as simple as pry bars and as complex as 4:1 block and tackle rigs. Keep a sharp eye out for these tools at farm auctions, estate sales, and wrecking yards. They can be tremendous labor savers and make seemingly impossible jobs possible.

SAFETY NOTE

Mechanical advantage is a wonderful thing that can allow one man to do the work of many, but using these tools necessitates showing great caution and common sense. Whenever using mechanical advantage, keep in mind that if you lose control (such as losing your grip on a rope or handle, a jack tipping over, or a cable breaking), things will start moving quickly. The law of gravity, with an acceleration rate constant of thirty-two feet per second, has no mercy. So carefully think through your rigging and the consequences of a slip or part failure *before* you employ mechanical advantage. Always have a Plan B, and most important—just like when felling a tree—an escape plan (with a clear path). Whenever you lift something heavy, you need to fully plan for the consequences if it comes crashing down. Use plenty of blocking and bracing, and lift things in gradual stages. And whenever you move something on anything but dead-level ground, keep acceleration in mind. Lastly, when you conduct your safety briefing, remind everyone present that human life and limb are more important than things, so if something starts to slide or fall, don't try to stop it. Just get out of the way, and let gravity have its way.

PRY BARS

A pry bar is the classic example of the use of simple leverage. The oft-quoted saying attributed to Archimedes is "Give me a fulcrum and a place to stand and I shall move the world."

SCREW JACKS

A screw jack is an amazing thing. A screw-type trailer hoist, for example, can allow an eight-year-old child to lift a two-thousand-pound trailer off of a ball hitch. Screw jacks have a tremendous variety of uses—everything from leveling the floor of a cabin or shed to straightening a post. There are thousands of small screw jacks that are sitting idle in the trunks of cars in automobile wrecking yards. These can be bought for little more than scrap metal prices. Buy them now, while they are inexpensive. And be sure to buy a few extras for barter and charity. One variation of the time-proven screw jack technology is a threaded chain tensioner. These have two threaded shafts with a steel handle set in the middle at a ninety-degree angle to the shafts. Although typically used for chaining down vehicles on trailers, these are actually quite versatile. Buy a pair of them.

BLOCK AND TACKLE

Once ubiquitous on farms and ranches, traditional block and tackle rigs have become scarce. This is because of the advent of electric winches. If we ever go back to an age of steam power, horse power, or human muscle power, then the older block and tackle rigs will become very valuable and sought after. Seek them out now, while they are still plentiful and relatively inexpensive. Look for steel blocks, rather that wooden. Also, look for a rig that can be swung open for cable rigging rather than solid blocks (which must be threaded through the pulleys), since this allows much more versatile rigging arrangements.

Limitations

One limitation is based upon the coefficient of friction and the concept of additive friction. Each source of friction in a pulley system is additive. This is why they don't make many six-gang pulleys; the accumulated friction is simply too great.

Another limitation is length of throw. Each doubling of mechanical advantage doubles the length that the free end of the rope or cable must be pulled. Hence, a 3:1 advantage block requires you to pull nine feet of rope to advance the block's position three feet. So if your rig will be used to move something over a long distance, then the length of rope or cable required can be considerable.

COME-ALONGS

Ratchet cable hoists (commonly called come-alongs) are crucial tools for life on a retreat and for off-road driving. They have umpteen uses, for everything from wire fence stretching to lifting elk carcasses for butchering. These should be purchased in pairs, for the greatest versatility. We now keep four come-alongs here at the Rawles Ranch: two that are two-ton capacity and two that are four-ton capacity. All four are American made, by Maasdam under the trade name Pow'R Pull (see snipurl.com/27m28hm). I highly recommend them.

Keep your ratchet cable hoists well oiled and out of the elements and they will give you many years of service. Inspect the cable after each use for any signs of fraying. Also, be sure never to attempt to apply force to a cable when the spool is nearly empty. Always have at least one and a half wraps on the spool before you crank. Otherwise, the cable terminating "button" might shear off and drop your load.

LEATHERWORKING TOOLS

Tandy Leather (tandyleatherfactory.com) provides one-stop shopping for leatherworking tools and supplies. Since leatherworking tools are fairly expensive when bought new and the quality of some of the imported tools has dropped noticeably in the past decade, I believe it is best to buy them used.

If you watch Craigslist regularly, you will often find sets of leatherworking tools that are being sold by folks who have either lost interest in the hobby or can no longer participate because of arthritis or carpal tunnel syndrome. These sets of tools often sell for just pennies on the dollar. Buy a large plastic fishing tackle box to keep all of your leather-working together and well organized.

FIBER TOOLS

Shearing, dyeing, carding, hand spinning, knitting, and felting are all skills that you can learn from a mentor and that require few, if any, printed references. But once you move up to weaving on a loom, some reference books are a must. My late wife (the Memsahib) was our family's expert on fiber tools, but I provide a basic list here.

SPINNING WHEELS

Ashford (of New Zealand) has the lion's share of the market for spinning wheels, for good reason. Their wheels are very well made. Unfortunately they've become quite expensive, so look for used ones at fiber fests or on Craigslist. For a practical spinning wheel (versus one for sake of home decor), I generally do not recommend buying an antique wheel. These were typically made long before the days of standardized parts. Not only are they more fragile, but they would be a challenge to maintain and repair. Buy an Ashford or a Louet. And if you plan to travel to any spinning events outside your home, then make it an Ashford Traveller. This is a compact, upright model that is much more convenient to carry in a passenger car than a traditional spinning wheel.

KNITTING NEEDLES

Buy a bucketload of needles that range in size from very small to very large diameter and length. Garage sales and estate sales are the best place to find them. You may have to mail-order some of the more specialized types, such those made specifically for knitting hats.

CARDING COMBS

Carding combs are a must to transition wool from fleece into "bats," which can then be hand spun. For larger-scale production, a drum carder is a good investment. We have one made by Ashford. These are built to last, but be sure to teach your children early on never to reverse the direction that you turn the handle!

LOOMS

The art of warping a loom (setting it up to weave) is the subject of entire books. But here are the basics: Large weavings require large looms. Cost goes up with size. If you want to weave more complex patterns, then you need a loom with multiple harnesses. Most handweavers would love to own a 36-inch (or larger) four-harness floor loom. But you can do a lot with just a simple 24-inch table loom with two positions. Here are some good references:

> *Weaving for Beginners: An Illustrated Guide*, by Peggy Os-
>   terkamp
> *Warping All by Yourself*, by Cay Garrett

Weaving Made Easy: 17 Projects Using a Simple Loom, by
   Liz Gipson
Hands on Rigid Heddle Weaving, by Betty Linn Davenport

Accessories and Spares

Once you begin spinning and weaving, you will quickly
learn about the requisite accessories and spare parts. These
include a Kromski niddy noddy (skein winder), a yarn ball
winding machine, and spare bobbins ("flyers") for your spinning wheel. (The late Memsahib preferred the jumbo size.)
Buy plenty. Also be sure to buy a couple of maintenance kits
for your spinning wheel. See snipurl.com/27ntmvy.

- **CHAPTER 15** -

LIFELONG LEARNING AND SKILL BUILDING

If a man empties his purse into his head, no man can take it away from him. An investment in knowledge always pays the best interest.

—Benjamin Franklin

Most of your knowledge of traditional skills and mastery of the use of tools won't come from reading a book or watching a DVD. Rather, this knowledge comes from *doing*, especially by working under an older and wiser mentor. Gaining this knowledge can take many years. The beauty of this is that you carry your most useful tools between your ears. Knowledge is portable. And you can in turn pass it on to your children and others, so it is transferable. But also remember that many of these skills require regular practice and hence are perishable, so I recommend keeping them sharp once you acquire them.

WHERE TO ACQUIRE SKILLS

An excellent resource is the elders in your community, including your own grandparents. Interview them using a digital recorder or a cassette tape recorder. Ask them about how they lived through the Great Depression and WWII, how they improvised, in what ways they were self-sufficient, and how they "pinched a penny." There is a wealth of untapped and underappreciated knowledge in retirement homes. This is where the skills that you thought were forgotten still exist. Are you lamenting the fact that you can't find a man to teach you how to sharpen and set your wood saw? Well, there probably is, but you may have to borrow him from the local rest home for a few afternoons. And believe me, you will both benefit from the experience.

Your local community college probably offers courses on welding, small engine repair, and other traditional skills. A few colleges even offer classes on horseshoeing, hoof trimming, and blacksmithing.

You will want to build a library (see Appendix A, Your Retreat Library). You will also want to develop a set of reference binders with the manuals for every piece of equipment at your farm, ranch, or retreat. For many skills there is no substitute for hands-on experience, but for a few, online and DVD courses will suffice.

Perhaps the best way to gain in-depth knowledge and skills is through apprenticeships. These can be either paid or unpaid, depending on the circumstances. In effect, you will be investing your time to gain skills that will last you a lifetime.

Some skills, like chain saw sharpening, can be learned in just a few hours. But more advanced skills such as barrel making, gunsmithing, locksmithing, cabinetmaking, bow making, and boatbuilding take *hundreds* of hours to master. For any trade that requires specialized tools, it is essential to get a start now, to allow yourself the time and money to acquire a full set of tools.

Even in lightly populated regions where you can't find paid apprenticeships, there is always volunteer work. Most notably, volunteer fire departments (VFDs) and EMT organizations teach many valuable skills. Beyond firefighting skills, VFD members are willing to share a wide variety of skills, such as maintaining and repairing vehicles and equipment. This knowledge almost always translates to other fields. For example, knowing how to rebuild a pump applies to irrigation just as well as it does to fire engines.

HOBBY CLUBS, GUILDS, AND GROUPS

Clubs and hobby groups are a good place to acquire skills. The mentoring that you will receive from elders with these organizations will be particularly important.

ARRL CLUBS

Your local American Radio Relay League (ARRL) affiliate club can pair you with an elder member (called an Elmer in the ham radio world). Many of these old gents have a tremendous wealth of knowledge on not just ham radio procedure and signal propagation but also how to breadboard your own electronics, troubleshooting, alignment procedures, SWR

A traditional hand-cranked bench grinder. Nineteenth-century tools and skills will have a place in your survival planning.

metering, antenna trimming, old-fashioned coil winding, and much more.

HISTORICAL REENACTOR GROUPS

One organization that you might have overlooked is your regional Society for Creative Anachronism (SCA) or other "living history" group. These include the Historical Maritime

Society (in the UK), the Vikings, Nova Roma, Mountain Man Rendezvous groups, and others. SCA folks do a lot more than wear strange costumes, drink ale, and bash each other with swords. They can teach you how to hand-spin and felt wool, how to make swords, fletch arrows, braid ropes (with a rope walk), and even make chainmail. See reenactor.net for details.

FIBER GUILDS

In many parts of the U.S. and Canada, there are groups of spinners and weavers who are organized into fiber guilds. These groups usually offer free classes or mentoring on a wide range of skills from sheep shearing to wool carding, wool dyeing, felting, hand spinning (with a rudimentary drop spindle or a more sophisticated wheel), hand knitting, and weaving on looms ranging in size from narrow arm-length belt looms to small table looms (roughly thirty-two inches square) to enormous four-harness floor looms, which take four men to carry.

WOODWORKING CLUBS

Mainly found in more populous regions, woodworking clubs vary widely in areas of interest and expertise. Some are devoted to small boatbuilding, while others are almost entirely focused on cabinetmaking. Just a few do wagon building and wheelwrighting. Most of them use power tools but a few are "hand tools only" purist groups. See woodworkingclubs.com.

SEWING AND LEATHERWORKING CLUBS

There are thousands of local sewing clubs in America. And despite the drop in popularity since its heyday, there are still hundreds of leatherworking clubs. These are great places to develop skills, to make mentoring contacts, and to gather useful tools. See sewinginamerica.com and tandyleatherfactory.com.

For raw materials, I recommend looking for fabrics and leather at thrift stores. You can often find capes, skirts, dusters, and trench coats that are made with good-quality leather, suede, or fabric available for far less than the cost of the garment material bought new "on the bolt." They are often donated to thrift stores only because the garments have gone out of fashion. Disassembling these (with scissors, a carpet knife, and a seam ripper) takes only a few minutes.

NOW GET TO WORK!

I trust that this book has inspired you to develop the skills and gather the tools to be able to handle the many tasks that may come your way in this uncertain world. Stock up, team up, and seek out the knowledgeable mentors in your community. Remember that an investment in tools is an investment in the future, and it's almost never a waste of resources. Many Americans have forgotten some crucial skills. They've left the use of many tools up to "certified" mechanics and tradesmen. Americans are now mired in a magnificent morass of mediocrity and inculcated into ingrained ineptitude. We can and should do better. Many of the old trade skills (such as brownsmith, cooper, wainwright, and wheelwright) have slipped away. Their day may come again.

Lastly, once you've developed useful skills, don't shirk the responsibility of passing them on to your children and others. As a twenty-first-century artificer, you may someday be instrumental in rebuilding a broken society, so take the responsibilities outlined in this book seriously. Now, get to work!

APPENDIX A

YOUR RETREAT LIBRARY

Tools are almost worthless without the requisite knowledge and skills to put them to good use. The following is a list of books I would recommend to deepen your knowledge and improve your skills.

Considering the underlying theme of this book, I would put this one near the top of my priority list: *The Complete Modern Blacksmith*, by Alexander G. Weygers.

You will also need manuals (a full set, operating and repair) for all of your vehicles, tools, and equipment.

The late Memsahib's top must-have book: *The Encyclopedia of Country Living*, by Carla Emery (get the tenth or later edition). This book is 845 pages of valuable how-to country survival knowledge. The Memsahib (1964–2009) wrote, "The first time that I butchered chickens, I used this book. When I needed 15 different ways to fix zucchini I turned to this book, when I wanted to make soap, pickles, jelly, bread from scratch, butter, and cream cheese, I found everything I needed to know in this book!"

Books Recommended by the Late Memsahib

Gardening When It Counts, by Steve Solomon

How to Survive Without a Salary: Learning How to Live the Conserver Lifestyle, by Charles Long

Small-Scale Grain Raising, by Gene Logsdon

The Family Cow, by Dirk van Loon

Raising a Calf for Beef, by Phyllis Hobson

Small-Scale Pig Raising, by Dirk van Loon

Raising Rabbits the Modern Way, by Bob Bennett

Raising Sheep the Modern Way, updated and revised edition, by Paula Simmons

Ducks and Geese in Your Backyard: A Beginner's Guide, by Rick and Gail Luttmann

The Complete Medicinal Herbal, by Penelope Ody

Storey's Basic Country Skills: A Practical Guide to Self-Reliance, by John and Martha Storey

Boston's Gun Bible, by Boston T. Party

Boston's Gun Bible stands alone as the very best all-around reference for firearms owners. Not only does it cover practical rifles, pistols, and shotguns in detail, but it also has a wealth of valuable information on related subjects such as optics, practical carry, training, legal issues, and legislative issues. The new expanded and updated edition (with two hundred extra pages) is fantastic! This weighty tome is an absolute must for all gun owners. At thirty-seven dollars it isn't cheap, but it is worth every penny. Boston's observations and conclusions about guns are precisely researched, scientific, and relatively dispassionate. Unlike many other writers in the firearms field, Boston has consistently shown that he is willing to change his mind when presented with logical evidence. This is a book that may very well save your life or that of a loved one. It is also a highly influential book that may contribute in the long run to the restoration of our constitutional republic and firearms freedom around the world. *Boston's Gun Bible* doesn't just whine about the decline of our God-given constitutional liberties. Rather, it shows practical solutions that individual citizens can and must take to ensure the liberty of future generations. It is nothing short of a monumental work of nonfiction! Don't just buy one. Buy two! You will soon find that you'll need an extra copy to lend out to family members and friends. By the way, if you already have the older edition, then I strongly suggest that you buy the latest, expanded edition. This has valuable new information, so it's well worth getting a new copy. As a published writer, I stand in awe of this important piece of nonfiction. It deserves a place of honor on the bookshelf of every freedom-loving citizen.

Survival Guns, by Mel Tappan

The Ultimate Sniper: An Advanced Training Manual for Military and Police Snipers (2006), by John L. Plaster

Flayderman's Guide to Antique American Firearms and Their Values, by Norm Flayderman *Armageddon Medicine,* by Cynthia J. Koelker, M.D.

Where There Is No Doctor: A Village Health Care Handbook, by David Werner

Where There Is No Dentist, by Murray Dickson

When Disaster Strikes: A Comprehensive Guide for Emergency Planning and Crisis Survival, by Matthew Stein

When Technology Fails: A Manual for Self-Reliance, Sustainability, and Surviving the Long Emergency, by Matthew Stein

Making the Best of Basics: Family Preparedness Handbook, by James Talmage Stevens

Ball Blue Book Guide to Preserving

Cookin' with Home Storage, by Peggy Layton and Vicki Tate

Nuclear War Survival Skills, by Cresson H. Kearny (available for free download)

The Alpha Strategy, by John A. Pugsley

Tappan on Survival, by Mel Tappan

Jim's "Second Tier" List of Recommended Specialty Books

Root Cellaring: Natural Cold Storage of Fruits & Vegetables, by Mike Bubel

Back to Basics: A Complete Guide to Traditional Skills, 3rd ed., by Abigail R. Gehring

Putting Food By, by Janet Greene

Stocking Up: The Third Edition of America's Classic Preserving Guide, by Carol Hupping

Emergency Food Storage & Survival Handbook, by Peggy Layton

Gardening When It Counts: Growing Food in Hard Times, by Steve Solomon

The Resilient Gardener: Food Production and Self-Reliance in Uncertain Times, by Carol Deppe

All New Square Foot Gardening, by Mel Bartholomew

Seed to Seed: Seed Saving and Growing Techniques for Vegetable Gardeners, by Suzanne Ashworth

Small-Scale Grain Raising, by Gene Logsdon

The Fifty Dollar and Up Underground House Book, by Mike Oehler

Emergency War Surgery (NATO Handbook: Third United States Revision, 2004, [or later]) , by Dr. Martin Fackler, et al.

The Merck Veterinary Manual, by Cynthia M. Kahn

Where There Is No Vet, by Bill Forse

The ARRL Operating Manual for Radio Amateurs

Outdoor Survival Skills, by Larry Dean Olsen

Essential Bushcraft, by Ray Mears

SAS Survival Handbook, by John "Lofty" Wiseman

The Survivor book series, by Kurt Saxon. Many are out of print in hard copy, but they are all available on DVD. Here, I must issue a caveat lector ("reader beware"): Mr. Saxon has some very controversial views that I do not agree with. Among other things, he is a eugenicist.

Nonfiction Books Recommended by My Readers

Crisis Preparedness Handbook: A Comprehensive Guide to Home Storage and Physical Survival, by Jack A. Spigarelli

Preserving Food Without Freezing or Canning: Traditional Techniques Using Salt, Oil, Sugar, Alcohol, Vinegar, Drying, Cold Storage, and Lactic Fermentation, by the Gardeners and Farmers of Terre Vivante

The New Organic Grower, by Eliot Coleman

Tom Brown's Field Guide to Wilderness Survival

Tom Brown's Field Guide to Nature Observation and Tracking

Tom Brown's Guide to Wild Edible and Medicinal Plants

Ditch Medicine: Advanced Field Procedures for Emergencies, by Hugh Coffee

Camping & Wilderness Survival: The Ultimate Outdoors Book, by Paul Tawrell

Engineer Field Data (U.S. Army FM 5-34). Available online free of charge with registration at Army Knowledge Online (AKO), and other sites, but I recommend getting a hard copy of the latest edition, preferably with the heavy-duty plastic binding.

Just in Case, by Kathy Harrison

A Comprehensive Guide to Wilderness & Travel Medicine, by Eric A. Weiss, M.D.

Rodale's Ultimate Encyclopedia of Organic Gardening: The Indispensable Green Resource for Every Gardener, by Fern Marshall Bradley (ed.)

Special Operations Forces Medical Handbook (it superseded the very outdated ST 31-91B)

Wilderness Medicine, 5th ed., by Paul S. Auerbach

Four-Season Harvest: Organic Vegetables from Your Home Garden All Year Long, by Eliot Coleman

The Modern Survival Retreat, by Ragnar Benson

The Merck Manual, by Robert S. Porter. The gold standard of medical reference books!

Last of the Mountain Men, by Harold Peterson

Primitive Wilderness Living & Survival Skills: Naked into the Wilderness, by John McPherson. His entire *Primitive* series of books is excellent. Also see McPherson's Web page, PrairieWolf.net.

LDS Preparedness Manual, by Christopher M. Parrett (ed.)

The Long Emergency: Surviving the End of Oil, Climate Change, and Other Converging Catastrophes of the Twenty-First Century, by James H. Kunstler

Principles of Personal Defense, revised ed., by Jeff Cooper

Survival Poaching, by Ragnar Benson

The Winter Harvest Handbook: Year Round Vegetable Production Using Deep Organic Techniques and Unheated Greenhouses, by Eliot Coleman

Jim's Recommended "Be Ready to Barter" Reference Book List

Flayderman's Guide to Antique American Firearms and Their Values

Blue Book of Gun Values

A Guidebook of United States Coins: The Official Red Book (latest annual edition)

Standard Catalog of World Coins (latest annual edition)

Antique Trader: Antiques & Collectibles Price Guide

Wristwatch Annual 2014: The Catalog of Producers, Prices, Models, and Specifications

Jewelry & Gems: The Buying Guide: How to Buy Diamonds, Pearls, Colored Gemstones, Gold and Jewelry with Confidence and Knowledge

APPENDIX B

RECOMMENDED GUNSMITHING SERVICE PROVIDERS

As my friend Tam over at the blog *View from the Porch* says, *"Armorer* does not equal *gunsmith."* I agree wholeheartedly. Most present-day "armorers" are just men who are skilled at changing gun parts. My favorite *real* gunsmith is John Taylor, at Taylor Machine in Puyallup, Washington. He is a master gunsmith who can do things like reline barrels and make replacement cylinders for revolvers from scratch. I once sent John an antique (pre-1899 production) 7.63mm Broomhandle Mauser pistol that was an absolute disaster, and he sent me back a perfectly functioning gun that had been rebored to 9mm Parabellum, equipped with an OBI detachable twenty-round magazine, and completely restored (with bluing expertly done by Mel Doyle's Gunsmithing). Thanks to them, it now looks gorgeous and it is just as functional as a modern pistol.

The following is a partial listing of suppliers and services. Note that many local gunsmiths offer bluing and a few do parkerizing. So you might be able to locate a local shop to provide these services, and thus eliminate the expense and delay of shipping a gun via common carrier.

My Favorite Gunsmiths

Mel Doyle's Gunsmithing
401 Ellis Lane
Plummer, ID 83851
Phone: (208) 686-1006
Specialties: Bluing, parkerizing, general gunsmithing

Taylor Machine
14119 Military Road E
Puyallup, WA 98374
Phone: (253) 445-4073
johntaylormachine.com
Specialties: Rebarreling, barrel relining, scratch-built
replacement cylinders, and other custom machining

Arizona Response Systems (T. Mark Graham)
16014 West Remuda Drive
Surprise, AZ 85387
Phone: (623) 556-8056 (by appointment only)
arizonaresponsesystems.com
Specialties: FAL, L1A1, and AK smithing as well as
METACOL finishes

The Robar Companies
21438 N. 7th Avenue, Suite B
Phoenix, AZ 85027
Phone: (623) 581-2648
robarguns.com
Specialty: Nickel/Teflon (NP3) coating

Miniature Machine Co.
606 Grace Avenue

Ft. Worth, TX 76111
Specialties: .45 Colt cylinders for .45 ACP S&W revolvers

H-S Precision
1301 Turbine Drive
Rapid City, SD 57703
Phone: (605) 341-3006
hsprecision.com
Specialty: Kevlar-graphite stocks

Some Gunsmiths Recommended by My Readers

Rifle Dynamics (Jim Fuller)
Las Vegas, Nevada
Phone: (702) 860-7774
rifledynamics.com
Specialties: AK-47/AK-74 family rifles

Trident Industries (David Schroeder)
1726 NW Kings Boulevard
Corvallis, OR 97330
Phone: (541) 760-5489
Specialties: Duracoating and general gunsmithing

Actions By 'T' (Teddy Jacobson)
16315 Redwood Forest Court
Sugar Land, TX 77498
Phone: (281) 565-6977
actionsbyt.com
Specialties: Pistol action and trigger tuning

Westwind Rifles (Dave Sullivan)
640 Briggs Street

Erie, CO 80516
Phone: (303) 828-3823
E-mail: westwindrifles@comcast.net
Specialties: Long-range and National Match
competition rifles

Brockman's
2165 South 1800 East
Gooding, ID 83330
Phone: (208) 934-5050
brockmansrifles.com
Specialties: Lever-action and bolt-action rifle gunsmithing

W. E. Birdsong & Associates
1435 Monterey Road
Florence, MS 39073
Phone: (601) 939-7448
black-t.com
Specialty: Custom finishes

Ohio Ordnance Works
310 Park Drive (P.O. Box 687)
Chardon, OH 44024
Phone: (440) 285-3481
ohioordnanceworks.com
Specialties: Class 3 (i.e., full auto, suppressors) and
military rifles

Springer Precision
60053 Minnetonka Lane
Bend, OR 97702
Phone: (541) 480-5546
springerprecision.com
Specialties: XD and XDM pistolsmithing

Guntech, Inc
942 NW 56th Street
Fort Lauderdale, FL 33309
Phone: (954) 776-4777
guntechinc.com
Specialties: Ultrasonic firearm cleaning and lubrication,
ramp polishing, rust removal, refinishing, sight installation,
broken screw extraction, part replacement, bore sighting,
scope mounting, and accessory installations

Benson's Minuteman Machine (Pat Benson)
8966 Cherry Lane
Nampa, ID 83687
Phone: (208) 467-2294
Specialties: General gunsmithing and machining

Gunning Arts (Charlie Maloney)
Catonsville, Maryland
E-mail: charliesarts@comcast.net
charliemaloney.com
Specialties: M1 Garand, M14, and M1A rifles

Gunsmithing LTD (also known locally as Mitch's)
3 Lacey Place
Southport, CT 06890
Phone: (203) 254-0436
Specialty: General gunsmithing

Vanden Berg Custom
15502 Galveston Road, Suite 218
Webster, TX 77598
Phone: (281) 480-3180
vandenbergcustom.com
Specialties: M1911s and AR-15s

Shooters Den (Ted Brown)
7025 Whitewater Drive
Jacksonville, OR 97530
Phone: (541) 899-8109
tedbrownrifles.com
Specialties: M14s, M1 Garands, M1 carbines, and M16s/AR15s

Sams Custom Gunworks (David E. Sams)
254 Columbia Road
Cartersville, VA 23027
Phone: (804) 375-3782
samscustomgunworksusa.com
Specialties: M1911s, Beretta 9mm Centurions, military service rifles

Bill Springfield
4135 Cricket Court
Colorado Springs, CO 80918
Phone: (719) 648-5725
triggerwork.net
Specialties: Rifle, pistol, and shotgun trigger tuning

Canyon Creek (Richard Dettelhouser)
2307 Teegardin Road
Streator, IL 61364
Phone: (815) 673-2515
canyoncreekcustom.com
Specialties: M1911 and XD/XDM pistols

Powder River Precision
3835 23rd Street

Baker City, OR 97814
Phone: (541) 523-4474
powderriverprecision.com
Specialties: Springfield Armory XD and XDM pistols

The Gunsmith, Inc. (Nelson Ford)
10210 North 32nd Street
Phoenix, AZ 85028
Phone: (602) 992-0050
thegunsmith.com
Specialties : Smith & Wesson revolvers, Colt .45 autos and clones, Browning Hi Powers, Marlin lever-actions, and Rugers

A W Peterson Gun Shop
4255 W Old US Highway 441
Mount Dora, FL 32757
Phone: (352) 383-4258
Specialties: General gunsmithing and antique guns

Chet Pauls Airgun Repair
4850 E. Cambridge Avenue
Fresno, CA 93703
Phone: (559) 251-9687
E-mail: c.pauls@comcast.net
Specialties: Air rifles and air pistols

Predator Custom Shop
3539 Papermill Drive
Knoxville, TN 37909
Phone: (865) 521-0625
predatorcustomshop.com
Specialties: Ceramic coating, AR-15s, precision rifles

APPENDIX C

THE PRE-1899 ANTIQUE GUNS FAQ

I coauthored a frequently asked questions (FAQ) article about federally exempt antique guns. (Guns made in or before 1898 are not considered firearms under U.S. federal law.) The FAQ includes some important data on serial numbers that can help you determine whether or not a particular gun was made in or before 1899.

Because some of the data in the FAQ changes frequently, I keep it regularly updated online:

http://www.rawles.to/Pre-1899_FAQ.html
or: snipurl.com/27s7k4z

APPENDIX D

Useful Formulas

This appendix includes two formulas for firearms bore-cleaning fluid. The first is optimized for removing carbon and primer fouling deposits. The second is an ammonia-based "decoppering" solution.

Ed's Red

A home-brewed firearms bore cleaner that is widely used in the U.S. and Canada is dubbed "Ed's Red." It was invented by Sturm, Ruger employee C. E. "Ed" Harris. This bore cleaner is much less expensive than commercially made products, and works just as well. Ed kindly published this formula in the public domain. It was adapted from Colonel Hatcher's Frankford Arsenal Cleaner No. 18 of the 1930s, substituting equivalent modern materials.

Mr. Harris wrote (in 1995):

Four years ago I mixed my first "Ed's Red" or "ER" bore cleaner. Hundreds of users have told me that they think this home-mixed cleaner is more effective than commercial products. I urge you to mix some and give it a fair trial, compared to whatever you have been using. Competitive shooters, gun clubs and police departments who use a gallon or more of rifle bore cleaner annually can save by mixing their own, and they will give up nothing in safety or effectiveness.

This cleaner has an action very similar to standard military issue rifle bore cleaner, such as Mil-C-372B. Users report it is more effective than Hoppe's for removing plastic fouling in shotgun bores, or caked carbon fouling in semiautomatic rifles or pistols, or in removing leading in revolvers. It is not as effective as Sweets 7.62, Hoppe's Bench Rest Nine, or Shooter's Choice for fast removal of heavy copper fouling in rifle bores. However, because ER is more effective in removing caked carbon and abrasive primer residues than other cleaners, metal fouling is greatly reduced when ER is used on a continuing basis.

I originally came up with this mix because I am an active high-power rifle competitive shooter and hand loading experimenter who uses a lot of rifle bore cleaner. I was not satisfied with the performance and high price of commercial products. I knew there was no technical reason why an effective firearm bore cleaner couldn't be mixed using common hardware store ingredients. The result is inexpensive, effective, and provides good corrosion protection and adequate residual lubrication so that routine "oiling" after cleaning is rarely necessary, except for long-term storage exceeding one year, or harsh service environments, such as saltwater exposure.

This formula is based on proven principles and incorporates two polar and two nonpolar solvents. It is

adapted from the one in *Hatcher's Notebook* for "Frankford Arsenal Cleaner No. 18," but substituting equivalent modern materials. I had the help of an organic
chemist in doing this and we knew there would be no
"surprises." The original Hatcher formula called for
equal parts of acetone, turpentine, Pratts Astral Oil and
sperm oil, and optionally 200 grams of anhydrous lanolin added per liter. Some discussion of the ingredients is
helpful to understand the properties of the cleaner and
how it works.

Pratts Astral Oil was nothing more than acid-free,
deodorized kerosene. I recommend "K1" kerosene of
the type normally sold for use in indoor space heaters.
Some users have reported successful substitution of civilian aviation-grade kerosene such as Turbo-A. I am
reluctant to recommend substitution of aviation-grade
kerosene, because the effects upon firearm components
of the additives required in aviation fuels are unknown. Some jet fuels are gasoline-kerosene blends
and absolutely should not be used, because of their in-
creased flammability.

An inexpensive, effective substitute for sperm oil
is Dexron (II, IIe or III) automatic transmission fluid
(ATF). Prior to about 1950, most ATFs were sperm oil
based, but during WWII a synthetic was developed for
use in precision instruments. With the great demand
for automatic transmission autos after WWII, sperm oil
was no longer practical to produce ATFs in the quantity
demanded, so the synthetic material became the basis
for the Dexron fluids we know today. The additives
in ATFs, which include organometallic antioxidants
and surfactants, make it highly suitable for inclusion in
an all-purpose cleaner-lubricant-preservative. Hatcher's

original Frankford Arsenal Cleaner No. 18 formula used gum spirits of turpentine. Because turpentine is expensive today, and is also an "aromatic" solvent, which is highly flammable, I chose not to use it. Safer and cheaper is aliphatic mineral spirits, a petroleum-based "safety solvent" used for thinning oil-based paints and also widely used as an automotive parts cleaner. It is commonly sold under the names "odorless mineral spirits," "Stoddard Solvent" or "Varsol."

Acetone is included in ER to provide an aggressive, fast-acting solvent for caked powder residues. Because acetone is an aromatic, organic solvent, it is recommended that users leave it out if the cleaner will be used in enclosed spaces lacking forced-air ventilation. The acetone in ER will evaporate, liberating volatile organic compounds (VOCs) into the atmosphere unless containers are kept tightly closed when not in use. The cleaner is still effective without the acetone, but it is not as fast-acting.

There isn't anything in Ed's Red that chemically dissolves copper fouling in rifle bores, but it does a better job removing carbon and primer residue than anything else that is safe and commonly available. Numerous users have told me that exclusive use of ER reduces copper deposits, because it removes the old impacted powder fouling left by other cleaners, which reduces the abrasion and adhesion of jacket metal to the bore surface, leaving a cleaner surface condition which reduces subsequent fouling. Experience seems to indicate that ER will actually remove metal fouling it if you let it "soak," so the surfactants will do the job, though you have to be patient.

Addition of the lanolin to ER bore cleaner mix is entirely optional. The cleaner works quite well and gives adequate corrosion protection and lubrication for most users without it. Incorporating the lanolin makes the cleaner easier on the hands, increases lubricity and film strength, and improves corrosion protection if weapons will be routinely exposed to salt air, water spray, industrial or urban corrosive atmospheres, or if you intend to use the cleaner as a protectant for long-term storage of over one year.

If you use other protective films for adverse use or long term storage you can leave the lanolin out and save about $8 per gallon. At current retail prices you can buy all the ingredients to mix ER, without the lanolin, for about $10 per gallon. I urge you to mix some yourself. I am confident it will work as well for you as it does for me and hundreds of users who got the recipe on the FidoNet Firearms Echo.

CONTENTS: ED'S RED BORE CLEANER

1 part Dexron II, IIe or III ATF, GM Spec. D-20265 or later

1 part kerosene—deodorized, K1

1 part aliphatic mineral spirits, Fed. Spec. TT-T-2981F, CAS #64741-49-9, or substitute "Stoddard Solvent," CAS #8052-41-3, or equivalent (a.k.a. Varsol)

1 part acetone, CAS #67-64-1 (optional up to 1 lb. of lanolin, anhydrous, USP per gallon; okay to substitute lanolin, modified, topical lubricant, from the drugstore)

MIXING INSTRUCTIONS FOR ER BORE CLEANER

Mix outdoors, in good ventilation. Use a clean one-gallon, chemical-resistant, heavy-gauge PET or PVC plastic container. NFPA-approved plastic gasoline storage containers are also okay. Do *not* use HDPE, which is permeable, because the acetone will eventually evaporate. It will also attack HDPE, causing the container to collapse, making a heck of a mess!

Add the ATF first. Use the empty container to measure the other components, so that it is thoroughly rinsed. If you incorporate the lanolin into the mixture, melt this carefully in a double boiler, taking precautions against fire. Pour the melted lanolin into a larger container, rinsing that container with the bore cleaner mix, and stirring until it is all dissolved.

I recommend diverting a small quantity, up to 4 oz per quart, of the 50-50 ATF-kerosene mix for optional use as an ER-compatible gun oil. This can be done without impairing the effectiveness of the remaining mix.

LABEL AND NECESSARY SAFETY WARNINGS

RIFLE BORE CLEANER CAUTION: FLAMMABLE
MIXTURE HARMFUL IF SWALLOWED.
KEEP OUT OF REACH OF CHILDREN.

1. Flammable mixture. Keep away from heat, sparks, and flame.

2. FIRST AID: If swallowed, DO NOT induce vomiting; call physician immediately. In case of eye contact,

immediately flush thoroughly with water and call a physician. For skin contact, wash thoroughly.

3.   Use with adequate ventilation. Avoid breathing vapors or spray mist. It is a violation of federal law to use this product in a manner inconsistent with its labeling. Reports have associated repeated and prolonged occupational overexposure to solvents with permanent brain and nervous system damage. If using in closed armory vaults lacking forced-air ventilation, wear respiratory protection meeting NIOSH TC23C or equivalent. Keep container tightly closed when not in use.

INSTRUCTIONS FOR USING ED'S RED BORE CLEANER

1.   Open the firearm action and ensure the bore is clear. Cleaning is most effective when done while the barrel is still warm to the touch from firing. Saturate a cotton patch with bore cleaner, wrap or impale on jag, and push it through the bore from breech to muzzle. The patch should be a snug fit. Let the first patch fall off and do not pull it back into the bore.

2.   Wet a second patch, and similarly start it into the bore from the breech, this time scrubbing from the throat area forward in four- to five-inch strokes and gradually advancing until the patch emerges from the muzzle. Waiting approximately one minute to let the bore cleaner soak will improve its action.

3. For pitted, heavily carbon-fouled "rattle battle" guns, leaded revolvers, or neglected bores, a bronze brush wet with bore cleaner may be used to remove stubborn deposits. This is unnecessary for smooth, target-grade barrels in routine use.

4. Use a final wet patch pushed straight through the bore to flush out loosened residue dissolved by Ed's Red. Let the patch fall off the jag without pulling it back into the bore. If you are finished firing, leaving the bore wet will protect it from rust for one year under average conditions.

5. If the lanolin is incorporated into the mixture, it will protect the firearm from rust for up to two years. For longer-term storage, I recommend the use of Lee Liquid Alox as a Cosmoline substitute. ER will readily remove hardened Alox or Cosmolene.

6. Wipe spilled Ed's Red from exterior surfaces before storing the gun. (While Ed's Red is harmless to blue and nickel finishes, the acetone it contains is harmful to most wood finishes.)

7. Before firing again, push two dry patches through the bore and dry the chamber, using a patch wrapped around a suitably sized brush or jag. First shot point of impact usually will not be disturbed by Ed's Red if the bore is cleaned as described.

8. I have determined to my satisfaction that when Ed's Red is used exclusively and thoroughly, hot water cleaning is unnecessary after use of Pyrodex or military chlorate primers. However, if bores are not wiped between shots and shots and are heavily caked from

black powder fouling, hot water cleaning is recommended first to break up heavy fouling deposits. Water
cleaning should be followed by a thorough flush with
Ed's Red to prevent after-rusting, which could result
from residual moisture. It is *always* good practice to
clean *twice, two days apart* whenever using chlorate-
primed (corrosive) ammunition, just to make sure you
get all the corrosive residue out.

This recipe is placed in the public domain, and may
be freely distributed provided that it is done so in its en-
tirety with all current revisions, instructions, and safety
warnings included herein, and that proper attribution is
given to the author.

—C. E. Harris

Ammonia-Based Bore Cleaner

SurvivalBlog reader W. S. provided instructions for making
his ammonia-based bore cleaner, which is a variant of a mixture used for more than a century. He begins by explaining:

There are a couple of main things you're trying to do,
or combat, with cleaning solvents: carbon fouling and
copper fouling. Carbon is a by-product of the burned
powder. Copper fouling is bullet jacket material that
has plated itself in the bore. If you used lead bullets,
you would have to contend with that, but this is tar-
geted at those who use copper-jacketed bullets. Carbon
is probably the toughest to get rid of. It is extremely
hard and stubborn. It can build up and degrade accuracy. The best way to keep it in check is to avoid letting
it build up in the first place, by cleaning when the

barrel is new and not shooting a hundred rounds before cleaning. But sometimes you have to deal with what you have now. Copper fouling does the same thing: It builds up in the barrel and just keeps getting worse. If you get a used gun and it is fouled badly, you may want to use something other than this cleaner at first. Abrasive cleaners (JB's, Iosso) do a good job of getting through this stuff. It takes some elbow grease to work it back and forth, and you need to keep changing patches, but it will get through it. Once the rough stuff is gone, then using this mixture will get the rest. [JWR adds: The consensus is to *avoid* abrasive bore cleaners, unless it is absolutely necessary. In my opinion, only a very pressing emergency would dictate that. Otherwise, nothing more abrasive than a brass bore brush should ever be used.]

WARNING: All of the usual precautions for handling caustic and flammable fluids must be taken, such as wearing goggles and rubber gloves.

So how to make an ammonia-based bore cleaner? There is an initial expense, but it goes a long way and my formula makes quite a bit. First, go to a GM car dealer and buy a few cans of GM Top Engine Cleaner. For many years it came in a fifteen-ounce can, but it is now sold in plastic bottles. This is the basis for the bore cleaner. It has the chemicals in it for fighting carbon deposits. [JWR adds: Very similar products are sold under various brand names and descriptions such as "upper cylinder lubrication and injector cleaner."] You can scale how much solvent you want to formulate in a batch by the number of cans of Top Engine Cleaner you buy. The second ingredient will be the hardest to get, and that is strong ammonia. Ideally, find a blueprint shop or a large printing shop, and ask if they have 28 percent ammonia. You may be able to find some strong ammonia at commercial janitorial suppliers. It comes in a gallon jug. Trust me, *don't* sniff it, as it will clean your sinuses like you've never known.

The next ingredient is Marvel Mystery Oil, which you can get in most auto parts stores. The final ingredient is regular hydrogen peroxide, which you probably already have. Get a colored glass container—brown, blue, something that is tinted. All of these solvents come in colored glass to keep out sunlight. Some whiskey, bourbon, and scotch bottles are brown and work fine. (Be sure to prominently label them POISON and include a description of the contents.) Add your ingredients:

- One 15-ounce bottle of Top Engine Cleaner
- 25 mL of ammonia
- 5 mL of peroxide
- 5 mL of Marvel Mystery Oil

Just pour it all in. It won't explode; don't worry. Shake it all up and you will have a top-notch bore cleaner. The Top Engine Cleaner goes after carbon deposits, the ammonia and peroxide attack the copper fouling, and the Marvel Mystery Oil penetrates and helps get under the deposits, keeping the bore conditioned. The ammonia reaction to copper fouling will turn a white cleaning patch blue, or rather the patch will pick up the blue tint from dissolving the copper. It's a good indicator of how well the barrel is cleaned. You don't have to get every last bit out, but if there are heavy deposits, the patch will be a deeper blue; when the bore is getting fairly clean, it will be a much lighter blue. I use this on all of my rifles and pistol barrels. Most of my rifles are bolt-actions, and cleaning is easy, but use a bore guide to keep the cleaning rod from damaging the barrel. If you have a lever gun or semiauto, you may have to clean from the muzzle. Beware that you can severely damage the end (what is called the crown) by letting the cleaning rod drag over the edges of the barrel. I would recommend getting a coated cleaning rod to help with this, but still, go slow and watch the rod position to keep it centered in the barrel.

I've heard that you can also use Mercury Quicksilver gear lube, which is made by the Mercury Marine outboard motor company. It seems to have the same properties as the Top Engine Cleaner. You can substitute Kroil penetrating oil for the Marvel Mystery Oil, although it's not exactly easy to find.

Additional Warnings: Ammonia destroys some plastics, so do not use any ammonia-based cleaner for Glock, Springfield XD, Kel-Tec, or other polymer-frame pistols unless you have first removed the barrel and are cleaning the barrel nowhere near any of the gun's plastic parts. Furthermore, hydrogen peroxide shouldn't be used on any aluminum parts, as it can induce corrosion.

GLOSSARY

Note: A few of the terms in this glossary are courtesy of Wikipedia. Those entries, marked "(WP)," are not copyrighted, per Creative Commons (CC) license terms.

10/22: A semiautomatic .22-rimfire rifle made by Ruger. Starting in 2012, a takedown variant became available from the Ruger factory.

1911: *See* M1911

9/11: The Islamic terrorist attacks of 9/11/2001, which took three thousand American lives

ABC: Airway, breathing, and circulation (medical acronym)

A-B-C: Fire classes A, B, and C; usually used to describe a combination class A-B-C fire extinguisher. *See* class A, etc.

ABS: Acrylonitrile-butadiene-styrene (black plastic pipe). *See also* PVC

ACH: Advanced combat helmet. *See also* ECH; Kevlar; MICH

ACP: Automatic Colt pistol

advancing: In the context of tools, synonymous with feeding stock into a machine tool

adze: An ancient edged tool dating back to before the Flood. An adze is used for smoothing or carving wood in hand woodworking, similar to an ax but with the head mounted perpendicular to the handle. Two basic forms of an adze are the hand adze, a short-handled tool swung with one hand, and the foot adze, a long-handled tool capable of powerful swings with both hands—the cutting edge usually strikes at foot or shin level. The blade of an adze is set at right angles to the tool's shaft (like a hoe or plane), unlike the blade of an ax, which is set in line with the shaft. A similar-looking (but blunt) tool used for digging in hard ground is called a mattock. (WP)

AED: Automated external defibrillator

AK: Avtomat Kalashnikova. The gas-operated weapons family invented by Mikhail Timofeevich Kalashnikov, a Red Army sergeant. AKs are known for their robustness and were made in huge numbers, so they are ubiquitous in much of Asia and the Third World. The best of the Kalashnikov variants are the Valmets, which were made in Finland; the Galils, which were made in Israel; and the R4s, which are made in South Africa.

AK-47: The early-generation AK carbine with a milled receiver that shoots the intermediate 7.62x39mm cartridge. *See also* AKM

AK-74: The later-generation AK carbine, which shoots the 5.45x39mm cartridge

AKM: Avtomat Kalashnikova Modernizirovanniy, the later-generation 7.62x39 AK with a stamped receiver

AM: Amplitude modulation

annealing: The process of heating and cooling a metal, most commonly used to soften

anodizing: Applying a controlled oxidation layer to the surface of aluminum

AP: Armor-piercing

APC: Armored personnel carrier

AR: Automatic rifle; generic term for semiauto variants of the ArmaLite family of rifles designed by Eugene Stoner (AR-10, AR-15, AR-180, etc.)

AR-7: The .22 LR semiautomatic survival rifle designed by Eugene Stoner. It weighs just two pounds, and when disassembled.

AR-10: The 7.62mm NATO predecessor of the M16 rifle, designed by Eugene Stoner. Early AR-10s (mainly Portuguese, Sudanese, and Cuban contract, from the late 1950s and early 1960s) are not to be confused with the present-day semiauto-only AR-10 rifles that are more closely interchangeable with parts from the smaller-caliber AR-15.

AR-15: The semiauto civilian variant of the U.S. Army M16 rifle

artificer: A person who creates or fixes intricate objects. In JWR's parlance, anyone who has eclectic skills in design, fabrication, maintenance, and repair of tools and machinery.

ASAP: As soon as possible

ASME: American Society of Mechanical Engineers

ATF: Automatic transmission fluid. *See also* BATFE

ATGATT: All the gear, all the time. *See also* EDC

AUG: *See* Steyr AUG

aviation snips: A variation of tin snips with a compound angle action that allows easier cutting than with standard-length handles or grips

AWG: American wire gauge

ax/axe: An ancient example of a simple machine: a type of wedge, or dual inclined plane. This reduces the effort needed by the woodchopper. It splits the wood into two parts by the pressure concentration at the blade. The handle of the ax also acts as a lever, allowing the user to increase the force at the cutting edge. Not using the full length of the handle is known as choking the ax.

B&E: Breaking and entering

bark spud: A traditional tool used to remove bark from felled timber; also known as a peeling iron, peeler bar, peeling spud, or simply spud

backsaw: A handsaw that has a stiffening rib at its upper margin, to provide a precisely straight cut; typically used in conjunction with a miter box

Bad Boy Buggie: A 48-VDC electric vehicle that combines the drive train of a golf cart with the suspension, tires, and winch of an ATV

ball: Depending on context, the round end of a ball peen hammer, or a full metal jacket bullet. *See also* peen

BATFE: Bureau of Alcohol, Tobacco, Firearms, and Explosives (a U.S. federal government taxing agency)

belt sander: A type of power sander with a sandpaper belt that is driven on wheels; typically used for rough finish work rather than fine cabinetry. If you are not careful, these powerful sanders can leave parallel sanding marks or even dig a channel. *See also* orbital sander

bench grinder: A treadle-powered, hand-cranked, or motor-powered grinding wheel (or pair of wheels), often mounted on a workbench that is used primarily for shaping metal objects or for sharpening tools. Goggles must always be worn when using a bench grinder!

bit brace: A brace (or brace and bit) is a hand tool used to drill holes, usually in wood. Pressure is applied to the top and the tool is rotated with a U-shaped grip, which is a kind of crankshaft. It gives the brace much greater torque than other kinds of hand drills. The front part of the brace consists of a chuck spindle with V-shaped brackets or clamps inside. Turning the spindle of the chuck in a clockwise direction tightens the drill bit in the chuck; turning it in a counterclockwise direction loosens the bit for removal. (WP) (See photo on page 69.)

black rifle/black gun: Generic terms for a modern battle rifle, typically equipped with a black plastic stock and forend, giving these guns an all-black appearance. Functionally, however, they are little different from earlier semiauto designs.

blacksmith: A metalsmith who creates objects from wrought iron or steel by forging the metal, using tools to hammer, bend, and cut (compare to whitesmith). Blacksmiths produce objects such as gates, grilles, railings, light fixtures, furniture, sculpture, tools, agricultural implements, decorative and religious items, cooking utensils, and weapons. Despite the incorrect common usage, a man who shoes horses is a farrier (although a blacksmith may fabricate the shoes). Many farriers have carried out both trades, but most modern or engineering smiths do not. (WP) *See also* smith; tinker

blacksmithing vise: A large, fast-opening and -clamping vise with a leg that extends to the floor to absorb the shock of hammer falls

blacksmith's hammer: A short, heavy hammer designed for metalworking. Typically these have one round face and an opposing face with a rectangular peen for shaping or bending steel. (WP)

BLM: Bureau of Land Management (a U.S. federal government agency that administers public lands)

BMG: Browning machine gun; usually refers to .50 BMG, the U.S. military's standard heavy machine gun cartridge since the early twentieth century. This cartridge is now often used for long-range precision countersniper rifles.

board foot/feet: A system of measurement for lumber. One board foot is equivalent to 144 cubic inches.

BP: blood pressure

brace: *See* bit brace

Break Free CLP: *See* CLP

breast drill: A hand-operated brace-type drill with a pad on the end that is pressed by a person's chest to increase the force that is applied. *See also* bit brace

brightsmith: A smith who works any shiny metal

broadax/broadaxe: A large-headed ax. There are two categories of cutting edges on broadaxes, both used for shaping logs by hewing. The double-bevel ax has a straight handle that can be swung with either side against the wood. A double-bevel broadax can be used for chopping or notching and hewing. When the ax used for hewing, a notch is chopped in the side of the log down to a marked line. This process is called scoring. The pieces of wood between these notches are removed with an ax in a process called joggling, then the remaining wood is chopped away to the line. (WP)

brownsmith: A smith who works copper or brass

BTU: British thermal unit

bubble level: *See* spirit level

bull's-eye level: A circular, flat-bottomed level with the liquid under a slightly convex glass face with a circle at the center (WP)

bucking: The process of cutting a felled and de-limbed tree into logs (WP)

bump key: A specially cut key designed for opening a variety locks with the same keyway. When used in conjunction with soft strikes from a mallet, the specially designed teeth of the bump key transmit a slight impact force to all of the bottom pins in the lock. The key pins transmit this force to the driver pins; the key pins stay in place, and the lock cylinder can then be turned. Also known as a jiggler key. (WP)

caliper: A device used to measure the width, thickness, or diameter of an object. A caliper can be as simple as a compass with inward- or outward-facing points. The tips of the caliper are adjusted to fit across the points to be measured; the caliper is then removed and the distance read by measuring between the tips with a measuring tool, such as a ruler. (WP)

cant hook: A traditional logging tool consisting of a wooden lever handle with a movable metal hook, called a dog, at one end, used for handling and moving logs. Unlike the similar peavey, the cant hook has a blunt tip, often bearing teeth. A cant hook is also sometimes called a cant dog. (WP) *See also* peavey

carpenter's vise: A bench vise that is optimized for holding lumber, typically mounted with the top of its jaws parallel to the workbench's surface. Also known as a woodworking vise.

CAT: Combat application tourniquet

CB: Citizens band radio, a VHF broadcasting band. There is no license required for operation in the United States. Some desirable CB transceivers are capable of SSB operation. Originally twenty-three channels, the citizens band was later expanded to forty channels during the golden age of CB, in the 1970s.

C-clip pliers: *See* circlip pliers

CETME: Centro de Estudios Técnicos de Materiales Especiales; best known as the maker of the Spanish army's predecessor of the HK G3 series rifles. Thousands of CETME rifle parts sets were imported into the United States in the late 1990s and rebuilt into semiauto-only sporter rifles.

chalk box: *See* chalk line

chalk line: A string—usually retractable into a chalk box—that is covered with chalk powder. When the line is stretched tight on a flat surface and flicked with the thumb and forefinger, it leaves a straight line marking. Usually blue chalk powder is used. (WP) (See photo on page 64.)

chasing: The process of cleaning up an existing screw or nut thread. Typically this is done with a tap, a die, or a screw thread–restoring universal sixty-degree angle file. (The latter is commonly called a chasing file.)

chuck: A specialized type of clamp used to hold an object, usually a cylindrical object. It is most commonly used to hold a rotating tool (such as the drill bit in a power tool) or a rotating workpiece (such as the bar or blank in the headstock spindle of a lathe). (WP) *See also* collet

circlip pliers: A type of mechanic's pliers used for fitting circlips or retaining rings. Two types are used: internal or external. Also commonly known as C-clip pliers or snap ring pliers.

circular saw: A handheld power saw used for crosscutting and ripping hardwoods, softwoods, plywood, and fiberboard. Commonly called a Skilsaw, which was one of the most popular early brands. Since these saws are fast, powerful, and handheld, they are famous for creating trips to the emergency room if used carelessly. (WP)

claw hammer: The ubiquitous carpentry tool with a hammer face on one side (for driving nails) and a claw on the opposite side (for pulling nails and other levering work) (WP)

class A: Fire extinguishers designed to fight traditional types of combustible materials such as wood and paper products. They are sized by the amount of liquid they hold.

class B: Fire extinguishers designed to fight fires of combustible liquids such as gasoline, grease, and kerosene. They are sized by the number of square feet of fire they can extinguish.

class C: Fire extinguishers designed to fight fires of an electrical nature, such as those from wiring, breakers, and outlets. These types of fires pose an electrocution hazard, so the extinguisher must produce a substance that is nonconductive.

class D: Fire extinguishers designed to fight combustible metals fires

class K: Fire extinguishers designed to fight cooking fat and oil fires (called class E in the United Kingdom)

CLP: Cleaner, lubricant, protectant; mil-spec lubricant, sold under the trade name "Break Free CLP"

CO: Carbon monoxide

CO_2: Carbon dioxide

cobbler: A person who repairs shoes, rather than manufacturing them. *See also* cordwainer

cold chisel: A traditional metalworking tool used for cutting steel; also useful for breaking mortar and concrete

collet: A holding device—specifically, a subtype of chuck—that forms a collar around the object to be held and exerts a strong clamping force on the object when it is tightened, usually by means of a tapered outer collar. It may be used to hold a workpiece or a tool. (WP)

combination square: A multipurpose square, made of steel; typically has a right angle, a forty-five-degree (miter) square, and a tool to find the center of a piece of stock. These often have a small scribe built in that can be withdrawn for use.

CONEX: Continental express; the ubiquitous twenty-, thirty-, and forty-foot-long steel cargo containers used in multiple transportation modes

CONUS: Continental United States

cooper: A person who makes wooden barrels

cord: A cord is a unit of dry volume used in Canada and in the United States to measure firewood. One cord is defined as 128 foot^3 (~3.62 m^3), corresponding to a woodpile 8 feet wide by 4 feet high of 4-feet-long logs. In the metric system, wood is usually measured in steres or cubic meters: 1 stere = 1 m^3 ≈ 0.276 cords. In the United States, the cord is defined by statute in most states. Wood is also sold by the "face cord" (sometimes called a rick), which is usually not legally defined and varies regionally. (WP)

cordwainer: A shoemaker; typically one who makes soft leather shoes. *See also* cobbler

cotter: A key that prevents a wheel from turning on its shaft

countersink: A conical hole cut into a manufactured object, or the cutter used to make such a hole. Typically a countersink is used to make a recess for a flat screw head, so that it does not protrude. (WP)

CPAP: Continuous positive airway pressure

CPR: Cardiopulmonary resuscitation

CQB: Close quarters battle

CRKT: Columbia River Knife & Tool

crocker: A synonym for *potter*

crosscut saw: A saw for cutting across the grain of lumber or timber. *See also* ripsaw

cutler: A maker of cutlery.

CW: Depending on context, continuous wave (an operating mode for amateur radio gear, used for Morse code), chemical warfare (NBC defense), or clockwise (mechanics and machining)

Damascus steel: A type of steel used in South Asian and Middle Eastern sword making; created from wootz steel, a steel developed in India around 300 BC. Modern Damascus steel is still used by a few contemporary custom knife makers. (WP)

diagonal cutters: A specialized hand tool with the outward appearance of pliers that is intended for the cutting of wire (generally not used to grab or turn objects). The plane defined by the cutting edges of the jaws intersects the joint rivet at an angle or on a diagonal, hence the name. Instead of using a shearing action as with scissors, diagonal cutters cut by indenting and wedging the wire apart. The jaw edges are ground to a symmetrical V shape; thus the two jaws can be visualized to form the letter X, as seen end-on when fully occluded. The pliers are made of tempered steel with inductive heating and quenching often used to selectively harden the jaws. Diagonal cutters are also called wire cutters or diagonal pliers, or simply dikes. (In common electrician's jargon you often hear the phrase "a pair of dikes" or "hand me those dikes.") (WP)

dial caliper: A caliper (either inch or metric) with an analog dial readout

dikes: *See* diagonal cutters

DIY: Do-it-yourself

DLA Disposition Services: Defense Logistics Agency Disposition Services; formerly DRMO (Defense Reutilization and Marketing Office)

DMV: Department of Motor Vehicles

DOA: Dead on arrival. Traditionally applied to cadavers, this acronym is now also used for describing a piece of mail-ordered equipment that doesn't work.

drawknife: A two-handed woodworking too used for shaping, primarily in cylindrical sections. A drawknife is used by boatbuilders, coopers, and wheelwrights. (See photo on page 65.)

drawknife bench: *See* shave horse

draw plate: A type of die consisting of a hardened steel plate with one or more holes through which wire is drawn to make it thinner. A typical plate will have twenty to thirty holes so a wide range of diameters can be drawn. (WP)

drill bit: A cutting tool used to create cylindrical holes, almost always of circular cross-section. Drill bits come in many sizes and have various uses. (WP)

drilling hammer: A short two-handed sledgehammer with front and rear faces that are usually identical. The short handle makes it suitable for use in close quarters. *See also* sledgehammer

ECH: Enhanced combat helmet. *See also* ACH; Kevlar; MICH

EDC: Everyday carry. *See also* ATGATT

EMP: Electromagnetic pulse

ER: Depending on context, emergency room or Ed's Red (rifle bore cleaner)

E-tool: Entrenching tool; a small military folding shovel

FAA: Federal Aviation Administration

FAL: *See* FN/FAL

FAMAS: Fusil d'Assaut de la Manufacture d'Armes de Saint-Étienne; the French Army's standard-issue bullpup carbine, chambered in 5.56mm NATO

farm jack: *See* Hi-Lift jack

farrier: A specialist in equine hoof care, including the trimming and balancing of horses' hooves and the placing of shoes, if necessary. A farrier combines some blacksmith's skills (fabricating, adapting, and adjusting metal shoes) with some veterinarian's skills (knowledge of the anatomy and physiology of the lower limb) to care for horses' hooves. (WP)

feed and speed: Refers to two separate velocities in machine tool practice: cutting speed and feed rate. They are often considered as a pair because of their combined effect on the cutting process. Each, however, can also be considered and analyzed in its own right. (Also known as speeds and feeds.) (WP) *See also* advancing

feeding: *See* advancing

feed stock: Raw or semifinished material that is advanced (or fed) into a machine tool. *See also* advancing

felling ax: An ax designed for felling trees; made either single- or double-bitted

FEMA: Federal Emergency Management Agency (a U.S. federal government agency). The acronym is also jokingly defined as "foolishly expecting meaningful aid."

fencing pliers: Pliers that are specialized for fence installation and repair. These combine a small pair of gripping pads, a hook for pulling staples, and a small hammerhead. (See photo on page 56.)

FFL: Federal firearms license

FFV: Flex-fuel vehicle

file: A metalworking, woodworking, and plastic-working tool used to cut fine amounts of material from a workpiece. It most commonly refers to the hand-tool style, which takes the form of a steel bar with a case-hardened surface and a series of sharp, parallel teeth. Most files have a narrow, pointed tang at one end, to which a handle can be attached. (WP)

fly-tying vise: A miniature bench vise, used for detail work

FN/FAL: A 7.62mm NATO battle rifle originally made by the Belgian company Fabrique Nationale d'Herstal (FN), issued to more than fifty countries in the 1960s and 1970s.

Now made as semiauto-only "clones" by a variety of makers. *See also* L1A1

foot-pound (ft lb): A unit of measure of force, defined as the amount of energy expended when a force of one pound acts through a distance of one foot along the direction of the force

forge: A specialized hearth used for heating metals, or the workplace ("smithy") where the hearth is located. The forge is used by the smith to heat a piece of metal to a temperature at which it becomes easier to shape, or to the point where work hardening no longer occurs. The metal (known as the workpiece) is transported to and from the forge using tongs, which are also used to hold the workpiece on the smithy's anvil while the smith works it with a hammer. Finally the workpiece is transported to the slack tub, which rapidly cools the workpiece in a large body of oil or water. If filled with water, the slack tub also provides water to control the fire in the forge. (WP)

framing square: A steel square with legs that are between eighteen and thirty-six inches, with measurements to an eighth of inch. These are used for squaring wood or steel projects, but they usually also have stair and roof truss layout tables inscribed on them.

froe: An L-shaped tool for cleaving wood by splitting it along the grain. It is used by hammering one edge of its blade into the end of a piece of wood in the direction of the grain, then twisting the blade in the wood by rotating the haft (handle). A froe uses the haft as a lever to multiply the force upon the blade, allowing wood to be torn apart with remarkably little force applied to the haft. By twisting one way or the other, the user may guide the direction of the split. Froes are used in combination with wooden mallets to split timber and to make planks, wooden shingles, and kindling; they are safer and more accurate to use than hatchets because the blade is not swung. Froes are also known as shake axes or shingle froes. (WP) (See photo on page 68.)

ft lb: *See* foot-pound

FTRSS: Flexible Temperature Range Sleep System

fulcrum: The support point about which a lever pivots

Galil: Israeli battle rifle, based on Kalashnikov action. Most were made in 5.56mm NATO, but a variant was also made in 7.62mm NATO, in smaller numbers.

GB: Gigabyte

GCA: The Gun Control Act of 1968; the law that first created FFLs and banned interstate transfer of post-1898 firearms, except "to or through" FFL holders

GFCI: Ground fault circuit interrupter

gimlet: A wooden T-handled tool with a metal spike and a small screw thread at the tip. Originally designed for pulling barrel bungs, these are used by carpenters for starting holes for screws or for making pilot holes for drilling.

glazier: A tradesman who cuts, installs, removes, and replaces glass panes

Glock: The popular polymer-framed pistol design by Gaston Glock, of Austria. Glocks are a favorite of gun writer Boston T. Party.

GMAW: *See* MIG

GMRS: General Mobile Radio Service, a licensed UHF-FM two-way radio service. *See also* MURS.

Gold Cup: The target version of Colt's M1911 pistol; has fully adjustable target sights, a tapered barrel, and a tighter barrel bushing than a standard M1911

GOOD: Get Out of Dodge; slang term for leaving an urban area in the midst of a disaster

GPM: Gallons per minute (water well and firefighting acronym)

GPS: Global positioning system

grain (gr.): The measure of mass used for firearm projectiles (bullets); a unit of lead mass measurement, roughly equal to ⅓ carat or 65 milligrams. Sixteen grains is roughly equal to 1 gram. Also used as a measure of mass for smokeless powder (nitrocellulose) propellant.

GTAW: *See* TIG

hacker: Before around 1970, this was a hoe maker. Now it refers to a software expert.

hacksaw: A handsaw for cutting metal and hard plastic with easily replaceable saw blades held by pins at both ends. Traditionally hacksaws had horizontal handles (parallel to the blade), but in the twentieth century their design evolved into pistol grip–style (nearly vertical) handles, for much greater leverage while maintaining precise control.

hand brace: *See* bit brace

hardening: A process usually involving heating and quenching certain iron-based steel alloys to a temperature within a critical range (WP)

hardware: Fasteners that are inserted into a piece of wood, bar stock, or a sheet metal part

heat treatment: *See* hardening

hew/hewing: The process of converting sections of a tree trunk from its round natural form into a form with more or less flat surfaces using primarily, among other tools, an ax or axes. It is an ancient method still used occasionally to square up beams for building construction. Logs are typically first marked with chalk line before hewing. (WP) *See also* broadax

HF: High frequency, a radio band used by amateur radio operators

high-speed steel (HSS or HS): A subset of tool steels, commonly used in tool bits and cutting tools. It is often used in power-saw blades and drill bits. It is superior to the older high-carbon steel tools used extensively through the 1940s in that it can withstand higher temperatures without losing its temper (hardness). This property allows HSS to cut faster than high-carbon steel, hence the name high-speed steel. At room temperature, HSS grades generally display high hardness (above HRC60) and abrasion resistance compared with common carbon and tool steels. (WP)

Hi-Lift jack: A heavy-duty utility jack/puller/spreader that uses a pair of walking pins to move a platform up and down a steel beam; also known as a sheepherder's jack and farm jack (see photo on page 29)

HK or H & K: Heckler und Koch, the German gunmaker

HK91: Heckler und Koch Model 91, the civilian (semiautomatic-only) variant of the 7.62mm NATO G3 rifle

hp: Horsepower

HRC: The Rockwell C scale for determining the hardness of steel. Sometimes expressed as just "RC" or "Rc." Named after the inventors, Hugh and Stanley Rockwell.

Humvee: High-mobility multipurpose wheeled vehicle

hydrometer: An instrument for measuring the density of liquids in relation to the density of water. Used to indicate the state of charge in lead-acid cells by measuring the specific gravity of the electrolyte. Also used in commercial food canning.

ID: Identification

idiot level: *See* torpedo level

IED: Improvised explosive device

JASBORR: Jim's Amazing Secret Bunker of Redundant Redundancy

jiggler key: *See* bump key

joinery: A woodworking process that joins together pieces of wood to produce more complex items. Some wood joints employ fasteners, bindings, or adhesives, while others use only wood elements. The characteristics of wooden joints—strength, flexibility, toughness, appearance, etc.—derive from the properties of the joining materials and from how they are used in the joints. Therefore, different joinery techniques are used to meet differing requirements. For example, the joinery used to build a house is different from that used to make puzzle toys, although some concepts overlap. Traditionally done with hand tools, most small joinery is now accomplished with specialized electric tools. (WP) *See also* mortise and tenon joint

JWR: James Wesley, Rawles

Kevlar: The synthetic material used in most body armor and ballistic helmets; also one nickname for the standard U.S. Army helmet. *See also* ACH; ECH; MICH

L1A1: The British Army version of the FN/FAL, made to inch measurements

lathe: A machine tool that rotates the workpiece on its axis to perform various operations such as cutting, sanding, knurling, drilling, deformation, facing, and turning, with tools that are applied to the workpiece to create an object that has symmetry about an axis of rotation. (WP) *See also* turning

lathe turning: *See* turner; turning

LC-1: Load carrying, type 1 (U.S. Army load-bearing equipment, 1970s to 1990s)

level: *See* spirit level

limbing ax: An ax designed for removing the limbs from felled trees. *See also* felling ax; bucking

log bucking: *See* bucking

LP: Liquid propane

M1A: The civilian (semiauto-only) equivalent of the M14 rifle

M1 carbine: The U.S. Army semiauto carbine issued during WWII. Mainly issued to officers and second-echelon troops such as artillerymen. Uses .30 U.S. carbine, an intermediate (pistol-class) .30-caliber cartridge. More than six million were manufactured. *See also* M2 carbine

M1 Garand: The U.S. Army's primary battle rifle of WWII and the Korean conflict. It is semiautomatic and chambered in .30-06, and uses a top-loading, eight-round en bloc clip that ejects after the last round is fired. This rifle is commonly called the Garand (after the surname of its inventor). Not to be confused with the U.S. M1 carbine, another semiauto of the same era, which shoots a far less powerful pistol-class cartridge.

M2 carbine: The selective-fire (fully automatic) version of the U.S. Army semiauto carbine issued during WWII and the Korean conflict

M4 carbine: The U.S. Army–issue 5.56mm NATO selective fire-carbine (a shorter version of the M16, with a 14.5-inch barrel and collapsing stock). Earlier-issue M16 carbine variants had designations such as XM177E2 and CAR-15. Civilian semiauto-only variants often have these same designations and are called "M4geries."

M4gery: A civilian semiauto-only version of an M4 carbine, with a 16-inch barrel instead of a 14.5-inch barrel

M9: The U.S. Army–issue version of the Beretta M92 semiauto 9mm pistol

M14: The U.S. Army–issue 7.62mm NATO selective-fire battle rifle. These rifles are still issued in small numbers, primarily to designated marksmen. The civilian semiauto-only equivalent of the M14 is called the M1A.

M16: The U.S. Army–issue 5.56mm NATO selective-fire battle rifle. The current standard variant is the M16A2, which has improved sight and three-shot burst control. *See also* M4 carbine

M60: The semi-obsolete, U.S. Army–issue 7.62mm NATO belt-fed light machine gun, which utilized some design elements of the German MG-42

M1911: The Model 1911 Colt semiauto pistol (and clones thereof), usually chambered in .45 ACP

MAC: Depending on context, Military Airlift Command or Military Armament Corporation

Maglite: A popular American brand of sturdy flashlight with an aluminum casing. Early models used traditional filament bulbs, but much of the recent production now uses LED.

mattock: A blunt tool, similar to an adze, that is used for digging in hard ground or clay. *See also* adze

MBR: Main battle rifle

MCD: Millicandela, the unit of measure commonly used to describe LED brightness. One thousand millicandela equals one candela (CD). The candela is a measure of how much light is produced as measured at the light source.

mcleod: A rake with a two-sided blade on a long wooden handle, designed specifically for firefighting. It is a standard tool used during wildfire suppression and trail restoration. The combination tool was created in 1905 by Malcolm McLeod, a U.S. Forest Service ranger at the Sierra National Forest, with a large hoelike blade on one side and a tined blade on the other. (WP)

mechanical advantage: A measure of the force amplification achieved by using a tool or mechanical device

mechanic's vise: A strong clamping tool with a screw-turning handle, usually mounted above bench-top height for gripping wood, plastic, or steel while working it. Modern variations often have pivoting heads and auxiliary pipe clamps, for greater versatility.

MICH: Modular integrated communications helmet. *See also* ACH; ECH; Kevlar

micrometer: A device incorporating a calibrated screw used for precise measurement of small distances in mechanical engineering and machining as well as most mechanical trades. Micrometers are similar in use to vernier calipers but are more precise. The slang contraction for micrometer (or the process of using one) is *mike*. (WP)

MIG: Metal inert gas (welding); also called gas metal arc welding (GMAW)

mike: *See* micrometer

milling: The machining process of using rotary cutters to remove material from a workpiece advancing (or feeding) in a direction at an angle to the axis of the tool. It covers a wide variety of different operations and machines, on scales from small individual parts to large, heavy-duty gang milling operations. Milling is one of the most commonly used processes in industry and machine shops today for machining parts to precise sizes and shapes. (WP)

mil-spec: Military specification

milsurp or mil-surp: Military surplus

mine ax: A short-handled ax designed for use in close confines. This is JWR's preferred tool for splitting short lengths of sapwood and cedar into kindling.

Mini-14: A 5.56mm NATO semiauto carbine made by Ruger

miter box: A guide for a handsaws, used to make precise miter cuts in small-dimension boards, such as moldings and picture frames; typically used with a backsaw. *See also* backsaw

miter (joint): A wood joint made by bevel-cutting each of two parts to be joined, usually at a 45-degree angle, to form a corner, usually a 90-degree angle. A disadvantage of a miter joint is its weakness, but it can be strengthened with a spline. (WP)

miter saw: A saw used to make accurate crosscuts and miter-joint cuts in a piece of wood (WP)

MOA: Minute of angle (1.047 inches at 100 yards), a measurement of rifle accuracy

MOLLE: Modular lightweight load-carrying equipment

Molotov cocktail: A hand-thrown firebomb made from a glass container filled with gasoline or napalm (thickened gasoline)

mortise and tenon joint: A joinery method in which a pin (tenon) cut from a piece of wooden stock is driven and/ or glued into a slot (mortise) (WP)

MRE: Meal, ready to eat

MSDS: Material safety data sheet

MTBE: Methyl tertiary-butyl ether, an oxygenating additive for gasoline

MURS: Multi-Use Radio Service, a VHF two-way radio service that does not require a license. *See also* FRS; GMRS

napalm: Thickened gasoline, used in some flame weapons

NATO: North Atlantic Treaty Organization

NBC: Nuclear, biological, and chemical

N.E.C.K.: No-nonsense emergency compact knife

nedder: Needle maker

needle-nose pliers: Hand pliers with elongated, narrow jaws, typically with a wire cutter at the back end of the jaws

NFA: The National Firearms Act of 1934; the law that first imposed a transfer tax on machine guns, suppressors (commonly called silencers), and short-barreled rifles and shotguns in the U.S.

NiCd: Nickel cadmium (rechargeable battery)

NiMH: Nickel–metal hydride (rechargeable battery); improvement of NiCd

NIMS: National Incident Management System

NRP: National Response Plan

OPSEC: Operational security

orbital sander: An electric power sander with a semi-random motion, to minimize parallel sanding marks. Also known as a random orbital sander or palm sander. Note that not all power sanders are orbital; some are reciprocating. *See also* belt sander

PASS: Pull, aim, squeeze, swipe (mnemonic for fire extinguisher use)

peavey: A log-handling tool consisting of a handle, generally thirty to fifty inches long, with a metal spike protruding from the tip. The spike is rammed into a log, then a hook (at the end of an arm attached to a pivot a short distance up the handle) grabs the log at a second location. Once engaged, the handle gives the operator leverage to roll, slide, or float the log to a new position. In the modern context, since logs are now rarely floated, peaveys and cant hooks are used to lift logs slightly above the ground so that a chain saw is not run into the ground while bucking a felled tree. The peavey (or peavey hook) was named for blacksmith Joseph Peavey, of Upper Stillwater, Maine, who invented the tool as a refinement to the cant hook in the 1850s. Many mistakenly use the terms interchangeably, though correctly a Peavey will have a spike in the end of the handle, and a cant dog will have a blunt end or possibly small teeth for friction. The Peavey Manufacturing Co. is still located in Maine and manufactures several variations. (WP) *See also* bucking; cant hook

pedal grinder/grindstone: A floor-mounted grinding wheel that is powered by pedals and, in later generation designs, with a chain. (The author's chain-drive pedal grinder is shown in the cover illustration of this book.) *See also* treadle grinder

peen/peening: The process of shaping metal by impact; also the nailing end of a ball peen hammer. *See also* ball

Pelosi: *See* plumb

pH (scale): The pH scale is a measure of hydrogen ion concentration. The scale runs from 0 to 14 with the middle point (pH 7) being neutral (neither acidic nor basic). Any pH number greater than 7 is considered a base and any pH number less than 7 is considered an acid. The strongest acid is 0 and the strongest base is 14.

plane/planer: A tool designed to cut or face off wood or metal. Traditional hand tools with this purpose are generally called planes, while their power tool equivalents are called planers. *See also* shave horse

pliers: A versatile hand tool with a scissorlike action, used for grasping, gripping, bending, and cutting. Technically, diagonal cutters are a form of pliers. (WP) *See also* Vise-Grip

plumb: An object that is exactly vertical, as established by a spirit level or a plumb line. If a board is truly vertical it is called "plumb" or "square to the world." If not, then it is deemed "out of plumb," or as we derisively put it in the Rawles Ranch parlance, "Pelosi."

plumber: Originally a trade name for a person who installed lead sheet roofing and who set lead frames for windowpanes. Only later, when the trade shifted toward lead water and drain pipes, did the meaning of the word change.

POV: Depending on context, petroleum, oil, and lubricants or privately owned vehicle

power sander: *See* orbital sander; belt sander

pre-1899: Guns made before 1899, not classified as firearms under federal law

prepper: Slang for prepared individual (a survivalist)

preps: Slang for preparations

pry bar: A leverage tool with a curved or angled blade that can fit between two portions of an object to separate them. The handle provides leverage to pry these portions apart.

PTO: Power takeoff, a physical mounting for running auxiliary equipment, turned by an engine. PTOs are found on most farm tractors and some trucks. They are used to power accessories such as post-hole augers, manure spreaders, and snow blowers.

Pulaski: A special hand tool used in wildland firefighting. The tool combines an ax and an adze in one head, similar to that of the cutter mattock, with a rigid handle of wood, plastic, or fiberglass. The Pulaski is a versatile tool for constructing firebreaks, as it can be used to both dig soil and chop wood. It is also well adapted for trail construction, gardening, and other outdoor work. As a gardening or excavation tool, it is effective for digging holes in root-bound or hard soil. (WP)

punch: A tool, usually less than eight inches long, that is struck with a hammer in order to make an impression or indentation, or to drive a pin

PV: Photovoltaic (solar power conversion array); used to convert solar power to DC electricity, typically for battery charging

PVC: Polyvinyl chloride (white plastic water pipe). *See also* ABS

pynner: A pinmaker

random orbital sander: *See* orbital sander

Rawles Ranch: The full-time home and retreat for the Rawles family, located in an unnamed western state. The ranch is small (less than a hundred acres) but has plentiful game and it borders public lands, providing the family a several-million-acre "big backyard." OPSEC dictates that we don't mention the location of the Rawles Ranch.

RC: Rockwell C (a scale of metal hardness for hard steels). *See also* HRC

RIG: Rust inhibitive grease (RIG is the brand name of one of the best greases on the market). *See also* silica gel; VCI

rigger: A person specializing in working hoist tackle or ship rigging

ripsaw: A saw for cutting parallel to the grain of lumber or timber. *See also* crosscut saw

roper: Rope maker, a maker of rope or nets

router: A rotary power tool that is used for cutting grooves or shaping the edges of wood stock; made in both handheld and table models (WP)

RPM: Revolutions per minute

RRA: Rock River Arms, an American maker of AR family rifles

S&W: Smith and Wesson

saddler: A person who makes and repairs saddles and bridles

sawyer: A person whose trade is sawing wood; also generically used for carpenters and lumbermen

SBR: Short-barrel rifle; legal term in the U.S. for a federally registered rifle with a barrel less than sixteen inches long

SBS: Short-barrel shotgun; legal term in the U.S. for a federally registered shotgun with a barrel less than eighteen inches long

SCA: Society for Creative Anachronism

SCBA: Self-contained breathing apparatus

Schumer: A euphemism for the stuff that the septic tank pumper truck hauls away (derived from the surname of Senator Charles Schumer)

scrollsaw: The generic term for a very fine-tooth saw that includes traditional handheld saws, nineteenth-century treadle scrollsaws, and modern electric scrollsaws

scythe: An agricultural hand tool for mowing grass or reaping crops. It was largely replaced by horse-drawn and then tractor machinery, but is still used in some areas of

Europe and Asia—particularly on steep alpine slopes where it is difficult for farm machinery to operate. (WP)

shave horse: A bench, usually with a seat, that clamps wood while for use with a drawknife or plane. A foot pedal actuates the clamp, leaving both hands free to work. Also known as a drawknife bench. *See also* drawknife

sheepherder's jack: *See* Hi-Lift jack

shingle froe: *See* froe

SIG: Schweizerische Industrie Gesellschaft, the Swiss gunmaker

silica gel: A granular desiccant, used to protect guns, tools, and other metal objects from rust. *See also* RIG; VCI

Skilsaw: *See* circular saw

sledgehammer: A heavy, two-handed hammer with front and rear faces that are usually identical. *See also* drilling hammer

SMAW: Shielded metal arc welding

smelter: Depending on context, a person who melts down ores, or a fisherman who fishes for smelt

smith: Generic name for a person working in any number of skilled trades. *See also* blacksmith

smithy: A smith's workshop

snap ring pliers: *See* circlip pliers

SOP: Standard operating procedure

spirit level: An instrument designed to indicate whether a surface is horizontal (level) or vertical (plumb). Different types of spirit levels may be used by carpenters, stonemasons, brick-layers, other building trades workers, surveyors, millwrights, and other metalworkers, and in some photographic or video-graphic work. Early spirit levels had two banana-shaped curved glass vials at each viewing point and were more com-plicated to use. In the 1920s, Henry Ziemann, the founder of Empire Level Manufacturing Corporation, invented the mod-ern level with a single vial. These vials, common on most or-dinary levels today, have a slightly curved glass tube that is incompletely filled with a liquid, usually a colored spirit or al-cohol, leaving a bubble in the tube. At slight inclinations, the bubble travels away from the center position, which is usually marked with lines. (WP) *See also* bull's-eye level

Steyr AUG: The Austrian army's 5.56mm bullpup infan-try carbine; also issued by the Australian Army as their re-placement for the L1A1

string line: A piece of string or more typically a piece of nylon fishing line that is stretched tight to establish straight lines, such as when laying out the partitions when framing a building

table saw: A woodworking tool consisting of a circular saw blade mounted on an arbor, driven by an electric motor (either directly, by belt, by flex drive, or by gears). The blade protrudes through the surface of a table, which provides support for the material being cut. In a modern table saw, the depth of the cut is varied by moving the blade up and down: In some early table saws, the blade and arbor were fixed, and the table was moved up and down to expose more or less of the blade. The angle of the cut is controlled by adjusting the angle of blade. Some earlier saws angled the table to control the cut angle. (WP)

tanner: A person who cures animal hides into leather

tap and die: Cutting tools used to create screw threads (a process called threading). A tap is used to cut the female portion of the mating pair (e.g., a nut). A die is used to cut the male portion of the mating pair (e.g., a screw). The process of cutting threads using a tap is called tapping, whereas the process using a die is called threading. Both tools can be used to clean up a thread, which is called chasing. (WP) *See also* chasing; threading

TEOTWAWKI: The End of the World as We Know It (coined by Mike Medintz), pronounced "tee-ought-walk-ee"

thermite: A powder used for an exothermic welding process that is a mixture of iron oxide powder and aluminum powder. It is most commonly used to join railroad tracks, using specialized molds and tooling.

threading: The process of cutting threads on a piece of stock to create a screw or nut. Typically this is done with a lathe, tap, or die. *See also* chasing

TIG: Tungsten inert gas (welding); also called gas tungsten arc welding (GTAW)

tinker: Originally a term for an itinerant tinsmith, who mended household utensils (WP)

tinkerer: In the modern context, anyone who tends to work on projects in a home workshop, and who employs tinkering skills

tinkering: The process of adapting, meddling, or adjusting something in the course of making repairs or improvements, a process also known as bricolage. Some modern-day nomads with an Irish, Scottish, or English influence call themselves "techno-tinkers" or "technogypsies" and are found to hold a romantic view of the tinker's lifestyle. (WP)

tin snips: Handheld, scissorlike shears for cutting thin sheet metal

tool steel: A variety of carbon and alloy steels that are particularly well suited to be made into tools. This suitability comes from their distinctive hardness, resistance to abrasion, ability to hold a cutting edge, and/or resistance to deformation at elevated temperatures (red-hardness). Tool steel is generally used in a heat-treated state. Many high-carbon tool steels are also more resistant to corrosion due to their higher ratios of elements such as vanadium and niobium. (WP)

torpedo level: A short spirit level that is used to establish a plumb or level surface over a short distance. Sometimes called an idiot level because it is not nearly as accurate as a full-length framing level.

TP: Toilet paper

treadle: The portion of a machine that is operated by the foot to produce reciprocating or rotary motion in a machine such as a weaving loom (reciprocating) or grinder (rotary). Treadles can also be used to power water pumps or to turn wood lathes. In the past, they were used to power a range of machines including sewing machines, looms, wood saws, cylinder phonographs, and even metal lathes.

treadle grinder/grindstone: A floor-mounted grinding wheel that is powered by a treadle and a connecting arm. (WP) *See also* pedal grinder

treadle lathe: A lathe that is powered by a treadle. These are usually wood lathes, and are most typically simple spring pole lathes (with a treadle beneath and a horizontal spring pole suspended overhead, for back pressure). Treadle metal lathes are now quite rare.

treadle loom: A multiple-harness floor loom that has its harness vertical motion actuated by treadles. Three- and four-harness looms are the most common.

treadle sewing machine: Many of the early sewing machines were powered by a foot treadle, which was operated by pressing down on it with a foot or both feet to cause a rocking movement. This movement spins a large wheel on the treadle frame, connected by a thin leather belt to a smaller driving wheel on the sewing machine. These machines were popular up until the 1920s. Common brands included Singer and New Home. Some modern electric sewing machines can be retrofitted to work on an antique treadle base. (WP)

trickle charge: Battery charging done at a low rate, balancing through self-discharge losses, to maintain a cell or battery in a fully charged condition

Trijicon: A maker of tritium-lit sights and rifle scopes

TSHTF: The Schumer Hits the Fan

turner: A lathesman

turning: A machining process in which a cutting tool, typically a non-rotary tool bit, describes a helical tool path by moving more or less linearly while the workpiece rotates. (WP) *See also* lathe

UPS: Uninterruptible power source

USGI: United States government issue

VA: Volt-amps

VAC: Volts, alternating current

Valmet: The Finnish conglomerate that formerly made several types of firearms

VCI: Vapor-phase corrosion inhibitor (a rust-preventive desiccant). VCI products are often produced as a coated paper, for metal parts storage. *See also* RIG; silica gel

VDC: Volts, direct current

VFD: Volunteer fire department

vise: A fixed-position clamping device, usually attached to a workbench or the bumper of a truck. *See also* blacksmithing vise; carpenter's vise; fly-tying vise; shave horse

Vise-Grip: Trade name for a variety of adjustable hand pliers that can both grip and lock

VOM: Volt-ohm meter

VW: Volkswagen

wainwright: A wagonmaker

WD-1: U.S. military–issue two-conductor insulated field telephone wire

WD-40: A commercial spray cleaner and lubricant, not recommended for most firearms cleaning tasks, in part because it deadens cartridge ammunition primers

wheelwright: A person who makes and repairs wooden wheels

woodworking vise: *See* carpenter's vise

wright: A skilled workman

YOYO: You're on Your Own

INDEX

Page numbers in *italics* refer to illustrations.

abundance-inspired waste, 18
*Accurate and Interesting Account
    of the Hardships and
    Sufferings of That Band of
    Heroes, Who Traversed the
    Wilderness in the Campaign
    Against Quebec in 1775, An*
    (Henry), 216
*Adaptive Curmudgeon's Blog,
    The,* 140
American Radio Relay League
    (ARRL), 235–36
ammonia-based bore cleaner,
    267–70
ammunition, 12, 18
    amounts needed, 184
anvils, 113–14
apprenticeships, 234
archery, 189–201
    arrows for, 198–99
    backyard range for,
        192–93
    crossbows for, 198, 199–201

equipment for, 198–99
    as gun substitute, 189–90,
        198–99
    instinctive shooting,
        190–91
    kinetic energy
        recommendation chart
        for, 196
    repair and maintenance in,
        191–92
    for self-defense,
        193–97
arrows, 198–99
artificers, xxiii–xxiv
ATGATT concept, 219–20
automated external
    defibrillator (AED), 212
automotive tools, 95–96
    jack stands, 96
    lockout, *see* lock picks and
        lockout tools
    mobility, 101–5
    securing in vehicle, 102

automotive tools *(cont.)*
   tire repair, 97
   tow chains and tow straps,
      97–98
axes, 21, *21*

backups and spares, 84–85
bark spud, 225
bartering, 23–24
bathroom gadgets, 79–80
batteries, 80–81
battery-powered hand tools,
   58–60, *59*
bench grinder, *236*
block and tackle rigs, 228
blowers, forge, 116
bolt cutters, 103–4, *104*, 105
Boston's Gun Bible (Boston T.
   Party), 151, 242–43
Brownfield, Derry, 149
bump keys, 109, 110, 111

canning, 11–14
   dry pack, 13–14, *13*
   equipment for, 11–12
canning jars, storing items
   in, 12
carding combs, 231
cars and trucks, 79
   buying, xxv
   tools for, *see*
      automotive tools
cattle, 34
chain saw, 23, 141–42, *141*
   care and maintenance
      of, 142
   safety gear for, 220
chalk line reel, 64, *64*

chisels, 60–62
clamshell digger, 34
clubs and groups, 235,
   237, 238
come-alongs, 229
communications equipment,
   80–81
community colleges, 234
Complete Modern Blacksmith,
   The (Weygers), 130, 241
computer, 80
Cooper, Jeff, 95, 188
countermobility tools, 105–8
crossbows, 198, 199–201
cutting tools, 57
   chain saws, *see* chain saw
   sheet metal snips, 63

Defoe, Daniel, 19
dehydrating, 14–15
dentistry tools, 212
digging bars, 35–36
Do Unto Others
   (Williamson), 49
drawknives, 65, *65*
drill bits, 69–70, *69*, *70*
drills, 68–70, *69*
   hand, 69, *69*
Duck Tape, 223–24
duct tape, 223–24

Ed's Red, 259–67
electrical projects:
   how-to videos and tutorials
      for, 87
   important rules for, 86
   safety with, 81–82
   soldering in, 90, 91

splicing cables in, 91
tools for, 87–94
electricity and electronics,
    xi–xii, 75–94
backups and spares, 84–85
cost-effectiveness and,
    83–84
efficiency and, 82
hybrid items, 81
necessities, 76–81
reliability and, 83
shared items, 84–85
Emery, Carla, 11, 241
EMT organizations, 235
*Encyclopedia of Country Living,
    The* (Emery), 11, 241

farming tools, *see* gardening,
    farm, and ranch tools
fences, 31–37
barbed wire, 31–32
braces for, 34–35
digging bars for, 35–36
gates for, 36, 108
"hot" wires on, 36
livestock, 33–34
post-hole digger for, 34
tensioning, 37
tools for, *33*
fiber guilds, 237
fiber tools, 230–32
files, 62
firearms, *see* guns
fire prevention and
    firefighting, 131–39
chimney, 137–38
flammability and, 17, 131
grease, 138

and science of fire, 136–37
tool sources for, 139
wildfires, 132–38
firewood, *see* wood
first aid kit, 202–12
basic, 204–6
container for, 209–10
nonmedical items in,
    208–9
rotating supplies in,
    210–11
flashlights, 98–100
Fleming, Peter, 38–39
food preservation, 11–16
canning, 11–14
dehydrating, 14–15
vacuum packing, 15–16
forge, 112–13, 115–16, 222
materials for, 113–14
Franklin, Benjamin, 233
Freecycle, xxvi
froe, 67, *68,* 225
fuel:
gasoline, 17
two-cycle, 23–24

gardening, 19–20
books on, 26–27
gardening, farm, and ranch
    tools, 19–37
for fences, *see* fences
hand, 20–26
Hi-Lift jacks, 28–31, *29, 33*
Plotmasters, 27–28
gasoline, 17
gates, 36, 108
glossary, 271–306
Glover, Thomas J., 60

gloves, 115
grandparents, 234
guilds, groups, and clubs, 235,
    237, 238
guns, 149–88
    5.56mm vs. 6.8mm vs. 7.62,
        180–81
    AK-47s as survival rifles,
        185–87
    ammunition for, 12,
        18, 184
    AR-10 and AR-15, 161–62,
        168, 169, 173
    archery equipment as
        substitute for, 189–90,
        198–99
    basic battery of, 151–60
    battle rifles, 160–62
    bore cleaners for, 259–70
    bullpups, 164–69
    common caliber for retreat
        rifles and handguns,
        175–80
    deer rifle as battle rifle,
        183–84
    exceptional logistical
        circumstances and,
        159–60
    FALs and L1A1s, 152–53,
        161, 168, 169–70
    Five Seven, 187–88
    gas piston AR-15s and
        M4s, 173
    handguns, 173–74
    HKs and clones, 162–64, 168
    inch vs. metric magazines
        in, 170
    legal loopholes and, 157–59

    magazine duplexing in,
        170–71
    pre-1899 antique, 257
    recommended, 160–62
    regional peculiarities and,
        156–57
    Remington, 154
    semiauto belt-feds, 171–72
    spare parts for, 162
    Springfield Armory
        M1A, 164
    standardization of, 174–75
    survival, 150–51
    survival, selecting, 151
    on tight budget, 181–84
    training in using, 188
    value and usefulness of,
        149–50
gunsmithing service
    providers, 249–55
gunsmithing supplies, 62

hammers, 66, 67
    blacksmithing, 115
hand drills, 69, 69
handguns, 173–74
    common caliber for retreat
        rifles and, 175–80
    see also guns
handsaws, 57
hardware, 58
Harris, C. E. "Ed," 259
H-braces, 34–35
heel bars, 62–63
helmets, 219, 220
Henry, John Joseph, 216
Hideyoshi, Toyotomi, 189
Hi-Lift jacks, 28–31, 29, 33, 96

historical reenactor groups, 236–37
hobby clubs, 235, 237
horses, 36
hot shop, 7–8
How to Survive the End of the World as We Know It (Rawles), xxiii, 9
Hurricane Katrina, x, xi

Indian Ocean tsunami, x

jack stands, 96

kitchen tools and appliances, 78–79
  knives, 10–11
knitting needles, 231
knives, 216–22
  American makers of, 220–22
  everyday carry, 216–18
  folding, 217, 218
  kitchen, 10–11
  multi-tools, 218
  neck, 217
  pocketknives, 218
  sheath, 217

levels, 64, 73
learning, lifelong, 233–39
  see also skills
leatherworking clubs, 238
leatherworking tools, 229–30
Leviticus, 10
library, 234, 241–47
lifting and pulling tools, 226–29

lightbulbs, 84
livestock, 24
  fencing for, 33–34
lock picks and lockout tools, 105, 109
  kits, 110–11
  practice with, 111
  vibration, 111
looms, 231–32
lumber, *see* wood

Mackay, Charles, 112
magazines, xxvii–xxviii
mallets:
  rubber, 66
  wooden, 67
Maslow, Abraham, 77–78, 79, 80
matches, 12
measuring and marking tools, 63–64
measuring tapes, 63, 64
mechanical advantage, 226–27
medical supplies and equipment, 78, 202
  automated external defibrillator, 212
  dentistry tools, 212
  first aid kit, *see* first aid kit
  surgery instruments, 212
Mikesell, Kory, 202–12
mobility tools, 101–5
multi-tools, 218

needs, hierarchy of, 77–78, 79, 80

News from Tartary (Fleming), 38–39

operational security (OPSEC) risk, 17–18

paper products, 17
Patriots (Rawles), 108, 214
Pearl of Death, The, 75
pencils, 64
pipe wrenches, 70, 72
plastic, cutting, 57
pliers, 55–56, *56*
Plotmasters, 27–28
plumb bob, *64*
plumbing tools, 70–71, 78
  pipe wrenches, 70, 72
plywood, 18
Pocket Ref (Glover), 60
post-hole digger, 34
pressure cooker, 12
pry bars, 62, 227
pulling and lifting tools, 226–29
punches, 60–62

radio, 235
ratchet cable hoists, 229
ratchet tensioner, *33*, 35
Rawles, Robert Henry, 175
rifles, *see* guns
Robinson Crusoe (Defoe), 19
rock boxes, 35–36
rubber mallets, 66

sanitation, 212–15
  in apartment buildings, 214
  outhouse, 213

septic system, 79, 213
  soap for, 214–15
sawhorses, 4
sawmill, 143–48
  getting to a finished product, 147
  hardest part of running, 145–46
  post-collapse considerations for, 144–45
  what tends to go wrong, 146
saws, 57
screwdrivers, 52–54, *54*, 55
screw extractors, 55
screw jacks, 227–28
screw thread restoring tools, 56–57
septic system, 79, 213
sewing clubs, 238
sewing machines, 39–48
  bobbin housing of, 44
  bobbin winder of, 45
  brands of, 47
  compound feed, 44
  important features in, 43–47
  reverse in, 44
  thread stand of, 45
  timing clutch in, 45
  walking foot, 43–44
  what to look for in, 40–43
  where to buy, 48
sharing resources, 84–85
shaving horse, 224
sheet metal cutting snips, 63
shelf life and deterioration, 16
shingle froe, *67*, *68*
shop, *see* workshop
shop tools, *see* workshop tools

shotguns, *see* guns
skills, xxiv–xxv, xxvi–xxvii
  building, 233–39
  where to acquire, 234–38
Smith, Jerry, 1
soap, 214–15
Society for Creative
  Anachronism (SCA),
  236–37
socket sets, 50
solar storms, xi–xii
Sowell, Thomas, 95
spares and backups, 84–85
spinning wheels, 230
splitting wedges, 224, 225
squares, 72, 73
stockpiles, 8–9
  of soft items, 16–18
surgery instruments, 212
SurvivalBlog.com, xiv, 105, 114,
  128, 140, 165, 185, 190, 199,
  202, 215, 221, 267
swords, 199

table saw, 4
telephone service, xi
television, xxviii
tensioning, 37
  tools for, 33, 35
tire repair tools, 97
timber, *see* wood
tongs, blacksmithing, 117
tools, xxviii–xxxi
  automotive, *see*
    automotive tools
  cutting, *see* cutting tools
  electrical project, 87–94
  fiber, 230–32

firefighting, 139
  gardening, *see* gardening,
    farm, and ranch tools
  handles of, 27
  improvised and
    handcrafted, 222–24
  keeping separate, 1
  knives, *see* knives
  leatherworking, 229–30
  maintaining and caring for,
    xxxi–xxxii
  plumbing, *see* plumbing
    tools
  pulling and lifting, 226–29
  sewing, *see* sewing
    machines
  training and, xxxii
  vises, 5–7, *6*, 116
  welding and blacksmithing,
    see welding and
    blacksmithing tools
  workshop, *see* workshop
    tools
tow chains and tow straps,
  97–98
training, xxvi
  tools and, xxxii
  see also skills
"Tubal Cain" (Mackay), 112
Twain, Mark, 202

uninterruptible power supply
  (UPS), 80
USB drives, 81
used items, buying, xxv–xxvi

vacuum cleaner, 77
vacuum packing, 15–16

vises, 5–7, *6*, 116
volunteer fire departments
    (VFDs), 235

water supplies, 78, 215
weapons, 199
    see also archery; guns
welding and blacksmithing,
    117–18
    with electric welders, 118–19
    motor oil in, 129
    references for, 129–30
    safety in, 119–23, 127, 129
    tips for, 129
    without grid power, 126–28
welding and blacksmithing
    tools, 112–17, 123
    anvils, 113–14
    blower, 116
    forge, 112–13, 115–16, 222
    forge materials, 113–14
    gloves, 115
    hammers, 115
    tongs, 117
    vise, 116
    welding rods, 123–26
Weygers, Alexander G.,
    130, 241
wildfires, 132–38
Williamson, Michael Z., 49,
    165–68
wire cutters, *56*
wire draw plates, 222
wood, 140–48
    chain saw for cutting, *see*
        chain saw
    sawmill for, *see* sawmill
wooden mallet, 67

wood planes, 65, *66*
woodworking clubs, 237
workbenches, 3–5
workshop(s), 1–9, 49
    benches in, 3–5
    essentials for, 3
    hot, 7–8
    safety in, 2
    separate, 1
    stockpiles for, 8–9
workshop tools, 49–74
    battery-powered, 58–60, *59*
    chalk line reel, 64, *64*
    cheap, 55
    chisels, 60–62
    cutting, 57
    drills, 68–70, *69*
    extraction, 55–56
    files, 62
    froe, 67, *68*, 225
    gunsmithing supplies, 62
    hammers, 66, *67*
    hand drills, 69, *69*
    hardware, 58
    heel bars, 62–63
    impact, 66–67
    levels, 64, *73*
    making, 73–74
    measuring and marking,
        63–64
    measuring tapes, 63, *64*
    miscellaneous, 72
    pencils, 64
    pliers, 55–56, *56*
    plumbing, 70–71
    pry bars, 62, 227
    punches, 60–62
    rubber mallets, 66

screwdrivers, 52–54, *54*, 55
screw extractors, 55
shaping and smoothing, 65, *65*, *66*
sheet metal cutting snips, 63
socket sets, 50
squares, 72, *73*
thread repair, 56–57

useful references for, 60
vises, 5–7, *6*, 116
wooden mallets, 67
wrenches, 51–52, 55, 70, *72*
wrenches, 51–52, 55, 70
  pipe, 70, *72*

Zerbe, J. S., xxiii

Also by James Wesley, Rawles

NATIONAL BESTSELLER

JAMES WESLEY, RAWLES
FOUNDER OF SURVIVALBLOG.COM

HOW TO SURVIVE THE END OF THE WORLD AS WE KNOW IT

TACTICS, TECHNIQUES, AND TECHNOLOGIES FOR UNCERTAIN TIMES

978-0-452-29812-5

PLUME
A member of Penguin Group USA
www.penguin.com